PENGUIN MODERN CLASSICS

Journey Through a Small Pl

EMANUEL LITVINOFF was born to Russian Jewish immigrant parents in Whitechapel in 1915. The second of nine children (and the brother of the historian Barnet Litvinoff), he left school at fourteen and, after working in a number of unskilled jobs, found himself down and out within a year. Drifting through Soho and Fitzrovia in the Depression, he wrote since-destroyed hallucinatory texts and survived on his wits. After enlisting in the army in January 1940, he served in Northern Ireland, West Africa and the Middle East. He quickly rose through the ranks to become a major at the age of twenty-seven. Litvinoff started to publish his poetry while in the army. His work was included in the Routledge anthology *Poems from the Forces* (1941). *Conscripts: A Symphonic Declaration* appeared that same year, and his first collection, *The Untried Soldier*, followed in 1942. The poems in *A Crown for Cain* (1948) were written between 1942 and 1946, mostly in West Africa and Egypt. After the war, Litvinoff worked briefly as a ghostwriter, before going on to produce novels of his own, starting with *The Lost Europeans* (1960), set in post-war Berlin, and also various plays, including some for the Thames Television series 'Armchair Theatre'. His memory of the Whitechapel ghetto of his childhood had been transformed by the Nazi genocide and, in the post-war decades, Litvinoff would devote much of his energy to campaigning against racism. In his poem 'To T. S. Eliot', he famously challenged the great Anglo-American poet for reprinting anti-Semitic lines, written before the Holocaust, in a new selection of his poems. Alarmed by what he saw when visiting Moscow with a British fashion delegation in 1956, Litvinoff joined the movement to counter anti-Semitism in the Soviet Union. For many years he was editor of *Jews in Eastern Europe*, the journal of that campaign, and he was also a leading witness in the Paris Trial of 1973, in which the Soviet Embassy, which had published a scandalously anti-Semitic article, was successfully sued for racial libel. Having edited *The Penguin Book of Jewish Short Stories* (1979), Litvinoff published his last novel, *Falls the Shadow*, in 1983. Written shortly before the Sabra and Shatila massacres in Lebanon, it questioned Israeli policy towards Palestinians. Since his retirement, Emanuel Litvinoff has lived quietly in Bloomsbury.

PATRICK WRIGHT's books include *Iron Curtain: From Stage to Cold War*, *The Village that Died for England* and *A Journey Through Ruins*.

EMANUEL LITVINOFF

Journey Through a Small Planet

With an Introduction by Patrick Wright

PENGUIN BOOKS

PENGUIN CLASSICS

Published by the Penguin Group
Penguin Books Ltd, 80 Strand, London wc2r orl, England
Penguin Group (USA) Inc., 375 Hudson Street, New York, New York 10014, USA
Penguin Group (Canada), 90 Eglinton Avenue East, Suite 700, Toronto, Ontario,
Canada m4p 2y3 (a division of Pearson Penguin Canada Inc.)
Penguin Ireland, 25 St Stephen's Green, Dublin 2, Ireland (a division of Penguin Books Ltd)
Penguin Group (Australia), 250 Camberwell Road, Camberwell, Victoria 3124,
Australia (a division of Pearson Australia Group Pty Ltd)
Penguin Books India Pvt Ltd, 11 Community Centre, Panchsheel Park, New Delhi – 110 017, India
Penguin Group (NZ), 67 Apollo Drive, Rosedale, North Shore 0632, New Zealand
(a division of Pearson New Zealand Ltd)
Penguin Books (South Africa) (Pty) Ltd, 24 Sturdee Avenue, Rosebank, Johannesburg 2196, South Africa

Penguin Books Ltd, Registered Offices: 80 Strand, London wc2r orl, England

www.penguin.com

Journey Through a Small Planet first published by Michael Joseph 1972
This edition first published in Penguin Modern Classics 2008
4

Journey Through a Small Planet copyright © Emanuel Litvinoff, 1972; 'Prologue: The Day the World Came to
an End' copyright © Emanuel Litvinoff, 2008; 'A Jew in England' copyright © Emanuel Litvinoff, 1967; 'A
Long Look Back' copyright © Emanuel Litvinoff, 1959; 'To T. S. Eliot' copyright © Emanuel Litvinoff, 1973
Introduction and editorial material copyright © Patrick Wright, 2008
All rights reserved

The moral right of the author and editor has been asserted

Typeset in Dante MT by Palimpsest Book Production Limited,
Grangemouth, Stirlingshire
Printed in England by Clays Ltd, St Ives plc

ISBN: 978-0-141-18930-7

Contents

Contents

'After a lapse of time, the past becomes a mythical country – a dreamscape. Memory is a literary exercise: it shapes our yesterdays into narrative form, an inevitably fictionalizing process.'
Emanuel Litvinoff, 2008

Acknowledgements

Emanuel Litvinoff wishes to express his warmest gratitude to his friend Patrick Wright, for the encouragement, tireless effort and long-term interest in his life and work; Marcella Edwards, Maria-teresa Boffo, Elisabeth Merriman and Nikki Sinclair at Penguin; Lesley Levene, whose attention to the text has been far more enthusiastic and informed than anyone would have right or reason to expect; his son Aaron for his dedicated assistance and involvement; and finally his wife Mary for her constant support.

Introduction
Brick Lane: Views from the Quayside

We were just a few hundred yards east of Brick Lane, in London's East End, and the narrow road stretched out between two rubble-strewn voids. The council had provided a new sign to confirm that this was indeed Fuller Street, but there was nothing left to see.

Not so, however, for the figure who stood on the pavement, his hands slicing the air as he hammered a world back into the emptied scene. He put a terrace of two-storeyed houses along both sides of the bulldozed street, and squeezed whole families into cellars beneath the road. Up at the far end he sketched in a taller tenement, named it Fuller Street Buildings, and then stared at it until it was fairly 'boiling' with humanity. Children started yelling, sewing machines rattled and there was a constant chatter of Yiddish. Exasperated neighbours took to banging on thin walls and ceilings with broomsticks, and the air was thick, even in the cold damp of winter, with the interfused smell of drains, sour pickles, garlic and overflowing dustbins in the backyard.

Who was this man – spry but of considerable age – who walked through a temporarily slumped corporation's building site, repossessing it as a village that was, in his own words, 'remote in spirit from the adjacent cosmopolitanism of the great city of London', and altogether more like the small Jewish towns that were once 'scattered across the lands of Eastern Europe', each one fatally 'hemmed in by ancient curses'?[1] And why – now just as then – do we know so little about him?

I wrote those words at the end of 1992, several decades after Emanuel Litvinoff climbed into his small Fiat convertible and drove to Fuller Street with the uproarious Swedish writer Alvar Alsterdal on a visit that prompted him to write the stories that would eventually be collected in *Journey Through a Small Planet*. Born in 1915, Litvinoff had lived in Fuller Street Buildings as a child, but I had met him a few miles to the west, in a small flat behind the grand façades of Bloomsbury's easternmost bastion, Mecklenburgh Square, where he resides in a building also used to house overseas students and their families. At that time, Litvinoff lived in an obscurity that owed nothing to geography or the length of the corridor leading to his door. To reach him, it was necessary to skirt the jostling vanity fair that is literary life in England, sidestepping the prize-giving ceremonies, the celebrity tennis matches (Julian Barnes was still playing Martin Amis in those distant days) and the chatter about Philip Larkin's dismal social attitudes then being adroitly publicized by his literary executors. Eventually, I pushed a numbered bell and the man who had once written a Thames Television play named 'The World in a Room'[2] peered out and, with a guarded smile, said, 'Come in.'

Litvinoff's books may have fallen out of print in the 1980s but some of them drew high praise before that, and a few have even sold rather well. In the late 1960s and early 1970s, he was one of Britain's best television dramatists: an accomplished exponent of the single studio play, a now all but extinct genre which Litvinoff often used to dramatize social prejudice. But television is, in his own regretful description, 'so much steam on glass' and no one should be expected to remember any of that. Yet Litvinoff has also been a contrary figure: insisting on asking awkward questions and never signing up for the compliances of the successful literary career. He was even a misfit stylistically, addressing fundamentally modern themes, but declaring that he did so as a storyteller ('you can't just jettison tradition or discount the problem of communication') and dismissing most avant-garde experimentation as the fashionable trickery with which self-indulgent writers attempt to make up for their lack of social imagination.

Having recently read *Journey Through a Small Planet* (1972), I had asked Litvinoff to show me around the place of his childhood. Warning that little trace now remained of the community he had known, except for a few 'occasional relics, such as you'd find after a volcanic eruption or an earthquake', he was prepared to go back nonetheless, and to follow the thread of his life through streets that, if they survived at all, now belonged in more recent immigrant worlds.

In the tube going east under the City of London, Litvinoff talked of his parents, who had journeyed to London from Odessa in 1913. Like many of the Jewish immigrants who came up the Thames, travelling 'steerage' in what might as well have been cattle boats, they had hoped to reach America but ended up in a Whitechapel ghetto that was already densely populated by Jews who had fled persecution in the Russian Empire – an emigration that had become a terrified mass exodus in the early 1880s, thanks to the brutalities licensed by Tsar Alexander III.

Emanuel remembers his father only as a tinted photograph on a vanished wall in Fuller Street Buildings. He was, apparently, a low-grade sweatshop worker who nevertheless thought of himself as an intellectual. Politically, he was an anarchist who had probably been involved in student activity in Odessa. He went back to Russia during the First World War: shipped off, like other male 'aliens' in Whitechapel, to join the Tsar's army in the East, he was soon enough caught up in the Russian Revolution.

Writing for the *Listener* in 1963, Litvinoff had recalled how 'most of the news' about these absent men had at first come from Tarot-reading fortune-tellers who 'promised every wife a swift reunion with her husband'.[3] Some eventually got back to London, but not Litvinoff's father: 'The things we know about him are extraordinarily romantic. He seems to have organized a band of freebooters, which minted money, and stole horses.' The group made its way north to Archangel and arranged passage on a boat leaving for London early one morning. Litvinoff's father arrived too late and was last seen on the shore, a receding figure waving frantically from the quayside. Obliged to fend for herself and her four sons alone, Emanuel's mother took to her sewing machine and worked as a home dressmaker. She haunts Litvinoff's pages as the 'resident ghost' of his childhood. Exhausted by endless drudgery and the five additional children that followed remarriage, she speaks out from a succession of grim flats (after Fuller Street, the family lived in Hackney's Mare Street and at 109 Sandringham Road in Dalston), issuing the despairing admonitions so vividly captured by the son she only saw going off the rails.

Emerging from Bethnal Green underground station, Litvinoff took his bearings from a terrace named Paradise Row and then launched off down Bethnal Green Road. He remembered how as a child he used to run up and down this street to visit Bethnal Green Library, fetching the books that, as an untutored but 'omnivorous' reader, he would choose by title alone.

After pausing to tug a weirdly shaped shop back into its pre-war incarnation as Smart's Picture Palace, where he saw the first talkies, Litvinoff turned to seek out the brick Victorian heights of the institution he knew as Wood Close School. The Jewish parents of that time stressed the importance of having 'a good trade in your hands', but the intelligent kids merely had to look at their own parents to realize that this meant being condemned to a life of 'humiliating drudgery'. The only escape lay in the local grammar school: it was 'through scholarship that you escaped the dread fate of the factory and sweatshop'. Litvinoff was on course for this elevation; indeed, as he walked around the school, glancing at Bangladeshi children in their bright red uniforms, he remembered winning the Bethnal Green essay competition on the theme of 'What I did on my holidays'. His tactic, as he explained, was 'to play on the sympathy of the judges at the beginning' by making it quite clear that his family had been in no position to offer him any holiday at all. But though he was at the top of the class, and generally something of a star pupil, he was defeated by the scholarship exam. Children were really 'fighting for their lives', and Litvinoff was ambushed by nerves – to such an extent that he couldn't even hold the pen. He failed repeatedly and the future disappeared.

Young Emanuel was sliding steadily into dereliction by the time we walked past the Carpenter's Arms, still seedily associated with the Kray twins. He had renounced his passion for reading, finding nothing in books but a painful reminder of lost opportunities. A trade scholarship checked his descent for a while, but, in what he would later describe as 'my first serious experience of anti-Semitism',[4] he was refused admittance to the school of lithography he hoped to attend ('The one question I did not apparently answer to the interviewer's satisfaction was that relating to my religion'). So he ended up learning shoe-making as the only Jewish student at Cordwainers Technical College near Smithfield meat market: a gruesome pork-filled institution that would become known to readers of *Journey Through a Small Planet* for the abiding stench of the offal yard next door, and for the cane-wielding headmaster who twisted mocking variations out of Litvinoff's alien name. Litvinoff left as soon as he was legally able and was soon sleeping rough, or in dosshouses. As he recalls, 'If you were down and out in the thirties, nothing existed for you. You could die on the pavements.'

It was in this condition that Litvinoff drifted westwards towards Soho. Having slept in the 'beggars' crypt' of St Martin-in-the-Fields, he would make his way over to the Cafe Royal in Regent Street, where he stole past the commissionaires for a free wash in the gentlemen's cloakroom, winning a smile on the way through from a knickerbockered George Bernard Shaw. He remembered catching an apprehensive glance from Wyndham Lewis, who was striding along Piccadilly in black cloak and wide-brimmed hat; and visiting a basement café named The Dive in Frith Street to scrounge a fourpenny plate of minestrone off Aleister Crowley, who sat there in tweeds, playing chess and looking altogether more like an English country gentleman than the notorious occultist, sexual pervert and diabolical 'Great Beast' of widespread reputation.

Jewish Whitechapel was a hard place, and ardent in its pursuit of redemption. Standing outside the chained and deserted building that once served as the United Workmen's Synagogue[5] at 21 Cheshire Street, Litvinoff observed that, while he had not been held by the rabbi with his Talmud and Hebrew lessons, he had certainly dallied with Zionism (he briefly espoused an 'extreme'[6] version similar to that associated with Jabotinsky and the terrorists of the Irgun in Palestine) and also with 'the red day of reckoning' promised by the ghetto's apocalyptic brand of Communism.

His next encounter with messianic impulses began when he was befriended in a Soho café, by a woman whose name he is still reluctant to divulge. Though only a little older than Litvinoff, maybe twenty-one or so, she seemed to live in a different age. She dressed in old-fashioned clothes and was, as he recognized only with hindsight, an uncompromising Jewish chauvinist. A skilled astrologer, she drew her acolyte into a world of esoteric divination reached through the exotically mixed media of Kabbalah, psychometry, automatic writing, meditation and seance-like attempts to re-enter past lives. It was, Litvinoff remembered, all a bit too much: 'I used to get the feeling that I could enter into madness. If you're an untrained young mind, struggling with the complexities of the Kabbalah, and if your sexual initiation is all mixed up with this . . .'

So there he was, trudging through the mid-1930s, a young man who had failed even the Jewish welfare organizations that tried to halt his descent: undernourished, often without food for days, and 'hallucinating' or having 'some kind of nervous breakdown' as he went.* 'I would be standing in front of a shop window, and suddenly it would feel dark. People would look spectral, and the world was spectral.' He remembers 'out of the body experiences', when a moment of time would suddenly seem 'stretched out to infinity', and other fugue-like occasions when he slipped through the historical fix of the city, 'stumbling into a little pocket of time'. He might be walking down the street, or perhaps approaching the Jewish soup kitchen off Bishopsgate, when he would look up and find the cars gone, and horse-drawn traffic in their place.

In this condition, he saw Jewish immigrants arriving from Russia, and tenements melting away mysteriously, to be replaced by older cottages with little gardens. He remembers asking a man the date and, on being told it was 1890, going into a

---

* In an unpublished letter to his younger brother Barnet, written on 9 July 1940, Litvinoff recalled, 'When I was nineteen the whole world flashed around my ears, all my false standards of values crumbled, everything that I had been sure of – the touch and quality of stone, the meaning of eating and sleeping and suffering, the texture of civilisation, all collapsed and left me in darkness. The world no longer existed. I was dead in some nightmarish way . . .'

haberdashery shop and looking at children's exercise books for verification. Litvinoff's first poem was among the spectral manifestations of that time. It appeared quite unexpectedly, when he was working in a furniture factory in Wembley. Perhaps it was down to the glue pot, with its 'rather extraordinary, intellectually aphrodisiac' fumes, but the romantic words suddenly appeared, as if from nowhere: 'Farewell O Queen of the Night, dark mistress of my cosmic dreams.' Litvinoff laughed at the memory of these overripe lines, quoted at the close of *Journey Through a Small Planet* as signs of the writer's life to come. While he had long wanted to be a writer, he had never been interested in poetry, knowing only the stuff he had learned by rote at elementary school: '"The boy stood on the burning deck," that kind of thing'.

He soon had a room over the Finchley Road and a piecework job as a fur nailer (he would wet the skins and nail them to the shape of a chalk outline), which enabled him to put in four or five hours a day, and devote the rest of his time to pursuing his renewed literary ambitions. He completed a long novel about the East End, written in 'a kind of fever' when he was just over twenty, and named *Of Time Wearied* after Thomas Wolfe's epic *Of Time and the River*. In one of many unpublished manuscripts, Litvinoff has described how Elias Canetti visited him in the darkened room where he would be sat at his long-carriaged Remington, 'typing out the interminable novel I was convinced was a work of genius that would win for me instant fame. Trance-like, I spoke of the need to shape one's life into an instrument through which the voice of God would utter, a trumpet of prophecy, of my dream that an angel stood at my shoulder while I wrote the story of my generation on to the page in illuminated letters like the Book of Kells.' Canetti listened and then declared the young author 'a schizophrenic artist', leaving him to hunt through dictionaries to find out just what this meant. Litvinoff burned that ambitious novel in a characteristic fit of embarrassment shortly after the war.

Although he has always lived in England, Litvinoff has never identified himself as an English writer. 'There has,' he told me, 'always been a parochialism about English writing' and Jewish Whitechapel demanded a different outlook. Certainly, *Journey Through a Small Planet* owes nothing to the customary English way of imagining tiny locales as worlds of epic scale.

It was Hilaire Belloc, a man of Anglo-French descent, who remarked, after visiting Ely in the first years of the twentieth century, that 'the corner of a corner of England is infinite and can never be exhausted'.[7] Belloc's friend G. K. Chesterton made related claims for the rural English locale. Arguing against Rudyard Kipling in the same decade, he declared that the imperial globetrotter actually lived in 'a smaller world' than the peasant who may know only a few fields and a village. Kipling did not belong to England, he declared, or indeed 'to any place; and the proof of it is this, that he thinks of England as a place. The moment we are rooted in a place, the place vanishes. We live like a tree with the whole strength of the universe.'[8] Then as now, there would be many who equated parochialism with spiritual cramp, deprivation and reactionary small-mindedness, but Chesterton was in no doubt that 'the "large ideas" prosper when it is not a question of thinking in continents, but of understanding a few two-legged men'. His symbolic fields and villages were cosmic locales because they had withstood the temptations and disturbances of modern history.

The cause of 'Little England' would find many advocates through the twentieth century. Like other attempts to define national society via ancient roots, it depended upon an organic idea of settled community, which was conceived as threatened by a vividly imagined battery of encroaching menaces. Variations of

'Little England' emerged on the left of the political spectrum as well as the right. In Conservative versions the 'England' in question might be the traditional hierarchy of the rural village, with its church and squire, its festivals and traditions of husbandry. Yet the inheritance at the centre of this vision might also be organized around the memory of the commons, the democracy of Magna Carta, the festive 'Merrie England' of the medieval guilds, Robin Hood and the republicanism of the seventeenth century. The defining threat of destruction varied too. The early twentieth century repertoire of encroaching modern forces included industrialism, urbanism and the spreading suburbs, mass culture and the standardizing accents of the BBC, property developers, capitalism and the finance system, socialism and the reforming edicts of the centralized state. In many versions, 'Little England' was also conceived to be threatened by human aliens, typically imagined as Jews.

Even without the immediate menace of Oswald Mosley's British Union of Fascists, and the 'biff-boys' with whom Litvinoff used to skirmish on the east London streets, Jewish Whitechapel was at odds with everything 'Little England' stood for. The 'small' of Litvinoff's title is simply factual: the Jewish East End consisted of only a few streets, organized along the spine of Brick Lane and pressed up against the adjacent City of London. However, if Litvinoff's Whitechapel was also a 'planet', this was not because it could make any deep historical claims to its place. Indeed, at the time when Belloc and Chesterton were praising their 'Little England' for such qualities, the Jewish East End represented all the fears codified by the Aliens Act (passed in 1905 in order to establish a new system of immigration control under the Home Office). The Jews of London's East End were unassimilated, proletarian and East European. Their community was defined by routes rather than deeply thrust roots. It was a planet not because it had withstood modern history unchanged, but because it was the product of violent disruption and the experience of that unsettling wider history now filled its narrow streets, along with the unruly hopes and fears of its Yiddish-speaking inhabitants.

Litvinoff recalls Jewish Whitechapel as a square mile where 'people spoke of Warsaw, Kishinev, Kiev, Kharkov, Odessa as if they were neighbouring suburbs'.[9] As he says of growing up in that two-roomed flat in Fuller Street Buildings: 'You were sitting in the kitchen or on your mother's knee, and what were they talking about?' He counts off a few possibilities: the failings of Kerensky and Russia's Provisional Government of 1917; the sayings of a much-loved rabbi in the Ukraine; the vividly remembered brutalities of a pogrom somewhere on the Black Sea; or the relative merits of Lenin and Trotsky, both of whom were said to be good for the Jews. 'You really imbibed with your mother's milk a sense of the wider world out there – a world that was still reaching in to touch you.'

None of this was calculated, or likely, to please the Little Englanders. In the surrounding society, the Jews of London's East End were perceived as violent conspirators of anarchy and international revolution (a fear that was famously articulated around the 1911 siege of Sidney Street). Anti-Semitic stereotypes were also confirmed by the fact that the area's modestly successful furniture trade was susceptible to incendiary outbreaks: in the 1920s many fires in the area were set by insurance fraudsters who felt little, if any, loyalty to the British society around them.

Adopting an English-sounding name was part of the Jewish survival kit in east London between the wars. Litvinoff remembers toughing it out as Len H. Lee, while his good friend Isaac Greyman passed as Reginald F. Grey. He suffered an Englishing of the eye too. As we wandered through the street market of Petticoat Lane, Litvinoff pointed to the Jewish physiognomy of some stallholders, and then proposed that one of the most insidious effects of racism is to make victims see themselves as their persecutors do. It may not really show in *Journey Through a Small Planet*, but Litvinoff himself left Whitechapel on a wave of self-loathing that he described, most memorably, in the 1960s: 'Every time a woman with a foreign accent made a scene on a bus, or two men argued loudly in Yiddish over a business deal, or a music-hall comedian got a few laughs by jamming a bowler-hat over his ears and retracting his neck into his shoulders, I was miserably ashamed.' He found the Jewish names on shop fronts

grotesque and provocative; the Kosher signs and Yiddish lettering were embarrassing advertisements of alienation; there was too much huckstering in street-markets; the flies crawling over exposed meat and groceries were proof of ingrained backwardness and squalor. I was equally affronted by the sight of a Hassid walking through the street in outlandish garb, impervious to the effect of his own strangeness, and of the herring-women down the Lane, plunging their chapped and swollen fingers into the open barrels of pickled fish.[10]

The Second World War changed everything. The disruptions effectively put an end to the Jewish East End as Litvinoff had known it, and the war also confirmed Litvinoff's own departure into a secular writer's life. Indeed, he would later remember travelling north with other new conscripts bound for an army depot near Glasgow, and describe the coming of the war as 'a kind of liberation for me'.[11] To begin with, he had registered as a conscientious objector, but he changed his mind as soon as Hitler's purpose became clear to him and urged the War Office to hasten him into active service. The authorities had different ideas, parking Litvinoff alongside other mistrusted 'aliens' in the Pioneer Corps, first in Ulster and later as an officer in West Africa and Egypt. Barred from directly fighting the Fascists, Litvinoff went to work on the poetic front. *Conscripts: A Symphonic Declaration*, published in 1941, retains some of the apocalyptic character of his early 'schizophrenic' period: the youthful khaki poet imagines the young rising up into 'the great open spaces of unthought where newness is', challenging 'the champions of unchange' and insisting on a 'prayer of human suffering' that rings out above 'the loud dogmatism of revolution / And of hucksters selling patriotism to the mob'. In 'Re-Dedication', he declaims, 'We saw truth shining through the shabby compromise / and closed our eyes'.[12]

A few pieces printed in an anthology, *Poems from the Forces*, brought a letter from Herbert Read, who then published Litvinoff's slim volume *The Untried Soldier* in the Routledge New Poets series. Some of his poems were broadcast by the BBC and there was further interest from John Lehmann, publisher and patron of young literary strivers from the East End. Litvinoff went to meet Lehmann at his residence in Park Lane, and was embarrassed to find himself being offered sherry and cigarettes by 'a blond Nordic giant with exquisite manners' wearing a silk dressing gown ('I didn't know where to put my hobnailed boots and soon departed'). He also heard from Dr Alex Comfort, at that time a young anarchist poet and novelist, with whom he was soon on good terms.

Yet Litvinoff's budding reputation as a neo-romantic poet did little to alleviate the difficulties of the late 1940s. He had married during the war, and had no idea that his wife would soon step out on to the catwalk as Cherry Marshall, a leading fashion model who eventually went off into a glamorous life of her own. The couple lived with their young children in a damp basement flat and Emanuel eked out a living by reviewing for the *Guardian*, *Tribune*, the *Spectator* and other papers. He tried radio too, proposing a series of short programmes inspired by a café philosopher named Schulberg, a 'Yiddish Socrates' known for his aphorisms ('If God made you a Jew you don't need a hobby', 'Every fool is convinced he is going to give birth to a genius', etc.), who worked as a dues collector for the Jewish Burial Society and frequented Goide's, a Whitechapel café favoured by East End Jewish intellectuals. His plans for a longer series named 'Harry's Delicatessen' were scrapped after July 1947, when a 'near pogrom mood' developed after British authorities in Palestine hanged three Jewish terrorists for an attack on Acre prison and two British sergeants were captured and hanged in retaliation.

Litvinoff was quickly reduced to ghostwriting – first the memoirs of an eminent surgeon, who recommended that his scribe should adopt a properly English name if he wanted to get on; and then more literary works for Louis Golding. The best-selling Anglo-Jewish novelist paid Litvinoff £10 a week to write three books, including *To the Quayside* (1954), a novel in which he took Golding's cast of Mancunian characters but used them to dramatize his own concern for the European Jews who, having survived Hitler, had faced new barriers as they tried to reach Palestine. Litvinoff would also try a comic novel ('everyone was writing one in those days'). Entitled *The Swello Girl*, this never-published satire was inspired by the ubiquity of tits and bums in advertising; it featured a buxom television presenter who became an instant celebrity after accidentally falling out of a low-cut dress.

Meanwhile, the once-repressed memory of Whitechapel kept reaching forward from the back of Litvinoff's mind. Reanimated by the shocking fact of Nazi mass murder, it intruded to pass stern judgements on his literary endeavours. As he once wrote, 'I had climbed out of that ghetto on a ladder of books, inadequately self-taught, only to settle into the myopic confines of a Hampstead rented room scribbling bad poems.'

In his post-war writing Litvinoff would range far and wide across Europe, but every road seems to lead him back to the rejected square mile of the Jewish East End. In his novel of post-war Berlin, *The Lost Europeans* (1960), we wander through the Communist eastern sector of Berlin (a city that Litvinoff had visited in 1955 and 1957), only to arrive at another 'claustrophobic tenement' which evokes the 'vulgarity, the noise and overspilling vitality' of slum life in Whitechapel, even though its poverty has a contrasting and far more pitiful 'picked-to-the-bone' quality.[13] In *To the Quayside*, Louis Golding's character Elsie Silver walks up the rue d'Hauteville in Paris and is suddenly surrounded by 'the smell of warm boiled brisket of beef, and chopped fried fish, and yellow cucumbers in great glass jars, and cheese-cake, and red horse-radish . . . It was home sweet home again.'[14] We turn to the first page of *The Bare Knuckle Breed*, a book of historical boxing stories that Litvinoff ghosted for Louis Golding, and find ourselves in the squalor of Whitechapel's Horse Shoe Alley, falling through successive time warps until the smell of fields and hedges is in the air and Bethnal is 'still somewhat Green'.[15] During these same early post-war years, Litvinoff wrote 'Prologue: The Day the World Came to an End', his extraordinary and previously unpublished account of an eclipse over the east London of his childhood (see page 150).

As we walked down Brick Lane, scouring the Bangladeshi detail for the odd remaining Jewish residue, I asked Litvinoff how he answered the charge of nostalgia. As a writer who came to identify so deeply with the lost world of Jewish Whitechapel, how did he avoid becoming as parochial as the English tradition from which he had felt so dislocated? Litvinoff conceded that you do indeed have to be very careful about the 'sentimentality' of a Jewish memory that lingers over bagels and herrings from the barrel, while choosing to forget that the East End was in many ways a 'frustrating and verminous' place which people wanted nothing more than to leave. Yet he also insisted on a 'real grief' at the passing of the ghetto. 'You've lost a world,' he explains, 'a living, vital, throbbing community, with enormous dignity, neighbourliness, fellowship and integrity.' Its demise, moreover, was like the 'death of a living creature': although it had the economic and institutional basis to have survived much longer, the Jewish East End was effectively killed off by the wartime bombing.

Litvinoff has never thought of himself as 'an East End writer' – resisting a category embraced by some of the left-wing Jewish novelists who wrote about Whitechapel in the 1930s and 1940s. He had been on the left, veering about between Zionism and the Young Communist League, but he stands back from Willy Goldman, author of *East End My Cradle* (1940) and *The Light in the Dust* (1944); and he shudders as he remembers the representation of Jewish Whitechapel offered in Simon Blumenfeld's *Jew Boy* (1935), screeching, "Twenty to eight!' in horrified mockery of the bawling mother who wakes the work-shy hero in the opening paragraph of that crudely realist novel. The settlement that kept returning to his mind through the post-war decades demanded a different kind of witness.

Litvinoff has long had an eye for the glowing Whitechapel fragment that lights up a wider history. In *Faces of Terror*, a much-praised trilogy of novels about the Russian Revolution and its consequences (initially commissioned by Thames Television as plays that were never made), he started with the 1911 siege of Sidney Street, in which the British authorities shot it out with Latvian Communists who were hoping to finance their revolutionary activities with the 'redistributed' wealth of British capitalists. The first book in the sequence, *A Death Out of Season* (1973), takes the siege and the violently miscarried robbery that precipitated it, and enhances the story with the help of old East End speculation – factually incorrect, but true in an imaginative sense – which turned the fugitives into anarchists and linked their activity to an abortive Tsarist plot to assassinate the British monarch, thereby closing the country to the exiled revolutionaries who gathered there. In the next two books, *Blood on the Snow* (1975) and *The Face of Terror* (1978), Litvinoff projected his company of locally gathered characters through the Russian Revolution and the Stalinist terror. A small, if much-fabled, Whitechapel experience is used to trigger a narrative that travels through the defining events of the early twentieth century.

If Whitechapel gave Litvinoff a day-to-day awareness of distant historical convulsions, it also bequeathed him abiding themes that would outlive the ghetto in which they were found: his sympathy for victims of all kinds and his concern with 'not politics per se, but a kind of morality that is often expressed in politics . . . You couldn't grow up in the Jewish East End without having also lived inside the necessity of that morality.' Unlike many more conventional figures of English fiction, Litvinoff's characters are displaced and often unable to integrate lives that have been broken and scattered by the continental shifts of twentieth-century history. Some have nothing left but hatred and bitterness: Litvinoff designates them 'the thin sour fruit of the ghetto'.[16] Others are threadbare idealists, overtaken and defeated by history's corruption of their cause. They crackle with the 'neurotic tension' of those who feel alien wherever they are. Litvinoff's Europe is seen from the quayside and prison cell: it has more frontiers than reassuring landscapes, and its cities are known less by their stately monuments than by tenement blocks and the shabby cafés in which 'all the world's foreigners' gather.

Halfway up Princelet Street, where, in 1992, one house was still a battered Bengali leather factory while the next glowed as an architectural icon restored and re-Englished by New

Georgian conservationists, we stepped through double doors into another pocket of forgotten time: a Huguenot weaver's house that had been converted to the tiny synagogue of a since-dispersed East European congregation. Litvinoff, who had not been here before, peered around in an amazed shock of recognition. Searching through the names painted on the balcony for families he might have known, he mutters that this dark place is indeed 'full of ghosts'. We climbed upstairs to visit the garret that was once home to David Rodinsky, an eccentric and, by posthumous reputation, somewhat prophetic figure who stayed on as caretaker after the closure of the synagogue. A student of remote and archaic languages who used to wander the streets pressing coins into the hands of the poor, Rodinsky was rumoured to have walked out one day and vanished, leaving behind the jumbled and evocatively time-warped room that had recently been cleared out in the interests of architectural restoration.

This gentrifying myth of the dematerializing immigrant was of little interest to Litvinoff, who understands Jewish disappearance in the incomparably greater terms demanded by the Holocaust. Such is the brute historical fact that really distinguishes Litvinoff's post-war rendering of Whitechapel, giving his response to the death of the ghetto a character quite distinct from merely sentimental nostalgia or the frisson sought out by 'Ripperologists' and 'psychogeographers' in more recent years. As Litvinoff explained at an Anglo-Israeli Writers' Symposium in Israel in 1966, the Holocaust had the effect of 'generalizing' his memories of Whitechapel, turning them into recollections of an extinguished 'tribal community'.

If the war re-formed Litvinoff's memories of Whitechapel, remembered now as part of the murdered Yiddish culture of Eastern Europe, it also reinforced his distance from the British mainstream. In explanation, he refers back to events that took place at a distant quayside during the Second World War. Litvinoff was stationed with the Pioneer Corps in Ulster when he heard about the *Struma*, an old cargo boat that had left Romania in December 1941, packed with nearly eight hundred Jewish men, women and children who had made their way to the Dalmatian coast in desperate flight from the Nazis.

Having broken down at sea, this overloaded vessel was eventually towed into Istanbul harbour, where its passengers hoped to disembark so that they could travel overland to Palestine, but the Turkish authorities wouldn't let them off the boat unless the British agreed to admit them to Palestine. Cabled in London, the British Colonial Office would have none of it, declaring the fugitives to be 'illegal immigrants' who 'exceeded the quota'. There were to be no concessions, even for the children. After weeks of hellish wrangling, a Turkish warship towed the *Struma* out of Istanbul harbour and abandoned it in the Black Sea, where in February 1942 it exploded and sank with only a single survivor. Many years later, it would emerge that the *Struma* had been torpedoed by a Soviet submarine acting on Stalin's orders. For Litvinoff, this shameful episode had the shocking effect of 'blurring the frontiers of evil'. The officials in London had become 'Hitler's accomplices' and there was only one conclusion to be drawn: 'Never again would I be able to think of myself as an Englishman, or face uncertainty about my identity.'

So Whitechapel lived on in Litvinoff's mind: not just an evocative lost world but an abrasive insistence on inconvenient truths and awkward questions. His most notorious clash with the English mainstream occurred in January 1951, when Sir Herbert Read invited him to perform at an inaugural poetry reading for the Institute of Contemporary Arts. A long-standing and even devout admirer of T. S. Eliot (he would later claim to have 'needed Eliot as a man needs food'[17]), he had been horrified when, in 1950 or so, he bought a copy of Eliot's recently published *Selected Poems* and opened it to find that it included a number of anti-Semitic verses written before the war. In the 1920s and 1930s, Litvinoff remarked, anti-Semitism was more or less endemic, but he was appalled, only a few years after the Holocaust, to find Eliot republishing his lines about 'money in furs' and the 'protozoic slime' of Bleistein's 'lustreless, protrusive eye'. After reading the book on the tube, Litvinoff had gone home and written a poem entitled 'To T. S. Eliot' – indeed, he remembered how it seemed to write itself in less than an hour. When he got up to announce the poem at the ICA reading, he was mortified to hear Read say, 'Oh good, Tom's just come in.' He nearly faltered when he looked up in time to catch Eliot's welcoming smile, but decided that 'the poem had a right to exist', and read it to the packed but silent room:

> So shall I say it is not eminence chills
> but the snigger from behind the covers of history,
> the sly words and the cold heart
> and footprints made with blood upon a continent?[18]

'All hell broke out' as soon as Litvinoff had finished. Sir Herbert Read, whom Litvinoff describes, with a sharp East End eye for compromise, as 'the anarchist knight', remarked that, had he known in advance, he would never have allowed the poem to be read: 'I have known Tom Eliot as a friend for many years and there is nothing at all to justify this crude and unprovoked attack.' Litvinoff's unpublished account of this event tells how Stephen Spender stepped in to say, 'As a poet as Jewish as Litvinoff, I deeply resent this slander.' David Gascoyne also rose to 'express dismay and amazement at the obscenity that had just been committed'. Shouted down as he tried to explain himself, Litvinoff decided that he couldn't just slink away, so he went and sat next to his wife as the storm raged. He admits to feeling 'a kind of regret about it . . . about the circumstances'. He also remembers Eliot getting up to leave, and one member of his adoring, dumb-struck entourage glancing at Litvinoff on the way out and spluttering in helpless outrage, 'Good God! He's with a beautiful girl!'

Litvinoff went home shaken. And that night his telephone kept ringing. Reuters had put the story on the wire and papers all over the world wanted to know more. Dannie Abse, who was at the reading, heard T. S. Eliot mutter, 'It's a good poem, it's a very good poem,'[19] but that judgement was not widely shared at the time. Indeed, Litvinoff found himself 'stigmatized as a talentless younger poet trying to achieve notoriety by attacking an eminent poet'.

His criticism of T. S. Eliot was sharply condemned on the letters page of the *Jewish Chronicle*, and there were further objections in 1960, when he published *The Lost Europeans*. The first to appear under his own name, this novel was concerned with Jews going back to post-war Berlin. People objected to its portrayal of Jewish hate, its supposedly tactless revival of animosities that were best let lie, and its use of homosexuality to suggest the artificiality of relationships in that guilty but already forgetful and divided city. Asked about these condemnations, Litvinoff told a joke. Two Jews are lined up in front of a firing squad and one of them starts protesting about his rights. He demands a last cigarette and the blindfold to which he is also entitled. But his companion takes him by the sleeve and begs him, in a pacifying tone, not to make trouble. Perhaps that was always how established Anglo-Jewry's advice sounded to the rude and noisy East European newcomers of the Whitechapel ghetto.

Yet, for a while, Litvinoff prospered. The film rights to *The Lost Europeans* were bought by Wolf Mankowitz, even though the film, which was to have starred Dirk Bogarde, never got made. There was a time when home was a six-bedroomed house in Abbots Langley, Hertfordshire, with a Swiss maid and a smart car in the drive. In 1966, Litvinoff told the Anglo-Israeli Writers' Symposium in Tel Aviv that he was content to live among generally 'mild, tolerant English people' in 'an urbanized English village' where he was 'not conscious of segregation from my neighbours'.[20] But while his second novel, *The Man Next Door* (1968), was all about English country life, it was an anti-idyllic affair hardly calculated to flatter those neighbours. It concerns a Jewish family who, having made good in the Whitechapel lingerie trade ('Alluriste Ltd'), move into Maidenford, a village that would have been quite charming were it not for the vast sausage factory that, in a reprise of the Smithfield market offal heap next to the Cordwainers Technical College, fills the air with the heavily symbolic stench of pork.

The arriving newcomers are studied by their neighbour, a middle-aged and all but redundant vacuum-cleaner salesman named Harold Bollam. Like Litvinoff, Bollam has spent time in West Africa and he comes equipped with the degenerate attitudes Litvinoff had found among some of his fellow officers during the war: men who humped their way through hot and sodden nights on long-suffering black girls and then woke up to enact a grotesque parody of colonial domination on the other unfortunate natives they were saving from barbarism. Bollam is a pastoralist of the racist variety, for whom the sight of 'pure countryside' communicates 'a deeply religious feeling as if you'd been cleansed through and through', and he greets his infuriatingly successful new neighbours with an escalating campaign of rape, arson and murder.

Litvinoff had been enthusiastic about Israel when it was formed in 1948. He remembers seeing the new state as a phoenix rising from the ashes of six million innocent victims. But his most sustained engagement with the post-war Jewish cause was actually prompted by a different experience some eight years later.

During a party at the London home of Litvinoff and Cherry Marshall, the actor David de Keyser announced that women in the USSR had 'absolutely nothing . . . No make-up, underwear, hats – not even a fashion magazine. They're starving for a glimpse of the Western world.'[21]

It was November 1955 and de Keyser had just visited the USSR with the Old Vic theatre company. His testimony prompted Marshall, who was at that time running one of the leading model agencies in London, and Litvinoff to imagine taking the first Western fashion show to the USSR. As Marshall would remark in her memoir *The Cat Walk* (1978), trade with Russia was customarily associated with 'heavy machinery and farm implements' and western clothes had hardly been seen in the Soviet Union since the revolution of 1917: 'We reckoned they must be pretty curious about fashion after forty years in proletarian drab, shoddier and more shapeless than had been our wartime utility.' Enquiries were made at the Russian Chamber of Commerce in London, which soon came back with the news that the Russian authorities were pleased with the idea. Indeed, they were, as Litvinoff remembers, 'amazingly happy about it'.

Marshall made an exploratory visit to Russia and adjusted her plans accordingly. Before going, she had envisaged showing a collection of 'practical, serviceable outfits geared as well as possible to their way of life'. But, like so many Western visitors before her, she found Russian women to be 'pathetically drab'. They had no make-up beyond perhaps the barest trace of lipstick and their clothes were 'so old-fashioned that I couldn't place them in time'. Marshall decided that they would really appreciate an unrestrained 'spectacle' of 'gay, colourful, feminine fashion', and certainly not another display of 'utility' clothing. So, in June 1956, she and six of her London models headed east, sponsored by the London Model House Group and various other British fashion companies Marshall had tempted into backing this 'tremendous publicity venture'. Emanuel Litvinoff squeezed himself on board as Cherry Marshall's 'business manager', added to the list at the last minute in case misunderstandings were caused by his surname, which was not just Jewish but coincidentally the same as that of Stalin's late ambassador to the USA and former Commissar of Foreign Affairs.

The 'English fashion delegation' flew to Helsinki in a plane (which the press quickly dubbed 'Cleopatra's Barge') stuffed with nylon stockings, model suits and dresses, frivolous lingerie, swimsuits, handbags and costume jewellery. Here they were picked up by their Russian hosts and flown on to Moscow, where the Soviet authorities had erected a special pavilion for them in Gorky Park, together with a huge catwalk, where the models would do their thing to the accompaniment of specially requested music by Ivor Novello.

The show proved vastly popular. Some 200,000 paying visitors were counted into the accompanying exhibition, housed in the pavilion, and crowds of over 60,000 people saw the models at work, greeting each one with rapturous applause as she stepped out on the catwalk. The Soviet authorities told Marshall that this was the most successful foreign trade show ever mounted. There would be little in return for the British fashion manufacturers who had helped cover the cost of this crusade against Soviet drabness. Not a single order was forthcoming from Russia, but the designs were enthusiastically stolen even if they weren't bought. Litvinoff recalls how Russians used to sneak into the pavilion at night, examining and measuring the clothes exhibited in the foyer with a view to creating copies for what was evidently going to be a huge black market.

Official outings were laid on for the 'English fashion delegation', who found themselves toasting their hosts at formal receptions ('We got squiffier and squiffier') and filing past the mummified corpses of Stalin and Lenin in Red Square, where they were led into an 'uncontrollable fit of nervous giggling' by the Welsh model Joy Slape. Emanuel Litvinoff participated in these light-hearted 'extensions' of the fashion show. Writing shortly after the trip, he remembered his wife gazing at the 'striped and star-studded' onion domes of St Basil's Cathedral and declaring 'What fun it would be to reproduce one in striped silk and take it for a walk down Bond Street.'[22] At one heavily lubricated reception involving representatives of such bodies as the All Union Chamber of Commerce, he even managed to warn the Russians that buying Western fashions would only put them on a treadmill: once started, 'it's got to be new fashions every year even if it bankrupts you'.

Yet the English fashion delegation's 'business manager' also ventured behind the official scenes on an excursion of his own. A little earlier in the year, on 4 April 1956, the Polish-Yiddish Communist newspaper *Folkshtimme* had published details of the imprisonment, torture and persecution of Soviet Jewish intellectuals, and the war against Jewish culture that had been under way between 1948 and 1952, when Stalin had many of the leading Yiddish artists and writers in the Soviet Union executed by firing squad.[23] Litvinoff may not have known the full story at the time, but he was well aware of the blatantly anti-Semitic trial of Rudolf Slansky in Czechoslovakia in 1952. He also knew about the notorious 'Doctors' Plot' – a fictional conspiracy of Jewish doctors bent on killing leading Communists (allegedly at the instigation of 'international Jewish and Zionist organizations'), which was 'discovered' in January 1953 and would almost certainly have led to more executions – and perhaps also a wholescale deportation of Russian Jewry to the Soviet Far East – had Stalin not died later that same year.

It had been possible to imagine that this resurgence of official anti-Semitism would come to an end with Stalin's death, but for Litvinoff among others the question remained open, to say the least. Much of the direct persecution had ended, but nothing was being done to restore Jewish life in the USSR. Indeed, many forms of political discrimination remained in place and Soviet Jews were still isolated and under intense pressure to assimilate.

News of Litvinoff's approaching visit to Moscow had reached Dr Nahum Goldmann, recently elected President of the World Zionist Organization. Hoping to be invited to Moscow by the city's Chief Rabbi, Dr Schlieffer, so that he could enquire into the condition of Soviet Jewry, Goldmann had given Litvinoff a letter, asking him to deliver it to the Chief Rabbi during the course of his visit. Litvinoff began by making enquiries through the British Ambassador, Sir William Hayter, with whom he remembers not getting on at all. Hayter unhelpfully referred him to Soviet officials stationed at the top of the hotel in which the fashion delegation was staying. His request was passed to the Foreign Ministry, which referred him to the All Union Chamber of Commerce, which passed his request to the Ministry of Trade, which passed it back to the Foreign Ministry. Tired of being 'kicked about like a football', he resolved to go to the synagogue himself. Having given notice of his visit, he approached a taxi driver, who helpfully passed him on to a Jewish-looking colleague who was prepared to drive him to the end of the street in which the synagogue was to be found, but no further.

So Litvinoff got out and set off on foot – he still shudders to remember the fashionable clothing he was wearing – and, in only a hundred yards, walked straight into 'the Soviet Jewish problem'. As he approached the Moscow Great Synagogue, he was surrounded by wraiths: a crowd of shockingly derelict Jews, many of them recently released from Siberia and hanging about the synagogue in the desperate hope of hand-outs from the charity box. Horrified, and feeling acutely aware of his luxurious leather shoes, Litvinoff entered the building to be greeted by a nervous attendant, 'a little fat man' who was 'sweating with anxiety'.

Litvinoff stepped in to find a service at its height. His visit coincided with the attendance of some visiting American rabbis, and the swollen congregation of elderly and sobbing Jews was being closely surveyed by two insolent and obvious secret policemen:

It gave me an almost melodramatic feeling of uneasiness. For the rest, it recalled irresistibly the closed chapter of Whitechapel Jewry, when Polish and Russian immigrants crowded the small Working Men's Synagogue off East London's Brick Lane, which is now a near-derelict ironmonger's warehouse, when the salty vigorous Yiddish tongue was the common language of the streets and the tenements, and one could buy loose Russian cigarettes in pennyworths, or a halfpenny portion of sunflower seeds.[24]

As Litvinoff left the synagogue, he found the truth still tottering on the steps outside. He was accosted by starving, stick-like spectres who whispered about 'Siberia, Siberia . . . they starved us there. They drove us with dogs.' Looking at these people who had survived Hitler only to have Stalin turn on them, Litvinoff recognized the faces he had seen in pictures of old Russian ghettos and 'in distant childhood memories of Whitechapel markets where the poor bought subsistence in pennyworths'. He remembers an old lady, her feet wrapped in rags and wearing a man's frayed vest, who asked, 'How is it with the Jews in England?' and then added ominously, 'as long as they live'. Speaking in Yiddish, the anxious attendant told him that things were 'good, good' for Jews in Russia, urging him to go away and not to listen to the others with their exaggerated and 'foolish' allegations. A rather well-dressed man followed him down the street and, speaking through the side of his mouth, guided him into the obscurity of a park, where he declared that the situation of the Jews is 'not good here. Soon there won't be any Jews left.' The point was underlined when he went back to meet the Chief Rabbi, who sat at his desk with three or four intimidating goons lined up against the wall behind him, and dismissed Dr Goldmann's request for an invitation, saying, 'He can come like any tourist.'

By this time, as Litvinoff recalled, 'my imagination was running riot'. And it was not calmed when, shortly after returning from Russia, he went to Paris to visit Manès Sperber, the Galician-born Jewish writer who had once been a high-ranking member of the Communist International. Now among the Soviet regime's fiercest critics, and a scourge of Western fellow-travellers, with their tactical silence about oppression in the Soviet bloc, Sperber was much concerned about the fate of Jews in Russia, fearing a repetition of what had happened in Nazi Germany.

So Litvinoff, who had gone to Russia still hopeful that the Soviet Union's 'Jewish problem' might have been solved by the death of Stalin, returned to London filled with a sense of alarm and determined to do something. He went to see Lord Sieff, of Marks & Spencer, who involved some wealthy Americans, and the British arm of the campaign for Soviet Jewry was launched shortly afterwards. In order to establish the legitimacy of this cause, Litvinoff would have to negotiate his way through the suspicions of people on both sides in the Cold War. He had to keep his distance from right-wing anti-Communists, who would happily have laid claim to his cause, and there were liberal and left-wing thinkers – Litvinoff met Bertrand Russell, Jean-Paul Sartre and many others – who needed to be convinced that he was not just an anti-Communist who had found a convenient new set of clothes.

In March 1958 Litvinoff published the first issue of the *Jewish Observer Newsletter*, relaunched eighteen months later as *Jews in Eastern Europe: A Periodical Survey of Events Affecting Jews in the Soviet Bloc*. Working from an office at 31 Percy Street in London's Fitzrovia, he edited this publication for years, scanning Soviet publications to record the revival of the medieval blood libel against Jews, the discriminatory rules that even banned the baking of unleavened bread, the burning of synagogues, cases of anti-Semitic murder, and the draconian sentences passed against all too many Jewish 'villains', 'parasites' and 'cockroaches'. He mapped the fate of Jewish communities in Russia: a little-known settlement of Mountain Jews at Balkaria, in the High Caucuses, and also the larger colony at Birobidzhan, the so-called 'Jewish Autonomous Region', established during the 1930s in the Soviet Far East, near the border with Manchuria, after a wave of earlier settlement supported by financial assistance (and even some emigration) from Jewish organizations in the West.

Though heavily persecuted by Stalin (the Jewish political and cultural leadership in the region was purged in 1937 and again in 1948), Birobidzhan would be much cited in post-war Soviet propaganda as proof that Soviet Jews had no reason to fear the future or, more to the point, dream of moving to Israel. As Khrushchev told a French reporter, Birobidzhan colony, which was actually situated in a bleak and inhospitable land of swamps, was a 'remarkable gift' of a place where 'tilling the soil . . . is pure joy. There's water and sun. There are immense forests, luscious soil, abundant minerals and rivers teeming with fish.'[25] Meanwhile, anti-Semitic conspiracy theories were being spread in the Arab world, and Israel was repeatedly attacked in articles claiming that Jews who had moved there from Russia were now desperate to return, having discovered what *Sovietskaia Kultura* called 'Hell in the Israeli Paradise'.[26]

Litvinoff was still monitoring this poisonous flow in the early 1970s, when he reported on the appearance of articles that lifted whole paragraphs from anti-Semitic tracts that had been used to trigger murderous pogroms in Tsarist times, reproducing them without change, except that the word 'Jew' had been replaced with 'Zionist'. It was a charge that was proven in 1973, when a French court (before which Litvinoff appeared as an expert witness) convicted the Soviet Embassy in Paris of publishing articles that amounted to an 'incitement to racial hatred and discrimination'.[27]

As editor of *Jews in Eastern Europe* and a journalist who placed some of his stories in the *Guardian* and other publications, Litvinoff shared the cause of Soviet Jewry with the government of Israel. He had contacts with Israeli intelligence, including Shaul Avigur, an elderly founder of Mossad, and much of his data about conditions in the Soviet bloc came directly from sources in Israel's embassy in Moscow. Yet the memory of the Whitechapel ghetto in which he himself had grown up would also come to stand between him and the more zealous champions of the Jewish state. While Israel commanded his loyalty as 'the land of the survivors', he had also, as he explained, always believed that the Jews 'belong intrinsically to the dispersal'. Litvinoff had argued this in the 1940s, but the differences had become exacerbated by August 1966, when he visited Israel to attend what was later described as the first symposium between Anglo-Jewish and Israeli writers.

Here Litvinoff found himself in open confrontation with the Zionist writer Moshe Shamir, who had spoken against the diaspora, insisting that only in Israel could there be 'Jewish trees and Jewish streams and Jewish rivers'.[28] Dismayed by Shamir's suggestion that Israel would 'liquidate the Exile', Litvinoff rejected the suggestion that Jews who were not in Israel were rootless, insisting that even without any geographic centre, the Jews were 'one of the most deeply rooted people in the history of the world'. The roots he cherished were to be found less in Hebrew, the revived language of the Zionist state, than in the Yiddish of Brick Lane, which he once described as 'a yeasty language, alive with experience of sorrow, exile, the knockabout humour of the market place; the language of Jewish peasants, artisans, and the emerging industrial proletariat dwelling in semi-feudal poverty in the vast territorial ghetto known as the Pale of Settlement'.

Like other diasporic Jews, including A. M. Klein, the Montreal poet who had visited Israel in 1949 and worried about the 'hard intransigence' of the writers he met there (he recalled a 'crew of chauvinists' who now yearned for 'the negation of the diaspora'[29]), Litvinoff was dismayed to find this tradition now held in contempt by secular Israelis, who spurned Yiddish as a stigma: 'a language of pedlars, of people who cringed, who were afraid of dogs and policemen and "goyim"'. This was the question that Litvinoff put to the 'dogmatic Zionist ideologists' who thought like Shamir: if you turn your back on the humour, the culture and the humanitarian values of the European exile, then what will your state become?

Litvinoff stayed with those values, exemplified by many of the works he would later gather in his *Penguin Book of Jewish Short Stories* (1979) – including those of Isaac Babel, who was once, as Litvinoff's mother had remembered, to be seen selling his stories on the pavement in the marketplace of Odessa. His disagreement with the more extreme Israeli Zionists grew as time passed. In his campaign against Soviet anti-Semitism, Litvinoff had repeatedly attacked the Soviet equation of Zionism with Nazism, especially a foul and much-repeated allegation, first 'publicly' aired during Israel's trial of Adolf Eichmann in 1960, that, in order to drive Jews to Palestine,

Zionists had actually assisted the Nazis in their slaughter of Jews in East Europe.[30]

Yet his last-published novel, a thriller entitled *Falls the Shadow* (1983), points in exactly that scandalous direction. It tells the story of a distinguished and apparently good Israeli citizen who is gunned down in the street and then found to have been a Nazi concentration camp officer who had escaped by stealing the identity of one of his victims. The idea of the Nazi Jew has become a formulaic cliché in recent decades (it has even turned up in ITV's television drama 'Inspector Morse'). But with Litvinoff it marks a reversal of a deeply shocking kind. There would be no Israeli edition of *Falls the Shadow*. Litvinoff knew that his book would be found provocative, but he wrote it because he was worried by the way Israel was by this time invoking the memory of the Holocaust to justify outrages of its own. Had he not written the book before September 1982, when the Israeli Minister of Defence, Ariel Sharon, consented, at the least, to the Christian Falangist massacre of Palestinians at the Sabra and Shatila refugee camps in Beirut, it would, as he once told me (long before Sharon became Israel's prime minister), have been even stronger.

There are writers who seem to choose their themes for strategic reasons – skipping from one massive historical event to another in order to demonstrate their command of a world that is rarely larger than their ability to endow it with significance. A year or so before our walk through Whitechapel, Martin Amis had chosen to revisit the Holocaust and, in *Time's Arrow* (1991), to throw time into reverse so that the gas ovens in Nazi concentration camps actually gave life to their murdered 'victims'.

Litvinoff declared himself horrified by the thought of this conceit. His themes have the heavy and perhaps old-fashioned quality of obsessions, curses, responsibilities that he is sometimes unable to shoulder. Sitting in the Market Café on Fournier Street, he recalled the unfinished work, the destroyed and discontinued manuscripts, the hundred ways he had found of cutting himself down from behind. Then he shrugged and repeated Orwell's observation that every life feels like a failure when seen from inside: 'I didn't have the ambition and drive you need if you want to be a noted author.'

Yet it was not entirely his fault that his experience could not easily be tailored into a steadily advancing literary career. As he once explained, the 'proletarian' life of Jewish Whitechapel had scarcely prepared him to get on even with the more 'deracinated' and flexible European Jews who would later turn up in London as refugees from Hitler – stylish, urbane and often strikingly 'erudite' newcomers who 'swam in the mainstream of European culture', and only needed a period of acclimatization to adjust themselves.[31] Certainly, this kind of 'failure' has been the lot of more than one writer from the inter-war Jewish East End. I mentioned Roland Camberton, whom Litvinoff thought he had probably last seen wearing a smart suit and disappearing, perhaps with some relief, into a job at Reader's Digest or some other such organization.

Camberton's novel *Rain on the Pavements* (published by John Lehmann in 1951) features a character named 'Uncle Jake'. Known as the 'bad lad' of the family, he had resisted both work and marriage, and spent his time talking socialism and anarchy, using his 'mortgaged bicycle' to pedal back and forth between the public library and innumerable meetings of left-wing political parties. Irreligious, unhoused and a 'perpetual student', Uncle Jake ends up as an education officer in the RAF: married with two children, living on the base and keeping his distance from London and the disavowed projects of his youth, including the single novel he had managed to get written and published ('a heart-breaking business undertaken in hopelessly unfavourable conditions') before giving up. Entitled *Failure*, this 'thin, ill-printed, yellow-wrapped volume' had proved entirely true to its name. It had sold only 300 copies, one of which could still be found at the British Library, providing unread testimony to the lost world of pre-war Jewish Hackney: 'the labour exchanges, the public libraries, the parks, the bed-sitting rooms, rain on the pavements, fog over the railway yards, and Uncle Jake in an old mackintosh cycling immortally, eternally, towards dreams more real than the reality in which they had been forgotten'.[32]

Litvinoff shrugged again, saying that one of the reasons he had devoted so much energy to the campaign for Soviet Jewry was because he didn't feel that his literary writing was an adequate justification for his existence. 'I suppose I've never stopped failing the scholarship,' he said, remembering those distant years, just up the road, at Wood Close School.

We walked on past the gaunt bulk of Hawksmoor's Christ Church, too late to investigate the old gentlemen's lavatory in front of the church steps: an underground amenity which had been bought as a potential wine bar by an Asian entrepreneur at the end of the 1980s and was then in sporadic service as an experimental art space run under the name of 'Strike'. Down near the southern end of Brick Lane, we turned east into Old Montague Street. This, as Litvinoff remarked, had once been the very heart of Jewish Whitechapel, and its vivid life has been transferred into his novels, where children still throw balls at old tin cans, bald mongrels wander about and the 'melancholy strain of evening prayers drifts across from the synagogue'.[33] In the *Faces of Terror* trilogy, a down-at-heel anarchist bookseller named Hoffman has his shop here, selling revolutionary literature to a shabby clientele that includes Special Branch detectives trying to pass as working-class intellectuals and Russian Embassy officials who come to keep an eye on émigrés considered to be 'the most dangerous agitators in Europe'.

Hoffman's shop is the site of heated argument between the anarchist tradition that was once so strong in the Jewish East End and the Bolshevik terror that would soon enough stamp it into the ground.

Here, as on Fuller Street, the evocative names of Green Dragon Yard and Black Lion Yard were preserved on brand-new street signs, but nothing else was left. 'There's no point going any further,' said Litvinoff, as the past evaporated in front of him. Yet we persisted, heading in the direction of one remaining place where Hoffman's struggle continues. We passed Whitechapel library, where Litvinoff had unveiled the blue plaque to the poet and artist Isaac Rosenberg, and turned into Angel Alley – an infamous slum in Victorian times, but now only squeezed by the expanded Whitechapel Art Gallery. At the end of this narrow way, we stepped through a cave-like entrance into a building that resounded with the noise of thrashing printing machines. The walls of the tightly curved staircase were covered with posters advertising diverse liberationist causes, and above that we stepped into the Freedom Bookshop – another tight little room, where the spirit of Kropotkin lives on.

Litvinoff had demonstrated that it is possible to straddle different eras and continents as you walk down a city street. But he now assumed the surprised look of a man who has suddenly been kidnapped by his own imagination. The books and pamphlets were piled high all around him. They expounded the anarchist theory of organization, and traced the belea-guered practice of mutual aid through the Spanish Civil War and then on into such unlikely refuges as allotments, holiday camps and alternative business networks. One offered a critique of the green theory of deep ecology, recommending that the plane trees of London – those purely decorative 'symbols of moral superiority' that Litvinoff sees from his own window over Mecklenburgh Square – should be uprooted and replaced by apples, which, in Henry Thoreau's phrase, are surely 'the most civilized of all trees'.

After pondering this unexpected place, Litvinoff approached the man behind the desk and asked for news of his old friend Alex Comfort, known here for what he was before 1972, when he turned his anarchism into a bestselling primer of carnal pleasures, *The Joy of Sex*.[34] Seeing a stack of imported books by George Woodcock, then still thriving as the grand old man of Canadian literature, he remembered another quayside proposition: when Woodcock was leaving for Canada, he had invited Litvinoff and his wife to join him in the anarchist literary commune he hoped to establish there.

After glancing at his watch and announcing that he had to meet his young son from school, Litvinoff remarked that he felt as if he had been in 'an extraordinarily intense dream. You could get home and find that the place you had just been had never existed.' Then he vanished into the underground at Aldgate East.

Patrick Wright

Notes

1. Emanuel Litvinoff, 'A Jew in England', in J. Sonntag (ed.), 'More Jewish – or Less? First Anglo-Israeli Dialogue', Special Issue, *Jewish Quarterly*, Spring 1967, p. 8. This introduction incorporates material from my earlier article about Litvinoff: see 'Ghetto Blaster', *Guardian Weekend*, 27 March 1993, pp. 16–23. A shorter version was published in Iain Sinclair (ed.), *London: City of Disappearances* (London: Hamish Hamilton, 2006), pp. 233–53. I have drawn on interviews with Emanuel Litvinoff held in November 1992, February 2002 and June 2007. I have also included quotations from unpublished manuscripts borrowed from Litvinoff, including *Travels in a Mind Machine*, an autobiographical sequel to *Journey Through a Small Planet*.

2. 'The World in a Room' was written for Thames Television's 'Armchair Theatre' and broadcast on 22 June 1970.

3. Emanuel Litvinoff, 'My East End Tenement', *Listener*, Vol. LXX, No. 1793, 8 August 1963, p. 199.

4. Litvinoff, 'A Jew in England', p. 8.

5. The United Workmen's and Wlodowa Synagogue was at 21 Cheshire Street, London E1, from 1901 to 1987.

6. Emanuel Litvinoff, 'They Made a Jew of Me', *Jewish Chronicle Literary Supplement*, 14 December 1973.

7. Hilaire Belloc, 'The Sea-Wall of the Wash', in *Hills and the Sea* (London: Methuen, 1906), p. 104.

8. G. K. Chesterton, *Heretics* (1905), in *The Collected Works of G. K. Chesterton*, Vol. 1 (San Francisco: Ignatius Press, 1986), p. 62.

9. Emanuel Litvinoff, *Journey Through a Small Planet* (London: Michael Joseph, 1972), p. 30.

10. Litvinoff, 'A Jew in England', p. 9.

11. Litvinoff, 'They Made a Jew of Me', p. vii.

12. Emanuel Litvinoff, *Conscripts: A Symphonic Declaration* (London: Favil Press, 1941).

13. Emanuel Litvinoff, *The Lost Europeans* (London: Heinemann, 1960), pp. 92–3.

14. Louis Golding, *To the Quayside* (London: Hutchinson, 1954), p. 222.

15. Louis Golding, *The Bare Knuckle Breed* (London: Hutchinson, 1952), p. 13.

16. Litvinoff, *The Lost Europeans*, p. 171.

17. Quoted from Raymond Gardner, 'Behind the Covers of History', *Guardian*, 21 May 1973.

18. 'To T. S. Eliot' is collected in Emanuel Litvinoff, *Notes for a Survivor* (Newcastle: Northern House, 1973).

19. Dannie Abse, *A Poet in the Family* (London: Hutchinson, 1974), p. 203.

20. Litvinoff, 'A Jew in England', p. 12.

21. Cherry Marshall, *The Cat Walk* (London: Hutchinson, 1978), p. 78.

22. Emanuel Litvinoff, 'A Visit to Moscow', *Midstream*, Autumn 1957, pp. 2–4, 102–6.

23. Emanuel Litvinoff (ed.), *Jews in Eastern Europe: A Periodical Survey*

of Events Affecting Jews in the Soviet Bloc, No. 1. Mid-September 1959, p. 27. For a detailed account of the campaign for Soviet Jewry, see Yaacov Ro'i, *The Struggle for Soviet Jewish Emigration 1948–1967* (Cambridge: Cambridge University Press, 1991).

24. Litvinoff, 'A Visit to Moscow', p. 4.

25. Khrushchev's interview with Serge Groussard was published in *Le Figaro* on 9 April 1958, and quoted in the *Jewish Observer Newsletter*, No. 2, July 1958, pp. 5–7.

26. Ibid., p. 7.

27. See Emanuel Litvinoff (ed.), *Soviet Anti-Semitism: The Paris Trial* (London: Wildwood House, 1974).

28. For this and the following quotations, see Emanuel Litvinoff, 'The Problem of Survival', in J. Sonntag (ed.), 'More Jewish – or less? First Anglo-Israeli Dialogue', Special Issue, *Jewish Quarterly*, Spring 1967, pp. 43–6.

29. A. M. Klein, 'The Dangers of Success' (18 March 1949), *Beyond Sambation: Selected Essays and Editorials, 1928–1955* (Toronto: University of Toronto Press, 1982), pp. 333–5.

30. See Litvinoff's 'Introduction' to *Soviet Anti-Semitism: The Paris Trial*, p. 4.

31. Litvinoff, 'A Jew in England', p. 10.

32. Roland Camberton, *Rain on the Pavements* (London: Lehmann, 1951), p. 135.

33. Emanuel Litvinoff, *A Death Out of Season* (London: Michael Joseph, 1973), p. 184.

34. For a consideration of Litvinoff's connection with British anarchy see Valentine Cunningham, 'Litvinoff's Room: East End Anarchism', in H. Gustav Klaus and Stephen Knight (eds), *'To Hell with Culture': Anarchism and Twentieth-Century British Literature* (Cardiff: University of Wales Press, 2005), pp. 141–61.

Note on the Text

Journey Through a Small Planet was first published by Michael Joseph in 1972. With the exception of a few minor corrections, the text is unchanged.

Appended articles/poems

'Prologue: The Day the World Came to an End' was written shortly after the end of the Second World War and is previously unpublished.

'A Jew in England' was published in J. Sonntag (ed.), 'More Jewish – or Less? First Anglo-Israeli Dialogue', Special Issue, *Jewish Quarterly*, Spring 1967, p. 8.

'A Long Look Back' was published in the *Anglo-Jewish Association Quarterly*, incorporating the *Jewish Monthly*, Vol. 5, No. 3, September 1959.

'To T. S. Eliot' was first published in *Poetry and Poverty*, Vol. I, 1953. It was reprinted in Litvinoff's *Notes for a Survivor* (Newcastle: Northern House, 1973).

Further Reading

Poems

Conscripts: A Symphonic Declaration (1941)
The Untried Soldier (1942)
A Crown for Cain (1948)
Notes for a Survivor (1973)

Novels

The Lost Europeans (1960)
The Man Next Door (1968)
A Death Out of Season (1973)
Blood on the Snow (1975)
The Face of Terror (1978)
Falls the Shadow (1983)

Memoirs/Short Stories

Journey Through a Small Planet (1972)

Edited Books

Soviet Anti-Semitism: The Paris Trial (1974)
The Penguin Book of Jewish Short Stories (1979)

Websites

www.emanuel-litvinoff.com
www.patrickwright.net

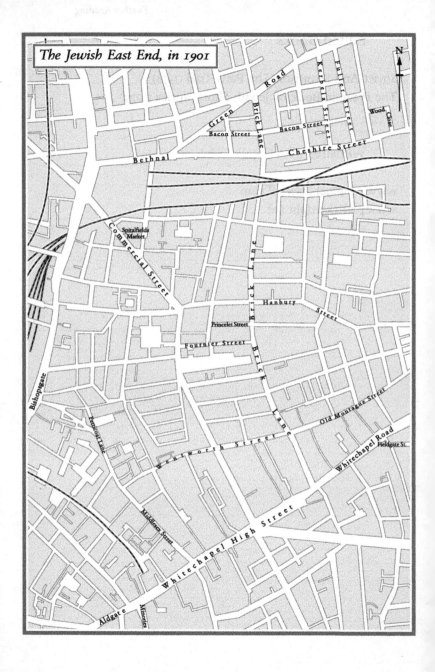

The Jewish East End, in 1901

N

Journey Through a Small Planet

For
Sarah
and
in memory of
Pinny,
and especially now, for my youngest son,
Aaron Emanuel Litvinoff

Contents

Author's Note

Until I was sixteen I lived in the east London borough of Bethnal Green, in a small street that is now just a name on the map. Almost every house in it has gone and it exists, if at all, only in the pages of this book. It was part of a district populated by persecuted Jews from the Russian Empire and transformed into a crowded East European ghetto full of synagogues, backroom factories and little grocery stores reeking of pickled herring, garlic sausage and onion bread. The vitality compressed into that one square mile of overcrowded slums generated explosive tensions. We were all dreamers, each convinced it was his destiny to grow rich, or famous, or change the world into a marvellous place of freedom and justice. No wonder so many of us were haunted by bitterness, failure, despair.

When I was about twenty, I tried to recreate something of this in a novel written at fever heat in dozens of cheap exercise books. Not knowing what else to do, I sent it to my old elementary school headmaster, who returned it with a stern note criticizing its unhealthy preoccupation with sex and squalor. Returning from six years of war, I carried the MS into the backyard and burned it page by page. The world it sought to describe had been bombed into rubble. Those of us who survived and were still young were moving eagerly into the universe of the future and had no wish to look back at the retreating past. I made two more false starts at an East End novel but finally said goodbye to all that with a short story significantly called 'The Day the World Came to an End'.

After many years the Swedish writer Alvar Alsterdal asked me to take him round the Jewish East End. One sunny afternoon, in no more than a mood of mild curiosity, we drove there from my house in Hertfordshire. The place seemed faded, nondescript, much like any other poor district of London at first sight. But as we proceeded on foot through the once familiar streets the change was startling. Clumps of Muslim men stood aimlessly on corners and there was a curious absence of women. Shrill, eerie music wailed in the heat of the afternoon. The odour of spices mingled with the stench of drains. Skinny little girls with enormous, solemn black eyes sat on doorsteps nursing babies. Outside a cinema crudely painted posters of veiled ladies and jewelled rajahs advertised a film from the sub-continent of India. Stubborn survivals of the past existed in the form of one or two small Jewish bakeries, or shops selling cigarettes, lemonade and long-forgotten brands of boiled sweets; but instead of the old Yiddish newspapers on the counters there were others printed in Urdu. In Old Montague Street, the very heart of the original Jewish quarter, nothing was left of the synagogue but a broken wooden door carved with the Lion of Judah.

The tenement I grew up in had somehow survived, shrunken by time but otherwise unchanged – the same broken tiles in the passage, the same rickety stairs, the pervasive smell of cats. I took my friend up to the first-floor landing window to show him the small yard with its overflowing dustbin. That, too, had not changed. Quite suddenly, a vivid memory returned. I was twelve years old: the news had come that once again I had failed the scholarship. Outside it was raining. I sat on the window ledge and carved my initials in the wood. When I looked, they were still there, jagged and irregular: 'E.L.'

The door of my old apartment opened and for one moment

I expected to see that same unhappy, resentful boy emerge to wander disconsolately into the street. A shabby, elderly man came out carrying a bucket full of refuse. He stared at us mistrustfully.

'Are you gennelmen from the Sanit'ry Department of the Tahn 'All?' he asked.

I felt indescribably bereaved, a ghost haunting the irrecoverable past. That evening when I returned to Hertfordshire I began a memoir, 'My East End Tenement'. This book has grown out of that beginning.

I

Ancestors

Although Mark Golombek was large, snub-nosed and red-headed, resembling a Ukrainian more than a Jew, he had a woman's dislike of violence. Back home he'd been a shipping clerk. The stevedores on the Odessa waterfront loved nothing better than vodka and a good roughhouse, so he'd been beaten a few times. But the hooligans learned to respect that tongue of his, which could lay about a man like a nine-thonged whip.

Golombek didn't do badly in London. Although work as a clerk was out of the question, him not knowing the language, he hated to be idle. For a time he pushed a barrow for Schwartz, an itinerant greengrocer who later opened a shop in Wentworth Street. Then he found a job as a tailor's presser, married a girl from Poland and settled down to raise a family. Things went well enough until the Kaiser invaded Belgium. Mark's blood boiled at the outrage to peace, but it wasn't a worker's war and he didn't intend to stand for it even if it meant plenty of overtime making khaki. In the pocket of every soldier's tunic that passed under his hissing iron was inserted a handwritten leaflet. Sometimes it read: 'Refuse to fire on your German brothers! Unite for Peace!' Sometimes, under pressure, the message was even more inflammatory: 'Turn your guns on your real enemies! Down with bloodthirsty Capitalism! (Signed) Workers' Committee For International Unity'. In addition to Mark, the Workers' Committee consisted of Gurevich, the glazier, and Cohen, the

upholsterer. The difference in the two messages reflected an
internal ideological struggle. Gurevich and Cohen withheld
the Committee's endorsement from the first message because
of its pacifist implications. For the same reason they refused
the Committee's approval of a small book of poems, *Finster
in Meine Oigen (Darkness Before My Eyes)*, which Mark wrote and
duplicated at his own expense.

Meetings, which were noisy, were generally held in Gurevich's
home in Spitalfields, above the small workshop where the glass
was cut and prepared, ready to be strapped to the frame he carried
on his back as he trudged the streets calling: 'Menjavinder! Menjavinder!' [1] in a high, complaining voice mimicked by all the children
of the neighbourhood. He was a short, emaciated, bandy-legged
young man with nervous hands and a stoop, partly scholarly,
partly a mannerism developed in protecting his brittle load from
slipping out of the frame. Bottle-thick lenses boosted his myopic
vision but created a strange distortion that made his gentle,
earnest eyes seem embalmed in the glass; when he removed
his spectacles one almost expected to find the eye-sockets of
his face empty. There was a Mrs Gurevich who sat in the back
kitchen nursing a puny child, but his principal love was the radical
literature of Diderot, Rousseau, Saint-Simon, Radishchev, Paine,
Locke and Karl Marx, whose abrasive pages had rubbed away his
vision but provided an apt quotation when a fellow member of
the Committee was inclined to argument. Gurevich was a born
conspirator. Slipping messages into military tunics was a strategy
he had devised over a glass of lemon tea in the Jubilee Street
Arbeter Fraint Institute,[2] the Socialist club for foreign Jewish immigrants. He also planted them in library books, placed them among
the leaves of toilet paper in public lavatories, scattered them from
buses, pushed them under doors and sent them through the royal
mails to members of Mr Asquith's war cabinet. But these pedes-
trian methods could not satisfy him and he dreamed of droves

of well-drilled pigeons flying in squadrons to the battlefields, of Nelson's Column painted from base to apex in revolutionary scarlet, of a thousand hidden megaphones trumpeting the battle hymn of freedom from the spires of Westminster Abbey.

Cohen, the upholsterer, third member of the Committee, was merely a disciple. He came from Vilna, the 'Jerusalem' of Poland, and the habit of orthodoxy was so fixed in him that he would never conspire on the Sabbath, which he devoted to prayer at the Machzike Adas synagogue. A bachelor of about thirty, he was worried about his prospects of marriage and spent much of his spare time at the Jewish Shelter in the hope of snaring a suitable virgin newly arrived from some East European *shtetl*.[3] But he had no luck. Perhaps it was the cough that bubbled in his throat, the result, he claimed, of horsehair stuffing and fibres of flock inhaled while filling sofas and mattresses; perhaps his workshop pallor was misunderstood as a deeper sickness, for no robust Jewish virgin ever willingly took a *kranker*, an invalid, for a bed-mate. Whatever the reason, Cohen regarded his enforced celibacy as an injury maliciously inflicted by society.

It was this bitterness which Gurevich fed, contrasting the loneliness of Cohen with the pleasure-sated rich embowered among beautiful corrupt women, offering him the comradeship of misery and the sweet of retribution. But Cohen was only intermittently ardent, the leaflets more often wearing to tatters in his pockets than performing their missionary function, and his principal value to Gurevich was that he provided a majority in the Workers' Committee when it was necessary to outvote the Golombek opposition.

One Sunday after work Cohen collected Mark for a meeting. 'I'll be back for supper,' the latter told his wife.

'I see she's pregnant again,' Cohen said enviously when the two men reached the street. 'Should one bring children into such a world?'

'When the young grow up they will look back at this as a time of barbarians,' Mark prophesied. 'The masters are so crazy with greed that they have begun to tear at one another's flesh.'

Cohen said: 'If I should have a wife and she should tell me, "*Nu*,[4] how about a baby?" I would put on the trousers and go.' He gaped yearningly at the ankles of passing women.

They trudged through the rotting debris of Spitalfields Market, Cohen stooping occasionally to search among the vegetable refuse for pieces of partly edible fruit which he stuffed into his coat pocket. A block from Gurevich's they separated, as a precaution, but met up again outside the glazier's shop, pretending that it was a chance encounter. Cohen knocked softly. The bolt scraped and Gurevich opened the door, beckoning them in with a gesture so absurdly secretive that any suspicious policeman would have walked off with an easy mind. In fact the furtiveness did not arise from fear of the law. Gurevich's old mother sat with her knees spread open before the fire, warming the insides of her thighs. 'Shah, the baby,' she said crossly. They filed sheepishly into the back bedroom, which was also the glazier's study. The place reeked like the body of an unwashed pauper. Books were piled in rickety heaps on the floor and the mantelpiece. Bearded religious Jews peered out of dim photographs on the walls, and there was only one chair and a bed covered with a huge feather bolster. Through the dusty glass of a small window a warehouse reared out of the gaunt and evil night.

An argument immediately broke out, not less intense for being whispered, over the protocol of reading minutes. 'Every meeting should begin by reading previous minutes,' Gurevich insisted. He held an exercise book with tables printed on the back, its pages filled with tiny writing in Yiddish. Mark Golombek disagreed.

Cohen agreed. 'You got to read the minutes,' he coughed,

clearing his throat by spitting into the empty fireplace. As if the matter was thus decided, he produced a half-mouldy apple, pared the rot away with a pocket knife and began to eat. But the argument went on with tactical shifts from procedure to ideology, from ideology to strategy, inevitably becoming deadlocked and personal.

'You're nothing but a dilettante,' said Gurevich. 'A café philosopher. Elegant conversation is for you everything.'

'And you, Gurevich?'

'I'm like Marx. I don't want to interpret the world. I believe in altering it. By revolutionary action.'

Rich blood rose in Mark's square face until it met the flaming red of his hair. 'So tell us how you went out in Kishinev and spat on the Cossacks' horses! Tell again a hundred times how you fasted twenty days in a Siberian prison! Take out your heart, Gurevich, and show the world how it bleeds for freedom, how it suffers!'

The old woman banged on the wall to stop the shouting.

'Please, please!' Gurevich implored. 'Am I insulting you? All I say is we should have action.'

'Action is necessary,' Cohen said.

'Action, yes! Violence, no!' Mark said, and pounded the table with his large fist.

The child next door cried briefly and its grandmother joined in with mournful curses. 'See, Golombek, you woke up the baby,' the glazier said unhappily. 'My wife nags enough.' He plucked distractedly at the loose skin of his forehead. 'Look, with all the leaflets did we save a single life or kill one enemy? A boy in the street, Solly Abramovich, only sixteen years old, didn't I give him your propaganda, the leaflet you wrote? Yet he runs off to the army. They only wipe their backsides with your leaflets, if you'll excuse me. Paper bullets, that's all! Paper bullets.'

Cohen coughed wetly and nodded. 'Every word is true,' he wheezed. 'By my mother's life.'

'Ideas are paper bullets by you?' Mark took out a cigarette and lit it with a trembling hand. He shook the spent match an inch from his adversary's nose. 'Violence! Can you think of nothing else?'

'Bombs are ideas,' Gurevich said, his myopic eyes watering with conviction.

'Bombs to me are impotence, bombs are despair, bombs are the arguments of imbecility.'

'No,' said Gurevich. 'The truth is exactly the opposite. Bombs are the only arguments understood by imbecility. Bombs are the refusal to accept despair. Bombs, Golombek, are the engines of revolution and those who flinch from violence are indeed dilettantes. How do you break down an empire or destroy a tyranny? By asking it politely to abdicate? Trample on tyranny, I say! Spit in its face! Cohen, you've also got an opinion. Why don't you speak up?'

Cohen rocked from side to side, as if trying to shift the question into a more comfortable position in his head. The discussion was beginning to make him uneasy. 'In principle, Gurevich, I think maybe you are right,' he temporized, 'but to be right is not everything. Sometimes it's possible to be right and wrong at the same time. As it says in the Talmud, do not unto others what you would not have others do unto you.'

'And doesn't the Talmud say truth is heavy so people don't like to carry it?'

'A small coin in an empty jar makes a great noise,' said Mark. 'I was also once a *yeshiva*[5] student. I do not understand why we are wasting our time arguing about bombs like Sidney Street anarchists.'

The glazier stood up restlessly and paced the floor. 'I am ashamed because we do nothing,' he said harshly. 'Are we waiting for God?' He glanced at the meek faces of relatives staring solemnly from their picture frames on the damp wallpaper. They were the faces of people who had waited a long time. 'My father coughed up blood when he was only thirty, but he believed God wanted him to spit up pieces of his lungs. God should have such lungs!' Cohen made a nervous gesture, but Golombek didn't notice. 'Men are being slaughtered like beasts, don't you see?' he burst out.

Mark had another try. 'The soldiers are all workers,' he said. 'One day they will realize they are all on the same side. The Germans, the French, the English, the Russians – they will say: "Why are we killing one another? What is it for? Who gains?"'

Gurevich smiled crookedly. 'How shall I write it in the minutes? That Golombek asks us to wait for a miracle?'

Mark was sitting on the pressing table, eating some sandwiches, when the tailor master's wife came to say he was wanted downstairs. The boss glanced angrily at the heap of khaki tunics awaiting the iron and grumbled: 'All right, five minutes.' In the passage was Cohen, still in a working apron, fibres of upholstery flock stuck to his gritty chin by a film of sweat. There was something terribly wrong. He looked sick and the pupils of his eyes were dilated in fright.

'It's Gurevich,' he rasped asthmatically. 'I ran all the way from the workshop. In the middle of dinner. We must finish with the Committee immediately! By a public announcement!'

'What are you talking about, Cohen? What announcement?'

'Leaflets is one thing, but breaking the law –'

Mark looked at him sharply and seized his arm. 'Come in the street,' he hissed. 'You want the whole house to hear?'

Outside in the cobbled roadway some young apprentices

were kicking a ball under the levelled forefinger of Kitchener. A shawled factory girl laboured past with a clumsy parcel and spat at their feet – two able-bodied men who wouldn't fight for the King.

'His missus came,' Cohen said. 'He broke two sheets of glass and singed his eyebrows, the madman! Don't you understand, Gurevich is making a bomb!'

Mark raced upstairs for his coat. The boss was outraged. 'You're going?' he shouted. 'Take my blood!'

'I'll be back soon,' Mark said. The boss seized an armful of tunics, threw them on the floor, and yelled: 'I should live so sure, if I let you come back!' Death was already gnawing at his stomach and he pressed his hand against the pain as he went back to the cutting bench.

The glazier had gone to the *schvitz*,[6] his wife told them. He would bring a catastrophe with his politics. Sometimes the child didn't have enough to eat, and he wanted to save the world. The world would see them all into their graves. Her voice followed them down the street.

At the Russian steam baths elderly men with nothing else to do lounged drowsily in the enervating heat. Mark and Cohen disrobed hurriedly and sat haunch to haunch on the scrubbed bench, awkward in their nudity, Cohen concealing his sex with a handkerchief. 'The steam, it's bad for my chest,' he complained fretfully. 'I'm going. Gurevich is not here.'

'Maybe he's in the hot room,' Mark said.

'I would suffocate in there,' Cohen protested.

Mark went in reluctantly: he was also not fond of heat. It came out in belches from vents in the stone floor and spun coils of boiling vapour around several fat men ritualistically flicking each other with damp towels. Someone said: 'How are you, Golombek? And Malka?' The steam irritated the tender flesh of his lungs and made his eyes smart. He nodded and

moved towards a bench already occupied by a skinny man
whose head drooped on the ridged stem of its spine. The man
raised his naked, defenceless eyes and stared at Mark without
recognition.

'Gurevich,' Mark said. 'It's me.'

Hands groping blindly in the steam, the glazier said: 'Who?'
He could not hear so well without his glasses.

'You know who!' Mark said sharply. 'What is going on? What
are you doing?'

'I am sweating,' was the laconic reply. A lopsided smile. 'It's
good for purifying the system. Even the mind begins to sweat.
The grease runs out, the dirt. Lumps of filth inside are broken
up and are flushed through the skin pores until nothing but
pure, clear water comes through.' He lifted his sinewy arm
and held it out. 'Look! It's purged already. You could drink me
like a river.'

Mark grabbed the slippery limb, but it eluded his grasp and
Gurevich disappeared, trailing a vaporous prophecy. 'Have faith,
Golombek. The end shall justify the means.'

And dare they speak thus to the armies of the doomed?
Mark dressed hastily and emerged into the early darkness of a
wintry afternoon. The street was almost deserted. Gas lamps
flared dimly behind curtained windows. Serge tunics the colour
of shit were piling up on the pressing bench of the workshop
and there would have to be a quick reckoning. He trudged off
grimly and stood a few yards from Gurevich's house. A chill
came off the pavement and numbed his feet, but as long as a
single life stood in danger he could not relinquish the vigil.

Not until the night turned black and frosty did the glazier
reappear. There was a bulge under his coat. Mark called after
him, but he pretended not to hear and walked swiftly away
with the characteristic stoop of his trade, as if a burden of glass
bowed his shoulders. In Aldgate ribald crowds clustered thick as

bluebottles around pubs, pieshops and painted girls. Gurevich was distracted by nothing, merely pressing his arm more tightly against the object concealed in his clothing.

A spasm of panic shook Mark at the thought of what a rough jolt by a passing soldier might cause. He hurried forward and placed a restraining hand on his comrade, who swung round alarmed.

'Go away,' Gurevich said. 'It's none of your business.'

'I'm a member of the Workers' Committee,' Mark said steadily. 'We have collective responsibility. What is under your coat?'

A tipsy lady came between them and placed her plump arms around their shoulders. 'Why ain't you little Yids in khaki?' she asked tenderly. Mark answered her in Yiddish. 'You pox-ridden trollop! Go away and rot!' She nodded, tilted her head coyly, and smiled. 'They'll make a man of yer, love,' she told him.

As he wrenched himself free, Gurevich was already darting through the traffic in the direction of the Minories. In their ideal society, it had been decided, men would exchange the fruits of their labour according to need and comradeship, not for profit. Was Gurevich planning a symbolic act of sabotage against that money factory, the Royal Mint? Resuming pursuit, Mark reflected that if one condoned acts of terrorism then it was not an unworthy target.

As one heard the story later, one was impressed by the glazier's facility for disappearance. First he was there, then there was nothing but an empty street, its silence unmarred even by a footfall. The East End of the time was honeycombed with darkness and Gurevich had the true conspirator's cunning, taking cover in lightless doorways, empty yards and deserted passageways where regiments could lurk in ambush. There was no sign of him or his package at the Mint, nor at the Tower, which, in any case, was patrolled by armed sentries rhythmically pacing the gate, the courtyard, the dry moat and river frontage. Mark turned away despondently, but as he crossed the road he glimpsed his terrorist in a small crowd gathered about a platform on the crest of Tower Hill where once the axe had fallen on the necks of nobles out of favour with the Crown.

'Armageddon is upon us,' the preacher was saying, repeating a sermon popular in those days. '. . . And they shall say in all the highways, Alas! Alas! The virgins and the young men are fallen by the sword.'

'It is done,' Gurevich said peacefully. The light gleamed on his bevelled lenses and he smiled without rancour. 'It was a question of principle, Golombek. There was nothing you could do to stop it. Now let's go home. We will read about it in the papers tomorrow.'

Mark looked at him in panic, then seized on a desperate idea. 'Ha! You think so,' he said, contriving a laugh with difficulty. 'There will be nothing in the papers. Nothing, I tell you!'

Gurevich spread his arms in a gesture of enormous tolerance. 'Such news you don't get every day. We will see how it will be. Look, my friend' – his glance was loving – 'why should we quarrel over a *fait accompli*? Please, we must go! Time is short.'

'Short? Ha! I should live so long!'

'Then they must say *kaddish*[7] for you in twenty minutes.'

'I followed you all the way,' Mark continued rapidly, praying that his tone carried conviction. 'I saw where you put it, and I threw it in the river.'

The glazier turned slowly on his axis and peered at him with myopic distrust. 'You followed me? Am I such a fool? Nonsense!'

'You'll thank me yet,' Mark said. 'I'm giving you back your conscience. Maybe your life, even.' With deliberate nonchalance he willed himself to walk away.

'Stop!' Gurevich screamed. 'You are telling me nothing but lies.'

'If you don't want, don't believe.'

'You think I care so much for life? Is it so precious? I would go tomorrow if it wasn't for my mother.'

'You have a wife, and a child also,' Mark said. 'They also have a right.'

The glazier lifted an anguished face as he trotted by his side. 'Shuva would be glad,' he pleaded. 'She is in love with her cousin. Is it my child, or his?'

There is suffering everywhere, Mark thought, hardening his heart. The sorrows of mankind.

Suddenly, Gurevich broke away and made for Tower Bridge. At first it seemed that the agitated man was contemplating a jump into the river. He ran along the centre of the bridge, made towards the side and stared fixedly down at the dark and freezing water. Then he looked quickly and furtively towards an overhanging parapet. Mark intercepted the glance, saw a small package placed unobtrusively against the metal railing. They both reached it the same time, grabbed simultaneously and wrestled to retain it.

And then he had it and was running away. The parcel felt unnaturally warm: Mark could sense the fearful explosive power inside. Never more frightened in his life, he hoped that if the bomb went off it would kill him instantly, not leave him blinded or otherwise mutilated. Intending to cast it into the water, he ran across the road to the far side of the bridge and was almost there when he tripped. The parcel leaped out of his hands as if propelled by its own dynamism, and Mark lay sprawled and helpless, waiting for the world to shatter. He was nothing special. In a time of many deaths, how could he grumble? Malka was young enough to remarry and the children would bear his seed into the future. But moments passed and nothing happened, only the throbbing of his grazed knee. He got up stiffly. Gurevich's bomb lay on the ground some yards ahead – fragments of splintered glass, a spilled heap of grey powder, wet stains that may have been acid, the broken mechanism of a clock.

'Traitor!' the glazier said. 'Tsarist lackey! Saboteur!' He spat on the pavement and walked away, shoulders hunched.

Mark went home to supper. He kissed his wife and stared for a long time at the sleeping infants. The incident cost him six shillings in wages, quite a tidy sum in those remote days. The war went on, of course, but the Workers' Committee for International Unity never met again and the Revolution – when it came – didn't turn out the way he'd hoped at all.

2

Growing up with Mother

His picture hung on the wall, pink of cheek and red of mouth, tinted masterpiece of the enlarger's art. He had a waxed moustache and eyes that hunted you all over the room, accusing you of being alive. No father was more totally absent: for a long time I wasn't even sure of his name. It was either Max or Mark, and, having brought three sons into the hungry world and planted a fourth, he'd gone back to Russia when I was still sheltering from everyone behind the vast skirt of my towering mother.

Our orphaned condition didn't bother me at all. Fathers – what I'd seen of them – were not much of a bargain. I classed them as an unfriendly species. They stank of sweat and strong tobacco; when they grabbed you in an unwanted embrace their rough beards rasped your skin; and big bad-tempered voices rumbled out of their stomachs like man-made thunder. I looked at my strong, clever and beautiful mother, who in those early days protected us against the whole world, glad for her sake that she was rid of such a creature. She'd been left, pregnant and twenty-two, with nothing but the three of us, a sewing machine and her skill in dressmaking. At first women brought her work as a good deed; they came back for the value. Anything bought in the smart shops along Whitechapel Road wouldn't have the quality or style she'd put into a dress at half the price in order to feed her children. Our own clothes were stitched up from any remnant available, and because our mother insisted on keeping us in long hair we were often annoyingly mistaken for girls. I once climbed on top of the wardrobe and hid for hours to avoid facing the East End Sabbath throng in a sailor suit of bright green velvet. Even worse, she never learned to cut trousers the right shape for a boy and we had the shameful choice of either taking them down to pee or trying to do it through a trouser leg without wetting our shoes and socks. The one thing we really envied in other boys was trousers with proper fly-buttons. Their fathers, if they had them, never came into it.

A lot of the kids in fact were in our position. Some fathers never returned from the war, others had been sent back to Russia and got mixed up in the Revolution. One of the few left behind in our tenement was Benny Zinger's, a twitching grey-faced man who'd made himself too ill to be a soldier smoking hundreds of cigarettes every day and living for weeks on bread and water. There were also wheezing old men and cripples whose legs and arms had been shot off. But as I crept more and more boldly out from behind my mother's skirts, it seemed to me that fathers were becoming more numerous. Unknown men tramped heavily up the stairs, shrieks of excitement came from one or another of the apartments, someone had a party. Next you knew, a boy who'd been running free was led off like a prisoner to school and synagogue classes and smacked if he was rebellious. They always made trouble, these fathers. Women sounded shriller, children wailed, neighbours banged broomsticks on each other's walls and ceilings. It reached a point where the arrival of a stranger at the entrance of the building filled me with panic in case it was our turn for trouble. Even when the newcomer entered turbulently into someone else's life my uneasiness remained. Next it might be the man in the picture, with his sad, sour eyes and waxed moustache, and he would stoop from his great height near the ceiling to rain hard and violent kisses on my only mother.

This was only the middle of the beginning. Perhaps I should

go back a few years earlier. My parents, who travelled from Odessa, the Russian city on the Black Sea, shortly before the 1914 war, were part of a vast migration of Jews fleeing from Tsarist oppression to the dream of America that obsessed poor men all over Europe. The tailors thought of it as a place where people had, maybe, three, four different suits to wear. Glaziers grew dizzy with excitement reckoning up the number of windows in even one little skyscraper. Cobblers counted twelve million feet, a shoe on each. There was gold in the streets for all trades; a meat dinner every single day. And Freedom. That was not something to be sneezed at, either.

But my parents never got to America. According to the mosaic I pieced together from half-hearted fragments over the years, this was why. Early one morning the emigrants were awakened in their foetid sleeping quarters by the sound of foghorns; they hurried on deck and peered eagerly through the mist. Where were the Statue of Liberty, the Brooklyn Bridge, the highest buildings on the earth? A laconic ship's officer – may he die of cholera and his children rot in the womb – said that anybody but a miserly lot of Jew-spawn would know the money they'd paid wouldn't cover the fare on a decent river ferry, never mind passage to New York. All the curses of men and the wailing of women didn't help. They were herded ashore and the sour smell of London choked their nostrils. They recognized it at once. It was the odour of a new Exile.

I was the second son, and by the time I was born America had gone the way of all dreams. My father, a vague recollection of a watch-chain spread across an inhospitable chest, soon followed. Life began for me in bewilderment and terror at the age of three with my first coherent memory, that of moving to our two-roomed flat and tiny kitchen in Fuller Street Buildings, Bethnal Green; with us were our sewing machine and a cart-load of second-hand furniture. I was bundled out of the van by two shaggy and ferocious men who spat on their palms and grunted under the weight of sofa, bedstead and massive wardrobe. And when I followed them up the stairs to the place which was to be my home for the next twelve years, an evil-smelling strangeness permeated from rubbish bins and lavatories in the yard. Then furniture was arranged, a kettle went on the gas and the women of the tenement came in to welcome us in a chatter of excited Yiddish, the language that to this very day speaks to me with the voice of my mother. We had joined our tribal community.

The tenement was a village in miniature, a place of ingathered exiles who supplemented their Jewish speech with phrases in Russian, Polish or Lithuanian. We sang songs of the ghettos or folk-tunes of the old Russian Empire and ate the traditional dishes of its countryside. The news came to us in Yiddish newspapers and was usually bad: a pogrom here, a tale of ritual murder there, a tyranny somewhere else. People who have since gone down in history were discussed in our tiny living room – not only Lenin and Trotsky, whom everyone said were good for the Jews, but also cruel anti-Semites like Petlyura, Denikin and the terrible Makhno, an anarchist bandit who waded through rivers of our people's blood. Letters from home were rare, arriving after weeks of delay snipped, stamped and thumbprinted by an army of censors; they spoke of famine and begged for food parcels which never got past the stomachs of hungry Soviet bureaucrats. One such letter, almost the last to reach us, told my mother that her fifteen-year-old brother, Mendel, had been shot dead, mistaken for a White by the Bolsheviks, and that after saying *kaddish* for the boy's soul her father went home and died. All day long, my mother lay on the bed crying over a torn photograph while we were taken in and fed by friends.

People spoke of Warsaw, Kishinev, Kiev, Kharkov, Odessa as if they were neighbouring suburbs. And the women kept the old folk ways alive; they shouted public gossip to one another over flapping laundry in the yard, screamed at unmanageable children, quarrelled, wept, cursed and laughed with exuberant immodesty. In the evenings they assembled in one another's kitchens, drawing tired infants on their laps to drowse and drink the milk of their words as they talked the day to sleep. So, drowsily, we absorbed our racial memories – stories of far lands we would never see with our own eyes, of wonder rabbis and terrible Cossacks spearing Jewish babies with their lances, of families cowering in cellars as mobs battered at doors shouting: 'Kill the Jews and save Russia!' But also anecdotes, marvellous and comic, about kings and cuckolds, beggars and millionaires.

Round the corner was Bacon Street, squalid even by our standards. Perhaps it was the name, but the only Jews I knew who lived there were an organ grinder and a cobbler who sat in the midst of a heap of run-down, stinking shoes that seemed hardly worth the mending. Until I was big and fairly robust I could only walk through Bacon Street by making myself invisible, crediting the simple folk down there with a malicious brutality that could only be circumvented by magic. When they emerged unsteadily from pubs, singing hoarsely and embracing one another over and over in amiable confusion, I heard the drunken mobs amok in the ghetto and fled. Their wild children greeted us with the chant: 'Abie, Abie, my boy,' and once when I was playing ball on the corner with my small brother we were pounced on by a big *yok*[8] with a runny nose who grinned ferociously and said: 'You killed our Lord, dincha? So I can pinch yer ball.' And he did. There was a mad gypsy woman over the road who gave off a musty smell like a barrow-load of old rags. All the workaday week she leaned on her windowsill, staring malevolently at the tenement with slitted black eyes; but on roaring Saturday nights she staggered out of the corner pub, shook her earrings in the lamplight and screamed, 'Christ-killers all of yer!' with a shrillness that pierced the dreams of sleeping children. We learned to take such melodramas for granted as fairly harmless, for violence of one kind or another was as familiar as the moods of the weather, living as we did from day to day, from shilling to shilling, and jostling for elbow room in our teeming brick box.

When I was four my mother bought me a pair of steel-shod boots, said we were going for a walk and dragged me screaming into the highest building I'd ever seen. Hollow noises came from all directions. I was handed over to a skirted monster in gold-rimmed glasses whose voice clashed and grated like the blades of a sharp scissors. To distract me she opened a picture book; but it was a trick, because when I looked round my mother had gone, disappeared. Gripping me so hard her fingernails dug into my flesh, the woman pushed me into a room with rows of staring faces. School! Incoherent with shock, I spent the entire day, swollen-faced and blubbering, kicking out like a caged animal at anyone unwise enough to try to pacify me. But before the first week was over I fell fiercely in love with the teacher, Miss Baker, a thin lady with a long, gentle horse-face, reddish hair and blue eyes as pretty as a doll's. It was my revenge against my treacherous mother.

To please Miss Baker in competition with forty other children greedy for approval was a task that drove me to paroxysms of goodness. When she ordered us to attention I'd sit with bulging eyes, holding my breath to be more at attention than anyone else. I'd rather wriggle and force my legs together than let her think I was the kind of boy who did anything as embarrassing as pee, and soon I was able to keep the flood in control by relieving its pressure with an occasional small squirt. It was harder to impress her with my scholarship, for I was a backward pupil. Letters refused to form words, words sentences, and my writing straggled erratically all over the paper. Part of the trouble was a goldfish in a bowl on the teacher's desk. Whenever I tried to do a sum the swimming fish disarranged the numbers and made it wrong.

It was the need to earn Miss Baker's praise that got me into trouble one day. She'd gone round the class asking everybody what work their father did. I sat there miserably, wishing she'd ask about our mothers instead. 'And you, Emanuel, what does your daddy work at?' I closed my eyes tight, partly to think about it, partly in the hope that it would make the teacher go away. Then I squinted at the goldfish. 'He catches fishes. Goldfishes.' Miss Baker held her head on one side and smiled with all her big white teeth. 'Now, you know that's not true,' she said. 'Goldfish come from China. Is your daddy in China?' The whole class stared. Digging my toe into the floor, I said: 'He catches fishes in Victoria Park.' Cissie Stoloff, who shared my desk, pursed her lips primly and put up her hand. 'Pleath, teacher,' she lisped, 'he'th got on'y a mummy.'

Miss Baker took out a tiny embroidered handkerchief from the sleeve of her dress and blew her thin nose. 'Oh dear!' she said. 'Was he a soldier, then? Did your daddy fall on the battlefield?' She spoke in such a silly small voice that I couldn't bear to look at her. Myriad specks of dust whirled in a shaft of sunlight, vanishing incomprehensibly when they reached the shadows. Words I couldn't properly read were stencilled around the walls. In the next classroom they were singing puzzling number songs. Miss Baker was waiting for an answer. I didn't know if my father was a soldier, or if a father in Russia was a proper father, or if he did indeed fall on the battlefield. It was vexing to be so ignorant. 'He fell down,' I said. 'But I think he got up.'

By the sad way she smiled and shook her head, it seemed I'd got it wrong. Grown-ups didn't fall unless they were drunk. She'd give me a bad mark for sure. Cissie Stoloff sat by my side, looking good and clever. Sliding my hand along the bench under her dress, I pinched her bum. She cried and cried until snot mingled with her tears.

'That was a very wicked thing for a little boy to do!' Miss Baker said, really angry. 'I'm thoroughly ashamed of you!' She wiped Cissie's nose with the chalk duster and sent her out to wash her face.

'*Shmackel!*'[9] I thought defiantly. Being wicked made me feel strong and dirty. '*Toochus!*'[10] Stinky feet! Smelly knickers!'

When class was dismissed I was kept behind. Teacher sat at her high desk, staring down at me from behind a vase of daffodils. She spoke severely, tapping a ruler against her ringed fingers. I would never pinch Cissie Stoloff again, promise! After an inner struggle, I promised. Nor any other little girl? she asked, more kindly. No, teacher, never. Miss Baker put out her arms and cuddled me. A lock of auburn hair brushed against my cheek and I felt the beating of her lovesick heart. She had a nice powdery smell. Badness, for some reason that must have something to do with my dim and vanished father, was being rewarded. To prolong the sweetness I forced a few tears into my eyes, which gave her much satisfaction. It was the nicest time I had with Miss Baker until I fell and broke my arm a year or so later balancing on the school wall.

A long time went by without a letter from my father, so we were taken to the office of the Bolshevik representative to see if he could give us any information. His name was Litvinoff, but not a relative. We carried a note for him from a man who lived in our street. 'I knew Maxim when he was still Meir Wallach,' he said. 'Just say it's from Motke Schwartz with my regards and he'll give you the blood from his heart. With pleasure!'

Whole families were camping in the Bolsheviks' waiting room. The air was thick with smoke from brown Russian cigarettes[11] and people shouted to one another across the room in Yiddish. We found a place next to a woman who shelled hard-boiled eggs and stuffed them tenderly into the mouths of her assorted children. Soon we were sharing sandwiches, looking at photos of all her relatives in Lvov, and listening while she read heartbreaking excerpts from her husband's letters. Whenever somebody appeared who looked like an official my mother rushed over to show him Motke Schwartz's note, but she was always waved away. Eventually an exhausted man entered, shoulders slumped as if the whole of Russia was weighted on his back, and business began. One by one people came forward, waved their hands excitedly and pleaded. He listened, shrugged, picked his nose, filled out forms. When it was our turn my mother insisted on seeing the boss himself. She had a note from his friend Motke Schwartz. Besides, with the same name, maybe he was a relative, after all.

The official rubbed his hand wearily across his eyes. 'Look, *Yideneh*,'[12] he groaned, 'I'm a Jew myself. I come from a *shtetl* near Przemszl. People like you I seen a thousand times. You think a big commissar like Comrade Litvinoff has got nothing else to do but find your husband? In person?'

'He could at least say a word,' my mother retorted. 'I'm a human being, no?'

By now the uncertainty was getting so much on her nerves she decided to consult a fortune-teller whose advertisement in *Die Zeit* offered advice on business, marital affairs, missing relatives and romantic prospects. Instead of the magician one might have expected, a man showed up wearing a bowler hat and a long black overcoat that reached to his ankles. He produced a portfolio of testimonials from satisfied customers, some of them having shredded like old love-letters. He settled on the hard chair and groaned wearily.

'Excuse me, missus. A bad back. You don't know how I suffer.'

'I know,' my mother said. 'Believe me!' She always knew about such things.

They both sighed heavily then, spreading a square of black velvet on the table, the fortune-teller produced a worn Tarot pack and invited her to shuffle. He licked his thumb and laid out the cards slowly with long pauses between each. Deep pleats formed in his forehead. We jostled to get closer, wondering what miracles he was seeing. '*Kinder, kinder,*'[13] he pleaded, interrupted in his concentration.

Preoccupied, our mother brushed us away, but we settled again like flies. I held her hand.

'*Nu,* is it good or bad?' she said, pressing my fingers tightly.

The fortune-teller raised one shoulder in a tentative shrug. 'For the moment, t'ank God, your husband is in good health. Maybe from rheumatism he suffers a little.'

'What are you, a doctor? Please tell me only one thing. Where is he? In Odessa, in Moskva, in Minsk, Pinsk, Dvinsk?' She emphasized each word with abrupt gestures. 'And when will he come back? I struggle for every piece of bread.'

'So young to carry such troubles,' the man remarked, rocking his head from side to side.

Another row of cards was set out slowly. As the last was laid he drew back and glanced nervously across the table. His hand hovered over the card as if to conceal it.

'If it's bad, say what it is,' my mother told him harshly. 'Lies I don't need.'

'Is a language from riddles. One listens not with the head – with the *neshumah*, the soul.' He seemed to descend into his own depths for inspiration. 'Your man, he struggles. He wanders. Sometimes a yuman beink is like a blind person who puts one foot after the other until he falls over the edge of the world into Gehenna.'[14]

'Gehenna,' she said bitterly. 'From such a place nobody comes back, even without rheumatism.'

The fortune-teller looked helplessly up at the ceiling. He folded the black cloth, gathered up his cards and put them in a small attaché case. A bread roll fell out of a paper bag. 'It's easy to tell a lic,' he said, picking it up and dusting it with his sleeve before putting it back. 'The answer is still hidden. But I promise one t'ing – not much longer will you live alone.'

She got up heavily and went into the kitchen to make tea. He watched her go, digging his teeth thoughtfully with a thumbnail, then followed. 'Is not easy, a young woman bringing up children mitout a fader. Maybe you need a good *fraint*, a man. To give the *kinder* a Jewish education.' He put his arm round her waist. 'Mister,' my mother said, pushing him away angrily, 'so long I can work with my hands, such advice I can live without.'

The stranger hurried out without waiting for his tea, but he'd left her with fresh worries. Yes, a Jewish education. After all, did we live on the moon? We were children of the community. She watched us angrily. Whenever one of us did something bad, she'd twist his ear and shout: 'You're growing up like the wildest *goyim*.'[15] At such times I was afraid she'd go out and bring us a father in sheer despair. But she found a temporary solution.

One Sunday morning a neighbour collected me and my older brother, Abie. He hurried us off to the market, fitted us with flat grey caps that settled well over our ears to our skinny necks, and enrolled us in the local *Talmud Torah*, the religious school attached to the Working Men's Synagogue around the corner.[16]

Our class was a small grimy room with barred windows and rows of boys declaiming Hebrew at the top of their voices in a shrill competitive gabble. Occasionally they kicked one another viciously under the desks, or threw surreptitious pellets, while an enraged old man hopped around waving a stick in his trembling fist. I sat at the extreme edge of a wooden bench, thinking it a hundred times more irksome than ordinary school. I didn't want to learn to be a good Jew, or wear my ugly cap, or be a big and Hebrew-gabbling boy like the others; but there was no choice, so I bent my head and slowly began to form the *Aleph, Bet*[17] of the ancient tongue.

3

'Call Me Uncle Solly'

My mother stuffed a bundle of clean rags into the front of her bodice and shaped it into two mounds. She looked thoughtful and determined, the way she did when her brown capable hands fitted a dress to a customer's body and her mouth was full of pins. Then she pinched her cheeks and examined the redness. My reflection flickered in a corner of the long mirror as I sneaked away. 'Big eyes!' she exclaimed, fretful with embarrassment. 'Why are you looking? Go downstairs with the other children.'

I stood in the corridor rebelliously. Dusk was coming through the grimy window overlooking the yard and the wind blew in through a broken pane, smelling of cat's piss and vegetable putrescence.

'There's nobody to play with!' I yelled through the closed door, then modified my voice to a plaintive whine. 'I'm cold, I'm hungry, my head hurts ...' She must suffer! The door opened, as I knew it would, and I crept in, trying to look thin. 'Show me your tongue!' she demanded, abruptly tilting my head towards the light. Next she pulled out my shirt, examined my naked chest for spots, spun me about and scrutinized my back. 'Did you do Number Two today?' I weighed the risk of being dosed with castor oil if I lied and reluctantly said yes. My mother mingled relief and exasperation in a prolonged groan. 'Oy! What is the matter with you all of a sudden? You

29

say you're sick. You go with a miserable face. Yesterday you made *pish*[18] in the bed.'

'It wasn't me,' I screeched in outrage. 'It was Pinny!'

'Pinny, too!' she retorted. 'Two great big boys of eight and nine. Are you so lazy you can't go to the pail in the night?'

I was shamed because her voice was loud enough for the neighbours to hear. 'Didn't! Didn't! Didn't!' I yelled, and she seized me by the ear.

'Don't shout at your mother! You'll drive me to an early grave, all of you! Shall I send you all to the Jewish Orphanage, like everybody says?' The thought upset her so she twisted my ear. 'Why do you aggravate me?' she said unsteadily. 'I was up till three o'clock last night finishing Lily Fleischer's wedding order and I'm also flesh and blood.'

My ear was burning and so was my heart. I started to cry. 'All right, all right!' my mother exclaimed in irritation, blowing her nose. She took a biscuit out of a tin and gave it to me. 'I don't know what it is with you all of a sudden, Manny, I don't know all of a sudden . . .'

It was the summer we became orphans, my three brothers and I. The news had come at last, eight years after my father had gone back to Russia in the company of other reluctant Jews faced with the alternative of dying on the Western Front or serving in the army of the Tsar. Soon after they arrived the Bolsheviks stormed the Winter Palace and gusts of that revolution blew with Siberian bleakness through our East End tenement. Now and then letters came begging for warm clothes, food, pictures of the family. We were taken one day to a studio, where we all held hands and stared in petrified alarm at the man crouching behind a black cloth. My father may have died with that photograph in his breast pocket, but no one will ever know because his letters stopped coming.

Then a few of the men returned, among them Roitman, an

old friend, and he gave a party upstairs in his flat. While others drank brandy and sang boisterous songs, he drew my mother aside and spoke to her quietly, his hand on her shoulder. Mrs Roitman took us into the kitchen and fed us cinnamon bread warm from the oven. She pressed our heads in turn against her heaving bosom, speaking a benediction in Yiddish. Downstairs my unreal father hung on the wall of the unlighted room and I knew now he would never come back from Russia.

Around that time we began to hear the name Paisky. Mrs Benjamin from next door mentioned it while sitting in our front room, reflectively chewing some black bread rubbed with garlic and washing it down with noisy gulps of lemon tea. She was a loud, friendly woman who had no need to enlarge her chest like my mother did. It began with bulges under her arms and lay like two soft pillows on the plump of her belly. She upholstered the atmosphere. I sat at the feet of the women, listening in a daze of content.

'And what's so bad about Paisky?' she wheedled. 'Is he a drunkard, a paralytic, has he got a wooden leg?'

My mother said: 'A bargain like Paisky I can live without, thank God.'

'You're twenty-nine, with four children, may they never suffer the Evil Eye. You want to be another eight years without a man?'

'Manny,' my mother said sharply, 'go somewhere and play.' I banged the front door, pretending to go out, but crept under the sofa in the next room. I could hear in the dark like a cat can see.

'Paisky is *meshuggah*[19] for you,' Mrs Benjamin was insisting. 'He'll take the four boys like his own sons. A first-class upholsterer like Paisky! Ask my Sam. You expect a Rudolph Valentino?'[20] Her stomach made a strange gurgling sound and she hiccuped loudly. 'Listen, Rosa, I'm speaking for your own good.'

One Saturday evening, instead of packing us off to bed, my mother scrubbed us extra clean, dressed us in freshly pressed white shirts, bow ties and velvet knickers, and led us upstairs to the Roitmans'. A card party was in progress, piles of copper heaped carelessly on the plush tablecloth with an occasional glint of silver. The men sat around in their braces and sweated with gambling fever, as much as five shillings at a time being staked in pennies. But the women and children crowded the rest of the room, talking and laughing as if it didn't matter who lost or won. A suckling infant kept losing the teat and howling, and the Roitmans' tethered duck, held ready for future slaughter, quacked in terror from the neighbouring bedroom.

One small fat man with gleaming gold spectacles grew pale as we entered and looked at my mother with a bulging, stricken gaze. Instinct told me it was Paisky. I tightened my grasp on her hand. Alec Roitman came over stroking his big moustache. There was mischief in the air. 'See, a wonderful family!' he boomed. 'Four lion cubs, eh, Paisky? If you tried for a hundred years, could you make such boys?'

My mother walked disdainful and erect, to the far side of the room to sit with Mrs Benjamin. Paisky detained us and tried to smile. A gold tooth twinkled in the ruined cavern of his mouth. '*Nu, kinder?*' he said, interrogatively. And then, again: '*Nu?*'

We returned a collective, unresponsive stare and droplets of sweat bubbled out of his skin. Roitman slapped him on the back, his narrow Tartar eyes sly with humour, and yelled: 'Show them, Berl! Show them you got a kind heart.'

'For sixpence, who will give me a kiss?' Paisky held up a shining coin and waved it tantalizingly.

My elder brother, Abie, grabbed the money before lunging forward with pursed lips. Barney, the youngest, went off to hide in mother's skirt. I was torn between greed, repugnance and a kind of unwilling fascination as Paisky pointed to his loathsome cheek and held up another sixpence. He leaned hopefully towards Pinny, our incorruptible, who shook his seraphic head, smiled his shy smile, then crawled under the table to sit among the booted feet of the men.

'A shilling!' Paisky pleaded. 'A whole shilling!' The lenses of his glasses magnified his near-sighted eyes, and I remembered what Mrs Benjamin told my mother. He was *meshuggah* for her. Now I could see he was really mad. I shuddered and said: 'No, thank you, Mr Paisky.' This politeness was histrionic, because I'd become aware that I was holding the audience. The card players rolled about, gasping, and the women were nudging one another, bosoms a-quiver with suppressed hilarity. 'I'll take it! I'll take it!' some of the children screamed and the noise startled the duck in the bedroom, which flew about, squawking frantically as its beak banged the wall.

Paisky's glance scurried around the room before returning to me, trapped. 'Two shillings, then,' he groaned, wiping his streaming face with the sleeve of his shirt. 'You can buy enough chocolate to be sick for a *gantze*²¹ month, God forbid.'

As I succumbed to temptation and stepped forward, eyes screwed tight, to administer the bought kiss, one of the men detained me. 'Half a crown if you don't kiss him,' he said. He was tall, with rich brown well-barbered hair and Charlie Chaplin moustache, smartly dressed in a Norfolk tweed suit and brogue shoes of polished ox-blood. They called him Solly the Englishman, and it was strange in that gathering to hear someone who didn't speak with a foreign accent.

I took his money. Paisky blushed, looked at my mother, and kept on looking, but she didn't seem to see him at all. She was watching the Englishman with an expression I'd never seen before. When we got home she slapped me for taking money from a stranger, and I had to share it with the others. So I slapped them in turn, because that was only fair.

Paisky came to our house now and then. He would knock on the door, slide in quickly and call: 'Are you busy, Missus?' As my mother stitched away on the machine he watched her the whole time, eager to hand her scissors, or thread, or a waxy piece of tailor's chalk whenever these were needed. There was usually some gift – a piece of Russian halva, a box of Pond's face powder, coloured balloons for the four of us. My mother always sighed when she thanked him. 'You shouldn't, Mr Paisky,' she'd protest, and he'd reply: 'It's a pleasure for me, Missus. A real pleasure!' When they stood together, Paisky strained to make himself look taller but was still hardly higher than her nose. Once Mrs Benjamin said: 'Have pity on him, Rosa. He suffers . . .' and my mother replied: 'It would be a *mitzvah*[22] for me if he didn't come already. What I can't feel in my heart, I can't feel.'

One night there was a terrible scandal. The Roitmans had a party and we'd been put to bed early. There was something about my mother's voice that could pluck vibrations from me even in the depths of slumber. Now it was late and she was speaking with quiet panic. 'Please, Mr Paisky! The children are sleeping! Go away, Mr Paisky, please!' There was a noise of snuffling and groaning, like a dog in pain.

I woke Abie and this disturbed the others. Just as Mrs Benjamin said, Paisky was mad. 'Rosa! Rosale! *Oy*, Rosale!' he panted hoarsely, both hands clutching her arms. His gold-framed glasses hung crookedly on his nose, and strands of the sparse, greasy hair he plastered so carefully across his bald crown had come adrift, enhancing the demented appearance of his blotchy face.

We started to pummel his fat behind, screaming for help. People came running from upstairs. Alec Roitman cursed softly, seized Paisky's collar and tried to pull him away. The cloth ripped in his hand. The sound was somehow shocking, like the garment-rending of Jewish mourners, and some of the women began to wail.

'*Schweig!* Silence!' Roitman shouted in a dreadful voice. 'Come, Berl!' he added sharply. Paisky suddenly became docile, permitting himself to be led away. Mrs Benjamin's great bosom heaved with compassionate convulsions. 'It's a shame, Rosa,' she said in a reproachful singsong. 'And don't think it's not your fault also. All right, Sam. Let us go already.' Her husband lifted his shoulders in resignation and followed her out. We heard their footsteps shuffling in the corridors, then it was quiet – dreadfully quiet.

One person remained after the others had left – Solly the Englishman. 'It's all right, kids,' he told us. 'You go back to sleep.' He closed the door of our bedroom. After a while my mother stopped crying. I lay in bed, staring at the yellow light of the street lamp outside the window until it grew blurry and disappeared.

That summer the world was full of hints I could not understand. Often I lay in bed as the evening light turned blue, listening to fragmentary voices drifting like torn newspaper on the blown pavements of the street. The nights were cavernous with disquiet. Once I woke with a pounding heart and my mother looked back from the sewing machine with the face of a witch. Late, always late, when we children were delivered to sleep, hard knuckles rapped against our dreams.

We began to see a lot of Solly Levy. He wasn't like any of the men in our building or in the rest of our street, soft-bellied tailors stooped from working with the needle, slow-moving men who hewed at wood, workers in fur who sneezed and coughed through all the seasons. Solly Levy was of another tribe of Jews, half Dutch in origin, not speaking Yiddish or Russian, as handsome and stylish as the Prince of Wales. When he walked down our street, jauntily swinging a malacca cane, the women used to fall silent, whispering eagerly to one another once he'd passed. He was only a machiner in the gents' trade, but he had once been a Royal Fusilier and a hotel manager in Jo'burg. He could ride a horse, killed Germans in Gallipoli and France, prospected for diamonds, strode once with the same nonchalance among the Kaffirs of the African veldt.

On Saturday evenings Solly Levy and my mother went to Smart's Picture Palace in Bethnal Green Road and scorned all envious gossip. He was twenty-seven, two years younger than she, and people said a man like that must be bad or mad to court a widow with four children. My mother sang Ukrainian melodies as she worked, her voice full of melancholy sweetness. Often she would gaze for a long time out of the window, sighing and smiling to herself. She stopped lighting the Sabbath candles for some reason, but still spoke as constantly to God, and Solly, who said he was a freethinker, also caught the habit. 'We'll go to the seaside some time,' he would say, 'please God!'

'Please God, why not?' she would reply. 'It will be nice for the children.'

One warm night, after they'd been for a walk, Solly came into the bedroom to see if we were awake. He gave Abie and me sixpence each to call him Uncle Solly while he sat on the sofa with my mother. 'I'm very fond of children,' he told her tenderly. 'I love the boys like my own.' There was a curious silence, then my mother got up and closed the door of our bedroom. He was there most evenings after that and one night didn't leave at all. My mother said: 'Uncle Solly is your new father, *kindelech.*' She hugged us and put us all to bed in the sitting room on the open sofa. One of us pished the bed that night; it was either Pinny or me. The next morning we watched Uncle Solly shaving at the sink in his combinations. He whistled cheerfully and made a playful swipe at us with the razor, because we all stood around gazing intently. It was the first time we'd really seen a man shaving. He drew the blade down his cheek, cutting a pink swathe through the foaming white lather, then delicately manipulated his nose as he trimmed the edges of his moustache.

'Will you live here always now?' asked Barney. He was only six and didn't understand.

Uncle Solly dabbed his face with the shaving brush and smiled.

When I got back from school that afternoon I noticed a change in the room. My father's picture had been taken off the wall. It couldn't be seen anywhere. I climbed a chair and looked on top of the wardrobe. It was lying there, face down, and I never saw it hung again.

4

The Geography Lesson

We were standing under the shelter during break, shivering in our jerseys. A water-logged morning, rain scudding under a nasty gale and the sky – what you could see of it – wrinkled and sodden like a sheet dipped in the wash. It was better to be jailed in class and we waited morosely for the bell.

Shmulevitch searched in his pockets and produced a grubby acid drop. 'On'y got one,' he mumbled, slipping it quickly into his mouth. He sucked noisily and wiped his nose with his sleeve: he disgusted me. I wandered hopefully over to a group of boys round Morry Schein who bought sweets by the pound when he was flush.

'*Oy*, Morry-boy!' I called, though I didn't like him all that much. His family kept a barber shop in Bethnal Green Road and he put on brilliantine. It only made him smell worse.

But Morry took no notice. He was in a state of excitement and so were the others. 'Yer telling a lie!' a boy said, running his tongue over his lips. 'Din' I tell ya I seen it?' Scheiny insisted, mouth dribbling. I drew closer, fascinated. 'Let's ask Litty,' someone suggested. 'E's a rill bookworm.'

'You fink they write about it in books?' Morry Schein said scornfully. 'No good asking ol' Four-Eyes. Never seen a tit, even!'

'What's the argument?' I enquired loftily, taking off my glasses.

'It's Morry's *shiksa*,'[23] Siddy Kravitz said. 'She let's 'im see 'er with no close. Starkers!'

'What about his *shiksa*, then?'

'Morry says the *knish*[24] is at the back, by the *toochus*. She sits on it.'

'Bollocks!' one of the boys exploded. 'I bet my sister don't!'

'Maybe *shiksas* is diff'rent,' Siddy argued. 'What d'you say, Lit?' He sat next to me in class and copied my sums, so my judgement was respected.

'Religion's got nothing to do with it,' I announced flatly. 'Everybody's got it in the same place, boys and girls. It's biology.'

Morry was enraged. 'I seen it, you didn't!' he shouted. 'Betcha hundred pounds I'm right! Betcha million!'

Shmulevitch ambled up and joined the argument. 'Joo know where the *knish* is?' Scheiny asked him. Shmuly looked puzzled. 'On a gal, you dope!' Scheiny yelled.

'Dahn 'ere,' said Shmuly. He touched himself between the legs.

'I'll prove it!' Morry threatened darkly. 'I'll letcha see.' We crowded round. 'When?' 'Ow can yer?' 'Don't berlieve!'

'Orlright, we'll see after school. I'll tell 'er to take off 'er bloomers an' bend dahn near the key'ole.'

When break was over, Parker, our master, distributed books and atlases for the geography lesson. He talked in a bored voice about Africa, surreptitiously picking his hairy nostrils. Outside the window, factory chimneys swirled in clouds of grit and trains trundling towards Liverpool Street Station vibrated the floor of the classroom. My forefinger traced the profile of Africa, lions prowling the forests of my brain. Suddenly Parker strode on spindly legs between the desks and thwacked his stick across my back. Siddy Kravitz, beside me, winced. 'I've got eyes at the back of my head!' Parker snarled into my startled face, but

39

he returned to the front of the class in good humour and told us we could read the geography books to ourselves as long as we ignored the pictures of naked black ladies. Baring his long teeth in a sinister smile, he went off for a smoke.

Morry Schein passed me a note. There was a drawing of something that looked like a vertical eye with a line down the length of it. Underneath was written: 'You.' I screwed it up, soaked it in the inkwell and chucked it at him. It hit the boy behind him on the head. He chucked it back and soon everybody was at it. Parker arrived while it was going on and enthusiastically caned six of us, including me.

Going home for dinner, I thought about Morry and the *shiksa*. The Scheins were rich and she was their servant, but I couldn't believe she'd let him actually *see* her without bloomers. He might have spied on her when she washed, or drilled a hole in the lavatory, but nobody had a *knish* where he said she did! I fingered myself and tried to imagine I was a girl, but it still seemed improbable. We'd just got a girl in our family a few weeks before and I'd watched my mother change its napkin, but all I ever saw was a kind of crease between its bandy legs.

It was a long day at school, and when it was over Morry Schein tried to sneak away. He'd always been a big mouth. We chased after him, Siddy Kravitz, Shmulevitch and me. 'Y'promised!' Siddy said indignantly.

'I changed my mind,' Morry said, breaking into a run. Shmuly caught him and put Chinese torture on his wrist, so he changed his mind again and said he'd do it after tea. But only for a minute. 'You better not be late,' he said. 'I gotta go ter Hebrew or my dad'll murder me.'

The three of us met by arrangement. Shmulevitch had to bring his brother along in the pram because their mother served on a fish stall during the evening busy. I was shivering inside and my face felt on fire despite the cold.

'I'm on'y going 'cause Morry dared me,' I said.

Siddy Kravitz looked miserable and excited. 'Yer,' he said, 'me, too.'

It was raining hard as we trudged up to Bethnal Green Road, getting splashed with mud as we steered Shmuly's pram into the gaps between lorries and buses to Schein's Gentleman's Hairdressing Saloon. It was quiet there at that time of the day. A man in a butcher's apron read a Yiddish newspaper, waiting while old Schein scraped soap off a fat man's chin, poured Levy's Patent Hair Restorer from a coloured bottle over the thin strands of ruffled hair on his pink scalp and gave him a friction.

Morry came to the door of the side entrance, looking shifty. 'You wanna play with my Meccano?' he asked in a low voice.

'No!' Shmuly hissed. 'We wanna see what yer said. The *shiksa*.'

The shop cat crept up stealthily and rubbed its back against Morry's leg. He picked it up and stroked the black fur. 'Look,' he said, 'this proves it,' and, lifting the animal's tail, pointed hopefully at the slit in its bottom.

'We didn't come 'ere in the bleaten rain just to see a cat's shitty arse!' Shmulevitch protested. 'I could a stayed 'ome an' done that!'

'Well, I don' know if she's in 'er room.'

Siddy Kravitz gave Morry a push. 'Gorn, let's go up, then.'

We parked the pram in the passage and followed Morry up the stairs, tiptoeing and giggling.

'Don' make so much soddin' noise!' Morry whispered frantically. 'It's right up in the attic.' When we reached it, he hesitated, then knocked timidly on the door. 'Jinny, are you in?' he called. 'Jinny, it's me, Morry.'

'Piss off!' someone said distinctly, a female. 'I'm busy.'

After some argument, the door was opened and he was admitted. We crept out of hiding and jostled to reach the keyhole. Siddy Kravitz got there first. He knelt on one knee and placed his eye against the aperture. 'C'n y'see?' Shmuly asked. Siddy shushed him.

Morry's voice came to us through the door. 'Do whatcha done last time, Jinny,' he coaxed.

We heard Jinny laugh. 'Dunno whatcha talkin' abaht.'

'Y'do know.'

'It's wicked. I'll tell yer dad.'

Shmuly began to get very excited. 'It's my turn,' he insisted, and after a brief scuffle replaced Kravitz at the keyhole. 'I kin see a bed,' he reported eagerly. 'Could see more if Morry wasn't in the way.'

The girl inside was laughing again. I got down and scraped my knees on the bare wooden floor but managed to get a peep into the room when Shmulevitch shifted. An unmade bed stood against the faded, flower-patterned wall and a skinny girl of about sixteen came into the line of sight. She sat on the edge of the bed and smiled wickedly.

'Who's yer darling, then?' she teased.

We heard Morry groan.

'Won't do it then. Y'gotta say it nice. Who's yer darling?'

'Aw, right!' said Morry. 'You are.'

'I'm what?'

I began to feel an irresistible tickle in my chest. There was some confused movement inside and I suddenly saw some flesh close up. 'She's done it!' I was awed and slightly scared.

Shmuly pushed me aside to see for himself. He gazed intensely for a moment, then said in outraged disappointment, 'It's Morry's knee!' When I laughed, he punched me. But he began to laugh himself and, after trying to stop us, Siddy found he couldn't stop laughing, either.

Morry's *shiksa* suddenly pulled open the door and she wasn't undressed at all. We scampered hastily down the stairs, making a terrible noise, grabbed Shmuly's pram and ran yelling into the rain. Old man Schein came out of the shop with a razor in his hand shouting Yiddish curses. We didn't stop running until we got among the evening crowds in Brick Lane market. Rain sizzled on the naphtha flares and gusts of wind flapped the tarpaulin covering of stalls. We didn't feel like laughing any more.

'Never saw nothin! Did we?' Siddy Kravitz said dejectedly. He stared defiantly at us. 'I'd a called 'er darling. Just to know.'

Shmulevitch, looking preoccupied, steered his pram close to the edge of the pavement. When he rejoined us, he lifted up the waterproof apron to show some apples lying by the fat legs of his little brother. 'Nicked 'em,' he said with huge satisfaction.

The kid woke up and began to cry.

5

The Battle for Mendel Shaffer

Mendel Shaffer lived in a flat on the third floor of our building with his grandmother and Mr Schulberg, the lodger, a small fat man of anxious countenance who was a collector for the Jewish Burial Society. His father, like mine, was away in Russia at the time and his mother had run off to America with a Lithuanian tailor so long before that the episode was little more than a scandalous legend in my day. Because of this there was hardly a Jewish mother in the street who did not melt with compassion at poor Mendel's plight or try to force some delicacy upon him when he passed with the shy and stricken look of one who would rather go unnoticed.

He was a quiet, studious boy of precocious gravity that came of living in the company of elderly folk. His grandmother, a devout woman, wanted him to be a rabbinical scholar, a musician or a doctor. Nobody thought her foolish in these lofty ambitions, for Mendel was both clever and talented. An old head on young shoulders, the neighbours commented approvingly, and oh! how he played the fiddle, like an angel – entirely self-taught. They would get him to perform at celebrations, drawing Yiddish melodies from the strings in a piercing, uncertain tone that made them snuffle into their handkerchiefs. The story of that fiddle was one of our folk legends. His grandmother got it from the rag-and-bone man in exchange for a leaking copper samovar. She took it home, polished it carefully, then held it out. 'Play, Mendel,' she said simply. Mendel had been playing ever since.

But what he did most was read, preferably encyclopedias. He liked to surprise us with stupendous facts. It was Mendel who first told me that King Solomon had seven hundred wives and three hundred concubines, that the female mantis consumes its mate in nuptial frenzy, that the Chinese alphabet boasts more than forty thousand characters, and other things that have stuck in my mind like burrs. He tried to learn a few stupendous facts like that every day, partly, I think, because ordinary conversation did not come easily to him and it helped to have something spectacular to talk about.

Mendel Shaffer's grandmother made buttonholes for a living. She worked at home on the bedroom table while Mendel read, practised the violin or lay at night dreaming eruditely under the hissing gaslight. Two evenings a week Susskind, the Hebrew teacher, left the cellar in Kerbela Street, where he lived, and gave the boy private tuition in the holy books. Afterwards, he drank a glass of lemon tea with Mr Schulberg and the grandmother, calling his pupil 'the little rabbi' and praising his precocity. The old woman listened shrewdly, counting the flatteries like the coins in her purse, while Schulberg noisily sucked his tea and confirmed the praise with ingratiating nods and eager grimaces.

There were other clever and talented boys in our neighbourhood, some of them now men of wealth and fame, but I cannot recall anyone who was nurtured so strictly as Mendel. His wasn't really much of a life for a boy of ten. When the rest of us were kicking a ball in the street, or wandering among the fruit stalls of the marketplace as rapacious as hungry foxes, Mendel was unable to move a hundred yards without being trapped by his grandmother's jealous vigilance. It was his soul she guarded as much as his safety. She kept him unnaturally clean in the eyes of God, both in person and in conduct, as if he were the son of the Chief Rabbi himself.

One stifling afternoon during some Jewish festival or other, when the brick streets of the East End gave off a more than usual stench of overcrowding and decay, I wandered around, bored and restless, looking for someone to accompany me to Victoria Park. After several rejections, I came to Mendel. I spoke persuasively of grass, trees, the cool water of the lake, my throat dry with grit and desperation. Eventually, he agreed to ask permission to accompany me. But when I went to call him, he was squatting disconsolately on the floor at home, his ankle tethered to the leg of a table by a ridiculously flimsy piece of string. Mr Schulberg, sweating with anxiety, tiptoed from the kitchen and hurried to the door, obviously fleeing from a domestic crisis. Just before he left, he waggled an admonitory forefinger in my face.

I sniggered with embarrassment, Mendel's lower lip trembled and he stared at me like an enemy. After a moment's agonized indecision, he untied himself and stood up just as the old woman entered the room, awesome in her black old-fashioned Sabbath finery. She trailed an atmosphere of claustrophobia and a smell of camphor balls. Her glance was like the wrath of Jehovah and I longed to escape from the cramped piety of the room into the pagan sunshine.

'Sit!' she ordered us harshly, pointing to an ancient horsehair sofa that gave off an odour like the rotted covers of old prayer books. We sat in guilty collusion, avoiding her eyes as she lectured us in a worn, plaintive voice of the need to be steadfast in our faith, to be good Jewish children and to remember how hard it was to bring up fatherless boys in a hostile world. Mendel scraped the scuffed lino with the toe of his boot resentfully. She took his face between her palms and said: 'Don't punish me, Mendel. How long have I got to live?' He began to cry. At the time I thought he was upset by the mention of her death, but now I believe it was the roughness of her hands that made him cry, reminding him of how she toiled to support them.

As I left she was crooning endearments, calling him her *feigele*, her little bird.

It was round about that summer that Mendel's father came home, a tall sick-looking man with a big nose jutting from his wasted face like a horny beak. All the children of the tenements were out, shrieking and jeering in their play, as he came limping along the street, a ragged figure with a military pack strapped on his shoulders who trudged past gossiping women and bawling infants with that glazed, exhausted indifference that is seen in soldiers after a long retreat. There was a feverish look in his eyes and we grew uneasy when he stopped and began to scrutinize us, his glance moving uncertainly from one to another. Then he saw Mendel, who was leaning against a window-ledge of the building, absorbed in a book. The Adam's apple in his skinny neck jumped spasmodically. He took the startled boy in his arms, kissing him over and over again with strange groaning sounds of joy. We all watched shamelessly. A woman sitting on a kitchen chair at her front door covered her face with her apron and wept. Bewildered by the unexpected embrace, Mendel freed himself and gazed mistrustfully at the stranger. Then the two of them stepped out of the sunshine and went together into the gloom of the building.

Mr Shaffer celebrated his return quietly. He was not, it was soon discovered, a particularly sociable man except with children. Instead of inviting the neighbours in for a party, he mixed a large can of ice cream and dispensed cornets to all the kids of the neighbourhood, smiling and tousling their hair as they came one by one for their free treat. The strains of Mendel's violin were heard in the apartment evening after evening. For a while, he enjoyed unusual popularity among us with stories

47

of his father's tribulation as a soldier in the Russian Revolution, of how he had eaten rats to avoid starvation, lost two toes on his right foot because of frostbite and spent years in Siberian exile for some political unorthodoxy.

But the sensation soon subsided. Mendel's father became Mr Shaffer, the cabinet-maker, and his drab comings and goings merged into the familiar pattern of the toiling adult world around us. People wondered if Mr Schulberg, of the Burial Society, would be permitted to remain in the cramped apartment, and if Mr Shaffer would consult the marriage-broker and seek out some young widow to espouse; but it was temporarily decided that he should share a bed with Mr Schulberg until the latter could find another cheap and hospitable lodging, an act of kindness, we thought, for few would wish to live constantly in the company of someone so intimately connected with death.

Acquiring a father unexpectedly like that could be either horrible or marvellous for a boy. In Mendel's case it was marvellous. You'd see the two of them walking hand in hand through the raucous streets, talking to one another as if no one else in the world existed. They went to museums, parks, art galleries, visited the Tower, climbed the Monument, inspected the Palace Guard, all things that Mr Shaffer must have dreamed of doing with his son during those long years of waste and deprivation in Russia. If the boy was happy, the man was ecstatic. I saw him one Sunday standing in the marketplace utterly dazed by the mounds of ripe fruit, barrels of shmalz herring and pungent strings of sausages, gazing at these and the stalls flowing with coloured silks and heaped with new-smelling leather, as if the wonder of the world was spread before his feasting eyes. And the way Mendel smiled up at the tall man you'd think he was the father, not the child.

Mendel was changing in all kinds of ways. He was the sort of boy who ran like a girl, flinging his legs out sideways; who couldn't catch a ball, climb a stack of timber or hitch a ride on the tailboard of a lorry. The more he tried to do these things, the clumsier he became, and he got into the habit of sitting around reading when the rest of us played games. Mr Shaffer observed this once or twice, then began to urge Mendel to join in with the others. Because his father was watching, we felt constrained to be more patient of Mendel's awkwardness. This gave him more confidence and, although most of us continued to outrun and outjostle him, he was soon quite a star in games that required mental agility as well as physical resources.

But in the meantime rumours of dissension in the Shaffers' apartment began to get around. Now that he was earning a living Mr Shaffer stopped the old woman making buttonholes, and the way she grumbled you'd think he had taken the very bread from her mouth instead of easing her labours. She was an obstinate, independent creature, designed by nature to rule a tribe, and all that resolute energy was expended on a solitary boy. Now even that was being made superfluous. More and more frequently the pacific Mr Schulberg was seen hurrying from the flat in a frenzy of apprehension. The women would stop him on the stairs and, with an elaborate pretence of incuriosity, ask him this, that and the other, but Mr Schulberg pleaded pressing business and made an agitated departure. It was a little while, therefore, before people discovered that the principal source of contention between the father and grandmother was the soul of Mendel Shaffer.

My mother got the first clue from me. One rainy evening, a few of us were sitting in the doorway of the tenement, staring at the reflection of street lamps on the wet, twilit pavements. This induced a sort of philosophic melancholy. As Mr Shaffer came by from work and gave us a tired greeting, the talk had got around to God. He was halfway up the stairs but paused and retraced his steps.

'There is no God,' he said.

'God is nonsense,' Mr Shaffer went on, gesturing vigorously with a folded Yiddish newspaper. 'The rabbis and the rich people talk about God just to keep poor people in their places.' His beaked nose stabbed at us, sombre eyes glowing with passion. 'Don't spend time on such rubbish, children! Learn science, study, think of the future! The world belongs to you, not to God.'

'What a nut!' somebody said when he'd gone.

During supper I told my mother that Mr Shaffer did not believe in God.

'How is it possible?' she exclaimed, and hurried to tell the neighbours.

The next time I saw Mendel I asked him why his father didn't believe in God. He hunched his shoulders and walked away without answering.

In our neighbourhood, religion was a kind of family affair, to be treated with irony and ambiguity. People made sly jokes about rabbis, and whenever things didn't work out well they addressed asides to the *Rabboine Shel Oilem*, the Lord of the Universe, chiding him for not contriving a better fate for His Chosen People. That is the way of the Jews. Since the time of the Patriarchs they have been on terms of familiarity with Jehovah.

There were also, of course, Anarchists, Communists, Bundists and Socialist Zionists who were outspokenly defiant of the Almighty. They smoked cigarettes on the Sabbath – except in public – and if they went to synagogue at all it was only out of respect for deceased parents, or because, after all, it was a social occasion. As for fasting on Yom Kippur, the Day of Atonement, they did so because it is good for health to give the stomach a rest once in a while. Sin had nothing to do with it.

In short, for some of our folk in those days God was still father and friend in a hostile world, for others He was merely the opium of the masses. Consequently, the affair of Mendel's soul touched everyone one way or another. There were those who gloated when Susskind, the Hebrew teacher, no longer came to give the boy private tuition; others, when it was learned that lessons were secretly continuing in the teacher's cellar. The score rose for some when Mr Shaffer took his son on a forbidden tram ride and was cancelled for others when the grandmother hurried to obtain absolution from the rabbi. She was not one to give up Mendel's soul lightly. At mealtimes, for each blessing Mendel would not speak in the presence of his father, she recited two. As fast as atheistic literature was brought into the house, she carried it down to the dustbin in the yard. In the women's gallery of the synagogue her lamentations rose insistently above the keening of the entire congregation.

Things went from bad to worse. Mr Shaffer and the grandmother ceased talking directly and addressed each other only through the boy. Their lodger, Mr Schulberg, got into the habit of spending his evenings in kosher restaurants meditating gloomily over a glass of lemon tea. As for Mendel himself, there were times when he seemed lonelier than any person I knew. He still took pleasure in his father's company, but he loved his grandmother, too, and the strain of remaining loyal to both left a hurt in his eyes for anyone to see. But he was not a boy to talk about such things except, perhaps, to his fiddle, which in those days made music of heartbreaking sadness. I think he was genuinely neutral in the struggle that was taking place over his soul. Looking back, I can see that he lived an interior life composed of the intense dreams of solitude, and in the soul of such a person there is room for everything.

It was about this time that the Slutskys moved away to America. They were a family with eight children, nearly all of them girls, and they had been so overcrowded in their two-roomed flat that there were children sleeping all over the place, even under the dining table. Chaim Slutsky had six brothers in Chicago and each of them contributed one hundred dollars to bring the family over. A day after they left Kramer, the furrier, moved into the empty apartment with his wife, two children and spinster sister, Freda.

In as close a community as ours, each newcomer added a now complexity, changing us all a little and sometimes even influencing the whole pattern of our fate. For Mendel Shaffer, the arrival of Kramer's sister, Freda, was momentous. She was a dark, lively woman of twenty-six who sang sentimental songs in a flat, adenoidal voice and laughed through a small opening in her mouth to conceal the loss of her back teeth. Apart from being very short and skinny, she was not bad-looking and it was soon observed that Mr Schulberg was paying some attention to her. He had a sly way of watching women, had Mr Schulberg. He would turn his head at an angle away from them and droop his eyelids as if half asleep, but in the narrow slits that remained the swivelled pupils were as sharply focused as binoculars. Still, his interest in Miss Kramer was perplexing, for he had never before come close to the objects of his admiration. Every time he saw her he doffed his shabby bowler hat with an ingratiating smile and held it to his chest like a bouquet of flowers.

Freda seemed flattered, although Mr Schulberg wasn't actually a young, or even middle-aged, man. It might even be that he was trying to sell her a plot in the cemetery. Therefore, her manner remained cool. She didn't even bother to keep her mouth closed when she smiled. Even so, the relationship progressed to the point where they were actually seen in earnest conversation in Mr Schulberg's favourite kosher restaurant. Assuming that he was pleading his suit, people were vaguely scandalized and openly derisive. There must be at least a hundred Yiddish jokes about the mating of old men with young women and at the time they used all of them. Later, when it became clear what

Schulberg had really been up to, they had to admit he was not such an old fool, after all.

For following on the restaurant episode the entire Kramer family became ostentatiously friendly to Mendel Shaffer. He rarely managed to pass their threshold without being molested in some way. Mrs Kramer would rush out with a piece of strudel, Freda pierced him with compassionate glances, Mr Kramer offered him as much as sixpence to run some simple errand, and the children urged him to come in and play. All this made Mendel intensely uncomfortable. He tried tiptoeing down the stairs, but was betrayed by his own awkwardness. The Kramers were out like a flash, picked him up, dusted him down and dragged him inside to have iodine dabbed on his grazes. He gave in: what else could he do?

Inevitably, therefore, the day arrived when Mendel's father was lured into the Kramers' apartment in search of his son. Naturally, he had to stay for a glass of tea, dispensed by Freda herself together with some delicious cakes of her own baking. Naturally, also, he could see with his own eyes that the Kramers had a nice family life, eating well and making pleasant company among themselves. The atmosphere must have been exceedingly comforting to a lonely man. Mr Kramer wound up the gramophone and played a Russian gypsy melody. It was casually disclosed that although he was related to the famous Sotmarer rabbis, he'd recently developed some doubts about religion. Perhaps Mr Shaffer had a few ideas on the subject . . . Splendid! Then why not drop in some evening, drink a little tea and enjoy a good intellectual discussion? Even tomorrow!

So that precious thing, a friendship, was born. After returning from work, Mendel's father would rinse his hands and face at the sink, sit down silently to supper, read the Yiddish paper or listen to Mendel practising his violin. An hour or so later he knocked at the Kramers' door. Freda always opened it to him, smelling of eau-de-Cologne and smiling the prim smile that made her seem shyer and less guileful than she was. The family enveloped him in a warmth as comforting as one of their fur coats. He would talk of religion, politics, hard winters in the Siberian plains, then, reluctantly at first but with growing passion, of Mendel and the way his scheming grandmother sought to make of the boy a hair-splitting Talmudist. The sinewy throat knotted and writhed. Freda Kramer bathed him with the balm of her womanly solicitude. When he returned home to bed misery had abated a little, and soon, no doubt, it began to occur to him how much better it would be if Freda lay in the place now occupied by the gently snoring bulk of Mr Schulberg.

In another corner of the bedroom, behind a sheltering screen that both protected modesty and blocked the draught of the window, the grandmother lay with Mendel cradled in the hollow of her arm. She, too, must have had her thoughts, listening to the creaking of the bed as her son-in-law turned restless in the dark. My mother once told me that if you know how to pray God will make one miracle especially for you. The old woman knew how to pray, but she did not rely on prayer alone.

So time passed and, as you can now guess, a day came when an announcement appeared in the Yiddish newspaper of the forthcoming marriage of Freda Kramer and Mendel Shaffer's father. With some reluctance, Mr Shaffer agreed to a religious ceremony. When he stood under the synagogue canopy, shy and solemn with the gravity of the occasion, beside his eager, diminutive bride, he was clad, like any other Jewish bridegroom, in a black homburg and neatly pressed suit. The ancient, sonorous responses came no differently from his lips than from others.

Marriage is a series of compromises. Freda moved into the Shaffers' apartment and Mr Schulberg moved out. She lit the

Sabbath candles and kept a kosher home as meticulously as even the grandmother could wish. A fertile woman, she was frequently pregnant, and with many mouths to feed Mr Shaffer had little time to worry about Mendel's soul. Mendel began to play the fiddle again, but couldn't do so often because it might wake the babies. No one cared any longer whether he played it or not. Most people were getting wireless sets in those days and everyone was crazy about dance-band music.

6

Uncle Solly's Sporting Life

All night they were quarrelling in my dreams and the next morning Solly came out of the bedroom with shell-shocked eyes. A burnt-out silence echoed in the house. The air was so bitter it hurt to breathe. My mother prepared breakfast as if it was a funeral rite and served our meagre portions with a wry and angry pity.

'Eat, eat!' she ordered harshly. 'Thank God we still got a piece of bread!'

Solly slid cautiously on to a chair and smuggled some food into his mouth as if performing a disagreeable duty merely to keep body and soul together. He sighed heavily and repeatedly to show he was aching with contrition.

'Rosa,' he said in a subdued voice, 'I swear by my mother's life, I didn't mean to do it.' The silence stretched and screamed as he waited for a sign. It failed to come. 'You won't even let me explain,' he resumed hopelessly.

She turned her lonely, obdurate gaze to the flaking distemper on the kitchen wall. 'Ask him, somebody,' she said remotely, 'can I pay the rent collector with explanations? Will explanations perhaps buy a piece of meat? What do I put on my children's feet – shoes or explanations?' Her nose turned red with the effort of holding in her tears.

Solly scraped his chair backwards and left the room in criminal silence. The front door closed and, after a moment, my mother got up abruptly and leaned over the gas stove. A choking noise came from her. We stared guiltily at our plates. Uncle Solly had done a terrible thing. The night before, straight after work, he'd stopped off at Mr Pippick's for a hand or two of rummy. Pippick had crooked teeth, the mark of a lucky gambler. When the game was over Solly'd lost a whole week's wages.

In a way, I was glad. My mother had recently embarrassed us by producing a girl baby out of her own body. I was, of course, old enough to know it came from between her legs. Until then I'd have killed anybody who said she did things in bed with Uncle Solly, although having seen the hair on his disgustingly naked chest I'd often felt very worried about what he might be doing to her. You could see he was a villain by his thin blue lips and pale staring eyes. He'd got round my mother by pretending to be nice: now the badness was coming out and she'd certainly send him away.

But Solly wasn't sent away and he didn't always lose. The ups and downs of luck made him rather unpredictable. One summer evening the sobbing of a melodious Italian voice arrested the street at its most crowded. Our local musicians didn't have such high-quality voices. 'A fine singer,' people remarked in surprise, maybe a war cripple who was once a famous opera tenor. And also trumpets, violins, a whole orchestra! From where could such a miracle come all of a sudden?

Uncle Solly appeared round the corner clasping in his arms a mahogany gramophone with an enormous green horn. Dancing children surrounded him and a moist, happy smile spread loosely over his rosy face. I stopped kicking my tin can in embarrassment, not sure how a boy of ten should react to the sight of his stepfather playing gramophone records in the street. One of the kids said: 'Your ole man's pissed,' which surely couldn't be true. A drunken Jew was as rare as a Yiddisher pork butcher.

57

I followed him into the building. Neighbours crowded every landing as Solly stood outside our flat, bearing his gift of music, waiting for my mother to open the door and show delighted appreciation. He smiled round at everybody and winked several times as if they all shared a nice conspiracy. But my mother seemed a long time coming and something queer began to happen to the singer's voice. It slowed, slurred, then groaned prodigiously. Solly put the machine on the floor to wind the handle, but his hat fell off as he did so. It caught the needle and the sound box came to a grinding end.

When the music stopped, the mood changed. 'It's a disgrace for the neighbourhood,' a woman muttered distinctly. '*Shickerve a goy*,'[25] said another, looking around for confirmation. 'And who suffers but the poor wife and *kinder*?' The mothers of the community rocked their heads from side to side in sorrowful condemnation. 'What can you expect when a widow with four sons marries an Englishman?' they whispered. Like in Poland, Galicia, the Ukraine such a disgrace could never happen.

Solly gazed round in bewilderment, not understanding why they had turned against him. He brushed the dust from his knees and straightened his trilby hat with an attempt at dignity. I was hiding behind a banister but he saw me and gave me a crooked smile. It caused me agony and shame. I turned away as if he was a stranger.

My mother opened the door, carrying the baby, the other kids peering round her skirt. The sight of Solly frightened her. 'Keep away from the children!' she screamed as he staggered in with the gramophone and made for the bedroom. We crowded at the doorway with excitement and fear. Drink drove people crazy and savage. Wild Solly.

He put on a new record, threw open the window and turned the horn towards the street. It played a song called

'The Laughing Policeman'. 'Mis'rable sods,' he said with satisfaction, glancing down at the gaping faces. 'Liven you all up a
bit!' he yelled. 'Bloody Peruvians!'[26] The gramophone chortled
'Ha-ha-ha-ha-ha' in a fat voice.

'In front of the whole world he wants to make a scandal,'
said my mother, horrified.

'It's got a beautiful tone,' Solly protested, waving his arms
like a conductor.

'There's enough noise in the house without such a katerinka.'

'Ha-ha-ha-ha-ha,' the horn chuckled fatly.

Solly began to laugh. She put the baby in its cot and slammed
the window down, which made him laugh even more. 'I'm
rich, Rosa,' he shouted, emptying his pockets. 'You married
luck when you got me.' Coins tumbled merrily over the floor
and pound notes floated about like torn paper after the Sunday
market.

'Such luck I wouldn't wish my worst enemy,' she said, picking
up the money. The katerinka went on playing.

My mother often spoke as if our stepfather was the worst
gambler who ever lived. As troubles at home piled up and
pregnancies followed each time they had a reconciliation,
gambling became one of her principal grievances. But usually
his speculations were modest, a few shillings on the dogs,
a bob or two with Charlie, the street bookmaker, an occasional game of cards for penny stakes. Sometimes, however,
recklessness got into him. He must have regretted what he'd
done to himself, giving up the life of a lord for half a bed
in an overcrowded flat swept by blistering quarrels and chill
blasts of misery. He'd go off hoping for the miracle of a big
win, hat at a jaunty slope, opulent shine on his sharp shoes,
pockets jingling with the rent money. And, more often than
not, the dogs he backed were doped to lose, or a boxer took

a dive, and we lived with that disaster till the next one came along.

'It's a mug's game,' he'd grumble on such occasions. 'Anybody gambling should be put in a straitjacket.'

For a while he'd sit around in the evening, shuffling and reshuffling a useless pack of cards, or read books on famous murderers, medieval tortures, life in Sing-Sing and other dreaded prisons, things that really interested him, or just fall into an irritable doze until it was time to go to bed. We children hated the bouts of remorse that kept him indoors, particularly in winter, when everybody bickered around the smouldering fire and Solly's huge, unpredictable arm could swing a knockout blow right across the room.

On one of those nights he lay on the sofa, half undressed, scratching reflectively at his hairy armpit and dribbling smoke from a hand-rolled cigarette. (It was slack in the tailoring and the place stank of cheap shag tobacco.) Spread over his chest was the racing edition of the afternoon paper. He'd been occupying himself working out how much could be won if he'd backed all yesterday's winners at Kempton Park on a ten-bob accumulator. It came to a fortune.

'It comes to a fortune, Rosa,' he said.

My mother was nursing Jacky, the latest baby. She shifted it from the breast, patted it until the burp came, then allowed it to seize the nipple again. A half-made-up dress lay on the living-room table and the money it would bring was already mortgaged to the grocer.

'Racing's the richest racket in the country,' said Solly. 'The sport of kings. Millions change hands every day. Did you ever think of that?'

'What else,' she said, 'have I got to think about from morning to night?'

'Must you be sarcastic about everything I say?'

The baby whimpered and pressed its nose into her flesh. '*Boobele*,[27] there is nothing left to suck but the bitterness of my life,' she told it.

Solly stood up and scowled through the window at the yard below, overflowing with rubbish and gross with the stench of its outdoor privies. 'What a pigsty. Wonder we don't all get consumption,' he remarked despondently. 'You'd think the sanitary inspector was struck blind when he comes round here. They're all in the pay of the landlord.' He looked at my mother accusingly. 'Your bloody landsmen.'

'The landlord is a Romanian,' she retorted. 'I take no responsibility.'

My brother Pinny took his thumb out of his mouth. 'What's conthumption?' I was lying on the floor reading a comic.

'Oh, it's only when you spit out blood.'

'My nose was bleeding yesterday,' Pinny said.

'Oh, shut up and let me read!'

Pinny sucked hard on his thumb and looked thoughtfully into the rusty glow of the fire. In the flat upstairs, stupid Hymie, built like a young bull, stampeded in rage after his shrieking sisters. A fine rain of plaster shook loose from the ceiling.

Solly grabbed the broom and jabbed it viciously upward. 'Keep quiet up there!' he yelled. 'Bloody savages!' But it was a waste of time. Hymie was only making his contribution. Mrs Benjamin, next door, scolded her husband to shrieks of studio laughter on the wireless and the whole building was strident with family disputations as on any normal evening. Solly had just never got used to it. 'It's like living in a bloody madhouse!' he moaned, glaring at my mother as if it was all her fault.

'So, the door is open. Go live in a palace.' She put the baby to bed and returned to the sewing machine to finish the dress. Sugarman, who lived below us, banged on his ceiling in protest against the noise so late at night.

'I won't put up with this for ever,' Solly threatened. He relit the damp stump of his cigarette and retreated to the sofa, resuming his study of the racing sheet to work out how to win a fortune.

The slack in tailoring persisted for weeks and half the street was out of work. My stepfather hung around Whitechapel Road with other idle needle-workers, many of whom were joining the Communist Party in the hope that it would get busy again after the Revolution, which had already nearly happened in Germany and could start at any minute in the Rhondda. Solly didn't join the Party. He remained a Labour supporter. 'What's yours is mine, what's mine's my own.' That, according to him, was Communism. Also, Communism was a mug's game. Better a swashbuckling private enterprise, was his line of thought.

In the meantime, my mother's wedding ring lay unredeemed in the local pawnshop and Solly seriously considering making some kind of a change in sheer desperation. He wasn't the sort of man to sell things off a tray in the market or push a fruitbarrow. It would have to be something that could offer spectacular possibilities. What none of us could have guessed was that for a long time he'd had the ambition to become a bookie.

'I'm thinking of becoming a bookmaker, Rosa,' he said one day.

'All of a sudden?'

'It's been in my mind a long time.'

'It's such a good business?'

'It's such a good business?' he mimicked in exasperation. 'Bookies make fortunes every day!'

She put it down as another of his foolish fancies and forgot about it. Tailoring began to improve, Solly went back to the machine, and we all started eating better again. With harmony restored, my mother began to get fat and soon there was another baby. There was hardly room to move in the house. 'Don't worry,' said Solly cheerfully. 'Soon we'll be able to move to a big house in Stamford Hill.' And how would such a miracle be achieved? It turned out he hadn't given up the idea of becoming a bookie after all.

Even so we didn't believe him. Bookmakers were fat men with cigars clenched between gold-capped teeth. They carried rolls of paper money fastened by rubber bands. They were also small bandy-legged men like Charlie, eyeballs darting from side to side on the lookout for a policeman as they stood on street corners collecting betting slips. It wasn't possible to see Uncle Solly in such a role. Since he came into our family, he'd lost crispness. There was a slight sag of the belly and a broadening of the behind from sitting at the machine. He no longer looked anything but a tailor. In any case, where was he going to get the money?

It turned out that he got it from his younger brother, Hermy, a high-class fur-cutter who had a marvellous post-office account. 'One thing you got to say about Hermy, he's a good saver,' my stepfather used to say, so with Hermy's money and his know-how they formed a working partnership. They picked up a pitch at Harringay Greyhound track from the widow of Rosenbloom, a deceased bookie. The deal included Rosenbloom's stand, a blackboard for chalking up runners, and a leather money pouch stencilled: 'Nat Pays On The Nail'. My mother made a special trip to Stamford Hill to see how she would like living in the neighbourhood.

The conversations that now went on in our house were all about the racing game. It was absolutely fascinating the things Uncle Solly told us.

'Betcha didn't know,' I said to Shmulevitch at school, 'kennel maids can earn a fur coat just by putting a powder in a dog's meat to make it run fast, or drop dead.' Shmuly was impressed and other boys crowded close. 'Mick the Miller, fastest dog in the world, had a splinter pushed up his backside and still came in second,' I said. 'At Tottenham, Nigger Joe, who didn't stand a chance, romped home at twenty to one. But he wasn't Nigger Joe at all. He was Parson's Nose, Silver Trophy winner, dyed black by the Syndicate. The Syndicate is a Liverpool Irish mob. They carve the shamrock on every welsher they catch.' Shmuly picked his nose thoughtfully and rolled a pellet between thumb and forefinger. He flicked it upwards with his thumbnail and said: 'We kin make a Jewish Syndicate and carve the Mogen Dovid.[28] Krr-krr-krr!' For a joke, he pushed me down to the ground, pulled up my shirt and did it in spit on my back.

The night Solly went off to set up his stand for the first time I was too excited to sleep. He'd spruced up with special care, pressed his trousers, trimmed his little moustache and donned a new check jacket with broad lapels like George Raft.[29] My mother went next door to sit with Mrs Benjamin and await his triumphant return. Her warm excited voice penetrated the plaster wall. As always when I couldn't sleep my senses reached out to the infinite possibility of the city, picking up the jagged syncopation of distant streets like the sound of an approaching brass band. Twisting restlessly, I listened for Solly's footsteps with an impatience that resembled love. He would return transformed, pockets jingling with good fortune, restored to the brilliance of his first appearance in our lives. We'd all like one another and be given bicycles. I'd win the scholarship and ride off each morning in a splendid blazer adorned with the crest of some famous school.

About eleven o'clock my mother came in from the Benjamins' and went to bed. The front door opening woke me from a shallow dream. A match scraped and Solly turned up the gas. As it puck-pucked into incandescence, I saw he was accompanied by Hermy, their expressions shifty and worried. Solly said: 'Better be quiet.

We don't want to wake the kids.' I was sleeping on the sofa with my three brothers and Abie's smelly feet rested on the pillow near my head. Pinny snored softly amid the tousled gold of his hair. My own feet rested in the softness of a stomach. It must have been Barny's: he'd burrowed into the bedclothes.

'Well, let's know the worst,' said Hermy. They made some calculations on the margin of a newspaper and it was so quiet the mice could be heard scurrying under the floorboards.

'It looks bad,' Solly remarked despondently. 'Fourteen quid down if we count four we gave the tick-tack men.'

'Fourteen!' Hermy's breath hissed as if he'd touched a hot poker. 'That's diabolical!'

'That last favourite done us. Otherwise we'd a been laughing.'

'We didn't hedge enough, Solly. I kept saying so.'

They went on whispering, rerunning all the races to see where they'd gone wrong. I screwed up my eyes against the gaslight and thought with incredulity of that stupendous loss. Fourteen pounds! The money turned into newly minted pennies spinning and tumbling, millions upon millions, into the bottomless purse of the dark.

Things never really went well. Bad luck resided in Rosenbloom's pouch: what it collected was returned with interest. Not all at once, there were some nights when the partnership showed a gain, but the only ones to profit in the end were the professionals, the tick-tack men. There was a story that Solly and Hermy left the track hurriedly one night after the third race on the card turned out badly for the book, but Solly used to tell it against himself and it may have been a joke. That was years later: at the time it was no laughing matter, only a source of endless family bickering.

'Money doesn't come from the sky,' my mother nagged. 'Maybe you'll learn it at last.'

Then an Italian ice-cream vendor drew the Derby winner in the Irish Sweepstake and collected £75,000. His picture with that of his vast, weeping family was seen in Pathé News and all the newspapers. An envious fever ravaged our neighbourhood. Women especially misappropriated shillings from their housekeeping to buy tickets. My mother formed a syndicate with Mrs Benjamin, Mrs Roitman, old Mrs Shaffer and Jinny Mundy, the caretaker's daughter, investing a florin each to win a fortune. Uncle Solly acquired a lucky ticket all to himself. When you added up the numerals they totalled the magic number, thirteen. And all without exception expected enrichment. The one thing you had to say about our people, we never lost hope. Not entirely.

7

Fanya

When I was growing up you could spend three hours in the gallery of a picture palace for fourpence and see two terrific all-star features. The living theatre couldn't compete: no wonder everyone said it was dying. Then Herschel Rosenheim broke Fanya Ziegelbaum's heart when the New York Yiddish troupe played a season at the Whitechapel Pavilion, and because I tasted a drop of that bitterness Rosenheim's Hamlet remained with me long after I'd forgotten *The Four Horsemen of the Apocalypse* or who played Al Jolson's sonny boy in *The Jazz Singer*.

Fanya first came to work for us when she was fourteen, a scraggy brown-faced orphan whose stockings wrinkled on her matchstick legs. She smelled of dirty knickers and aroused all my nine-year-old mistrust of girls. My mother took her as an apprentice because it was a *mitzvah*. She lived with a stingy aunt in a tall barrack-like building in one of the worst streets off Commercial Road. The aunt economized on Fanya's food to stuff the mouths of her own four fat children. She and her husband made a living out of watching corpses, a ritual requirement, augmenting their income by selling the deceased's clothes to a second-hand dealer with whom they had an arrangement. Such an environment could have a dreadful effect on a young girl, but Fanya had the remedy in her own hands. Quick to pick up the essentials of dressmaking, after a year or so she went up West with my mother's blessing to earn good money in the high-class trade. Still, she was always ready to help out with a big wedding order or in other emergencies, and so never become a stranger.

Every time she returned, skinny Fanya seemed to grow plumper, particularly in the tender region of the chest and behind, where the flesh curved like twin full moons. She'd left her aunt to lodge with a young widow, a saleslady in the cosmetics trade who knew a lot about being smart. As a result, the change in Fanya became startling. She walked around in West End dresses copied from ladies' magazines and stitched by her own hand. Her mouth pouted 'kissprufe' lipstick the colour of raspberry jam. She scented her breath with cachous and did something to her eyes to make them large and brilliant. In short, she'd suddenly turned into a beauty, and although not everybody approved – some of the women said she'd made herself look common – most people agreed that such a picture as Fanya was sure to find a marvellous boy, maybe even with his own business. I hoped so too because she was one of the first girls I really loved.

The summer my mother was pregnant with David,[30] Uncle Solly's third child, Fanya came over to help out most evenings. She was a stimulating influence. Abie, nearly fifteen and rather cocky because his wages were a pound a week, hung around her speaking in a gruff voice and blowing smoke from Player's Weights through his nostrils. Uncle Solly practically stopped going to boxing or the dog track. He talked restlessly of old times in South Africa before he was married, or even further back in the trenches, pulling up his trouser leg to show us his shrapnel wounds and letting Fanya feel the metal under the skin. As for my mother, for whom things were going well at the time, she sang as she treadled the sewing machine, remembered Odessa, spoke seriously with Fanya about love, and occasionally turned towards Solly with the eyes of a young girl.

Late one night, about eleven o'clock, I was detailed to walk Fanya home. Her route led under the railway arch, where *goyim* were supposed to lurk, maddened with drink and lust. My mother wouldn't let her go alone, nor with my stepfather, nor with Abie, for that matter. Not that she didn't trust them exactly, but she was inclined to believe the *dybbuk*[31] of temptation haunted certain dark and evil places and I suppose it seemed less likely that the fiend would seize a sexually unready boy of thirteen. For my part I was flattered to play the protector of so lovely a girl and felt older every minute as we walked side by side.

There were no unusual signs of debauchery when we came to the railway arch, although couples grappled against the dripping walls and tramps lay around parcelled in old newspaper. The evil of the place was in its gloom, its putrid stench, in the industrial grime of half a century with which it was impregnated. The sinister possibilities excited me: I was not immune to the *dybbuk*, after all.

'We're walking past the scene of Jack the Ripper's most famous murder,' I announced. 'It was a foggy night. The woman came out of a pub when she saw this figure in a black coat. He dragged her under the railway arch and slashed her so much, the blood ran down the gutter.'

'You're trying to frighten me.' Her eyes were black and enormous. 'I'll tell your mum.'

I hadn't realized that scaring girls was so thrilling. 'God's honour, Fanya. He was a famous doctor who got a disease and became a sex maniac. That's why he cut up women. You can read all about it in the library.'

'They haven't got things like that in the library,' Fanya said, beginning to go faster. 'It wouldn't be allowed.'

'But, Fanya –'

'I don't want to hear any more!' She spoke in a severe,

grown-up voice, so I shrugged and let her walk on alone. She'd only gone a few yards, glancing back at me nervously, when two men lurched round the corner, roaring drunk.

They staggered along the narrow pavement towards us singing a dirty song. We clung together for mutual protection, pressing close to the wall. The softness of her was a shock of illicit delight; my pressure became urgent. As our bellies touched my boy's cock strained towards a premature maturity and even when the men had gone, we did not immediately separate. We were about the same height. She had a rich dark smell like a pungent animal. Our mouths came together clumsily and I tasted the sophistication of cachous on her breath. A sinful corrupt, oriental flavour.

She wrenched herself away. The night throbbed with darkness and shame. We walked along in silence, interminably. At last we reached the lights of Whitechapel and exchanged a sideways glance. Electric music came out of pin-table saloons. Young men with heavily padded shoulders swaggered by, whistling aimlessly. Fanya was obviously anxious to get rid of me as quickly as possible. I understood her embarrassment. She didn't want to be seen promenading with a boy in short trousers, especially after what had happened. As she hurried away a youth with brilliantined hair called out in an American drawl: 'Hey, sugar, what's your hurry?'

I went home very slowly, remembering the shape of that softness and confused by it. Undressing for bed, I looked at the hair that had started to grow below my thin belly. It reminded me that I must inevitably inherit the hairiness of men, their grotesque, depressing lusts. And all night long I burned with a shameful fever.

The New York Yiddish Theatre opened its London season that autumn with what the drama critic of our building, a watchmaker named Shmulik, described as a daring translation of Gotthold Ephraim Lessing's *Nathan the Wise*. I heard him discussing it with old Mrs Rosen, the grocer, while she was at her daily task of weighing sugar into blue paper bags. Lessing was an assimilationist of the worst kind, according to Shmulik, and consequently he made his heroine, Recha, fall in love with a *goy* of exceptional vulgarity, a *sheigetz*.[32] Mrs Rosen shook her head with disapproving vigour, her ritual wig almost slipping into the sugar. Even at the best of times *Nathan the Wise* wasn't Shmulik's favourite play, but on top of everything he had the bad luck to sit next to a woman who didn't stop eating fried fish the whole performance. She must also have been a critic, he remarked sourly.

The failure of *Nathan the Wise* was redressed by the next production, a Goldfaden comedy, the title of which I have forgotten. It succeeded because it made people laugh and cry and remember the past, all at the same time. And even though one always heard how bitter everything was in the past, the old people were still crazy to relive it. After the triumphant first night, there was a stampede for the box office by every class of Jew, from master tailor to underpresser. The moneyed rolled up in taxis all the way from Park Lane and Stamford Hill but mingled on equal terms with class-conscious proletarians. Toothless crones who could barely hobble to the market-place raced along Whitechapel as if rejuvenated and used their stick-like elbows to reach the front of the uproarious queue. Trampled peanut shells and discarded sweet papers made the pavement look like Victoria Park on a Bank Holiday. There were vendors selling hot beigels, baked potatoes, fruit, chestnuts, fizzy drinks. Down-at-heel rabbinical types with matted beards solicited alms for *yeshivot* in Vilna or Jerusalem. Street musicians who hadn't played the fiddle for years scratched out their rusty tunes. Everybody said it was like the old days at the Pavilion and elderly intellectuals in Goide's restaurant, squeezing the last drop of lemon juice into their tea, predicted a miraculous revival of Yiddish culture.

All this, of course, hardly affected the younger generation and Fanya Ziegelbaum might never even have met Rosenheim if the American troupe's costumes had not needed constant running repairs. She was introduced to the wardrobe mistress by a mutual friend. On her very first evening Rosenheim strode off-stage wearing buckskin breeches and cavalry boots. He was full of fire and tenderness, still under the influence of his romantic role. Fanya went down on her knees to stitch up the split seam and as she did so, she was later to tell my mother, the actor put out his hand to stroke the back of her neck. He must have been pleasantly surprised by her youth and freshness, for even *ingénues* in the Yiddish theatre were performed by actresses who'd already married off their own daughters. As for Fanya, she must have been parched for the touch of such a hand, and from then on there was nothing in life she wanted more than to stand under the *chuppah*[33] and become Mrs Rosenheim. The second Mrs Rosenheim, in fact, the actor soon confessed, but certainly, he promised, the last. When the season in London was over, he'd take her back to America and there make her his own little angel bride.

Afterwards, when the damage was done, everybody said they'd known it would end badly, but if so they were careful not to say it to the girl's face. Whenever she came round to us, the neighbours were never short of an excuse to drop in. Suddenly they ran out of sugar, or were in need of change for the gas meter, or just looked in as they were passing. The springs of the sofa sagged as one by one they settled down comfortably to stay for a cup of tea.

Fanya was excited and talkative. 'Such a cold audience last night,' she would say, 'you wouldn't believe!' Or, with evident satisfaction: 'Six curtain calls yesterday.' All of a sudden she was an expert. The future of the Yiddish theatre worried her. People would rather go to see any rubbish at the movies nowadays. And where were the playwrights, the new Sholem Aleichems? The public no longer had respect for a Jewish actor. They spat in his face. Harry – that was what she called Herschel Rosenheim – had turned down offers to play the biggest roles on Broadway, but how long could he go on making such sacrifices?

The women would surely have preferred to hear less of Rosenheim the actor and more of Rosenheim the lover. It was hard for us to believe actors were real people. Did they bleed real blood, experience real suffering, go to the lavatory? Musicians, yes. Prizefighters also. But actors? Fanya was young, foolish, she had romantic notions. Maybe it wasn't even true about Rosenheim: it could be an exaggeration. And even if it was, an ordinary working girl, what did she want with an actor? About such people one thing was sure, morals they didn't have.

My mother said: 'An orphan like you, without even a mother or a father, you have to be careful somebody doesn't take an advantage.' Everybody knew what that meant. Two minutes' pleasure, nine months' pain, and unspeakable ruin. 'After all, how long do you know him? Practically from yesterday! Sometimes a man pays a compliment. He makes a flirtation. Marriage,' my mother said heavily, 'is for a whole lifetime.'

Fanya was a serious girl. She thought for a while before replying, then looked into my mother's face with the solemn eyes of one who had seen her destiny. 'Sometimes you can be sure in a single minute,' she said with sombre conviction, and added humbly: 'I don't know why I should be so lucky. Once Harry danced with Gloria Swanson. At a charity ball. I don't know what he can see in me.'

One Sunday morning I was standing in a crowd in Middlesex Street market, absorbed in watching a small Irishman working the three-card trick. 'All you got to do is keep your eye on me hands,' he confided out of the corner of his wide rubbery mouth. 'Now watch it, sports!' He showed us the lady and dextrously shuffled the cards on a folding green-baize table.

At that moment Fanya came out of Strongwater's delicatessen holding a brown paper bag. She was with a man in a curly-brimmed hat worn well back on a thatch of red hair. I could tell he was an actor by the elegant way he smoked his cigarette. Otherwise he looked no different from a tailor. Excited, I was just about to follow when the Irishman grabbed hold of me. 'There's some o' you wouldn't trust an Irish feller wid the price of a drink,' he said gloomily. 'Now look at this young laddie, a face of innocence like a holy choirboy. Put your finger on that card, lad. Now, listen! If I was to say this boy's digit is on the lovely Queen of Hearts, would any of you sports venture to believe me for ten bob?' No one ventured. Disconsolately the Irishman turned up the card. It was the Queen and I hurried away.

Fanya leaned against Rosenheim and kept turning her head with quick nervous movements as if she wanted to catch people looking at them. She was wearing a yellow sleeveless dress and her long hair gleamed like rich mahogany. Men stared at her, as they always did, but no one gave Rosenheim more than a glance. He was probably only acting the part of an ordinary person and I admired this modesty, although his lack of height disappointed me. I'd imagined him a tall, commanding figure, but without his hat he'd have been shorter than Fanya.

In Fieldgate Street I slipped over to the opposite pavement to get a good view of the actor's profile and they saw me. I gazed intensely into a watchmaker's window at a man fishing for tiny cogwheels with a magnifying glass screwed into his eye and pretended to be there accidentally. They came over.

'Well, stranger! What are you doing in this district?' Fanya said, in a modulated voice, as if we were as far afield as Oxford

Street at least. I looked round and gave a simulated start of surprise. Rosenheim's hand rested on the soft inside of Fanya's upper arm and he stroked the skin musingly with his forefinger. She told him who I was. They'd obviously discussed her connection with our family because he looked at me with interest.

'I hoid a lot about your mudder and fader,' he said. The accent was just like a Chicago gangster's. 'What Fanya tells me, dey is marvellous pipple.' His pale grey eyes blinked with sincerity. 'Especially your mudder. She look after dis young goil like her own dotter.' He squeezed Fanya's plump arm and she gazed back adoringly. '*Nu*, ve gotta go. Give my best to your pipple, sonny,' he said and, as they were about to leave, remarked as an afterthought: '*Liebchen*,[34] bring the boy vun efening. Maybe he's interested to see the backstage. Vy not?'

Frankly, I didn't expect much from the Pavilion – a Jewish theatre was not the London Palladium, after all – but it was a shock to discover that the stage door led into a building as filthy, neglected and unromantic as the corridors of our tenement. Fanya took me into the costume room. There was a treadle machine and a bench for pressing clothes. A yellowed Ministry of Labour poster on the whitewashed wall was prosaically concerned with fire regulations and you could smell the toilet next door. Mrs Myers, the wardrobe mistress, was a heavy-breasted woman whose square face disappeared into the folds of her neck. But she was nice and gave me a mug of syrupy coffee. A remote drone of voices reached us from the direction of the stage, a sound that resembled the kind of argument one heard at home through the walls of a neighbouring apartment.

They were doing *Hamlet*. Mrs Myers told me the plot, although she'd never actually found time to see the play right through. It was about a Prince who had a mother, a monster. Together with his uncle, the King's brother, she poisoned his father, her own husband, then married with the murderer. From this the Prince had such aggravation, he turned against the whole world. Even to his fiancée, a beautiful girl, he behaved so badly that she drowned herself.

Mrs Myers described it all so vividly, I could hardly wait to see the drama for myself.

In semi-darkness, Fanya led me to the wings. Her hand was hot and I could feel it trembling. In a sunken well that made him look like a trapped grey mouse, an elderly man peered along his pointed nose at a copy of the play text. Battlements rose to the rusty grinding of pulleys and were replaced by gloomy palace chambers. A man in baggy trousers picked his teeth with a matchstick held in one hand and moved a spotlight with the other. I couldn't quite follow the Shakespearian Yiddish. It wasn't in the slightest like the iambic pentameters spoken in our classroom through the pinched Gentile nostrils of Mr Parker, my schoolmaster, and it didn't sound like anything my mother said. Only when Rosenheim, gravely pacing the stage and plucking at his chin, began the famous soliloquy, did I start to get the gist of things.

'*Tzu sein odder nisht tzu sein, Dos is der frage,*'[35] said Rosenheim in a slow, perplexed but remarkably resonant voice.

Fanya gazed at him with petrified eyes as if afraid he might make the wrong decision. Her lips were parted like a listening child's and she responded to Rosenheim's voice as the strings of a piano vibrate to pressure on its keyboard. As he declaimed to the half-empty auditorium, she clenched her small hands and breathed faster. Her bosom was palpitating like a small, agitated animal and I had to restrain the temptation to stroke it into calmness. Nothing that happened on the stage, not even Hamlet's grief over Ophelia's drowning, moved me so much as the madness of Fanya's love.

But soon I became terribly bored. It was more diverting to eavesdrop on the actors who stood around smoking between scenes, scratching their itching faces to avoid smearing the greasepaint and grumbling about the audience. Hamlet's mother, the famous Esther Friedenthal, nibbled a chopped liver sandwich, talking to another actress about her son in New York, who had sensibly decided to study business administration.

One by one the actors stubbed out their cigarettes and went on stage to be murdered. When it was Rosenheim's turn to die, he jerked and quivered for a long time. The final curtain descended to scattered applause and the cast bowed and smiled a couple of times, exchanging supercilious glances when Rosenheim stepped forward to receive solitary homage. Patches of sweat showed on his tunic as he spread out his arms and drooped his flaming head in a crucified gesture. The sound of crunching peanut shells could be heard all over the theatre as the audience stampeded towards the exits. He stood motionless until the curtains swished together.

Fanya hurried to him. 'Harry,' she said, 'darling . . . that was so . . . marvellous! I can't tell you.' Rosenheim squeezed her hands without a word, too moved to speak, then left the stage. As he brushed past me I got a close-up of his face. It was pale, wrung out, ecstatic. 'He really suffers,' Fanya said tearfully. 'When he plays, he gives his heart and soul.' She ran after him and disappeared into the dressing room.

There was nobody around. I advanced stealthily into the centre of the empty stage. 'Ladies and gentlemen, people of the world,' I said quietly in deep tones, gesturing towards the auditorium. Then, louder, '*Tzu sein odder nisht tzu sein?*' My voice went squeaky in the middle of a word. From pit to gallery, empty rows of seats gave me their attentive silence. I felt as if at any moment a terrible eloquence would burst from my mouth and fill the whole city with resonance.

'I . . . am . . .' my voice began. 'I . . . am . . . am?' What? I would soon be fourteen. I wore glasses and had failed the scholarship. There was nothing to say.

Rosenheim's door stood slightly ajar. It was very quiet in there. A corner of the room, tilted at a crazy angle, was reflected in the dressing-table mirror and Fanya was drowning in the kisses of her red-haired Hamlet.

At home, the King, my father, was also dead, and his usurper was in a bad mood. 'Where you been till twelve o'clock, eh? Eh?' he demanded. I pierced him with the glitter of my sword-sharp eyes.

The New York Yiddish Theatre ended its season and departed. I never saw Rosenheim again. The reason he couldn't take Fanya with him right away was because as soon as the actors returned to New York they would have to go on a tour of all the places in America where Jews lived. She begged him to take her along. After all, it was useful to have someone who was handy with the needle. But, no. Such a dog's life of travel, cheap boarding houses, draughty public halls she should never experience, God forbid. Rosenheim wanted her to come to him like a princess. For this everything had to be made ready – a nice apartment, wall-to-wall carpets, a good air-conditioning so summer and winter would be always the same. Maybe, even, a coloured maid in a frilly apron. For his angel bride-to-be, nothing but the best. The whole of New York, America, the world, he would give to her – but it would take a little time, a little patience.

Fanya was disappointed for she only wanted Rosenheim, not the world, but love gave her strength to wait. She brought round a postcard he sent from New York. Over the towers of Manhattan he had written in Yiddish: 'My love is bigger than the Empire State, tallest building in the whole earth, Your Harry.' From Chicago, at the back of a picture of Lake Shore Drive, were the words: 'I miss you, sweet angel, and my tears fill the lake.' The message from Pittsburgh was shorter. 'Thinking of you always.' There was a gap of some weeks, then a card from

San Francisco. 'The "Examiner" writes "Rosenheim's Hamlet a triumph". Wish you were here to see.'

Next time Fanya came to tea she was wearing an old dress and her face without make-up looked as thin and hungry as when she first came to be an apprentice. My mother gazed at her keenly and led her into the bedroom. They talked in low voices, then Fanya rushed out and left, drowning in tears.

'Of course she's pregnant,' my mother muttered to Mrs Benjamin next door. 'Anybody can see.' She leaned back in the chair, hands clasped over her own big belly.

Mrs Benjamin stared in horrified delight. 'Pregnant? From him? From the actor?'

'How else? From a wind in the stomach?'

Mrs Benjamin slapped herself on the cheek and rocked from side to side. 'Aie, aie, aie! Such a bandit, that Rosenheim. You should never trust a ginger, Rosa. In a ginger the blood boils like in a kettle. And when,' she added eagerly, 'is she expecting?'

'Tomorrow I'm taking her to see Fat Yetta.' Tears dripped from my mother's nose. She'd unsuccessfully visited Fat Yetta on a couple of occasions herself. 'Please God, it should work. That poor child is like my own daughter.'

Fat Yetta was at first reluctant to take the case, my mother told Mrs Benjamin the following day, when it was all over. She'd agreed to do so only out of pity for the plight of such a young girl. My mother got up heavily and closed the living-room door so that none of us should hear the shocking details. So, of course, we eavesdropped.

'It was terrible,' she said in an agonized whisper that penetrated the wall. 'A living child was torn from her body. Each fingernail was perfect. And the *neshumah*, the soul, was struggling to breathe. If I live to a hundred, I'll remember it all my life . . .' There was a prolonged silence before she resumed speaking. 'It should be put in a coffin and sent to . . . that murderer!' my mother declared in a terrible voice. She opened the door. 'Go out, children. Go out and play!'

When I came back in, Mrs Benjamin had left and the whole place was filled with the spicy aroma of boiling chicken. My mother filled a jar with soup and sealed the lid with wax paper. She told me to take it to Fanya.

It was one of those leaden Sunday afternoons in January. I carried the soup under my jacket against my breast and its warmth was the only comforting thing in a bleak walk along Brick Lane. Shreds of a poster advertising New York's brilliant Yiddish players still adhered to a board outside the Pavilion. The poster was still there months later when Fanya Ziegelbaum moved up to Manchester, where no one knew of her disgrace. Night times, passing under the railway arch, I thought how different it might have been had I been older, uncommonplace, enhanced by the glamour of strangeness.

8

Enemy Territory

Mr James, the trade school master, had a square, freckled, open-air face with a cleft chin like Johnny Weissmuller. The look of a good sport. 'Sit down anywhere,' he said in a jolly voice as we shuffled into the classroom and sniffed the unfamiliar air. Some deep racial memory stirred the sediment of disquiet: fear of the uncircumcised. 'We'll sort out the sheep from the goats later,' he threatened, grinning matily.

The animal metaphor was unfortunate. A strong carnivorous smell filtered in from neighbouring Smithfield Market, which I'd seen for the first time as I walked to school that morning past rows of refrigerated pigs, agony frozen in their tiny slitted eyes. Worse still, the stench of an evil brew permeated the playground from an adjoining building where cauldrons bubbled with offal ripped from the flesh of slaughtered beasts. It was a disquieting place for one convinced of his own goatishness to begin a new education.

The Headmaster came striding in on short fat legs.

'All together, boys,' Mr James said, lifting his arm with the flourish of an orchestral conductor. 'Good morning, sir!'

The face of a rosy, bald-headed schoolboy of sixty ballooned over the Headmaster's wing collar. He cleared his throat, spat daintily into a large clean handkerchief and examined the result before folding it away. 'As 'Ead of this college, it's my privilege and duty to greet you with a few words of welcome.' He paused to ensure he was receiving full attention. 'What we hexpect of our pupils is hobedience and guts. Hobedience means when you're told to do something, do it, don't lark about. Guts is don't go moaning to your mums when you get whacked across the posterior because you didn't.'

Folding his short arms behind his back, he strode up and down the dais for a few moments, chin meditatively resting on his chest. 'I'm stressing that point,' he went on, confronting us again, 'because you 'ave been selected to learn a honourable and hancient craft – practised, if I might say so, by one of the holdest guilds in the kingdom. The British boot, like the British hinfantryman, is the finest in the world. And that's something to remember with pride. We marched to victory on British leather!' The recollection of patriotism stiffened the Headmaster's podgy frame and made us all sit up straighter. 'Righto!' he said threateningly. 'We'll now call the register. When you 'ears your name jump hup smartly and reply "Present".' He opened a large book, bending back the covers till the spine cracked, and unscrewed a thick fountain pen. The roll call in alphabetical order proceeded briskly. Each boy stood up as commanded, was duly scrutinized, and resumed his seat. The first interruption occurred when the name Leoni, G. was read out. A sallow boy with close-cropped black hair stood up. He had a long thin nose and hairy wrists protruding from the short sleeves of his jacket. The Headmaster examined him for several painful seconds.

'What's the G. stand for, lad?' he asked eventually.

'Giuliano, sir.'

'Dad an ice-cream merchant, his 'e?'

'No, sir.' Leoni's dark eyes flinched. 'My father's a waiter.'

The Headmaster exchanged an amused glance with Mr James and said: 'Righto, sit down, Lester, R.'

My own name seemed a long time coming and I prepared for the shock of it by pressing my knees together to control their trembling. I knew with hopeless certainty that I should never have come to this school. When the official letter from the London County Council offered me a place at Cordwainers' Technical College it seemed a reprieve. Otherwise, at fourteen, like any other unsuccessful boy, I'd be dressed up like a man of forty sawn off at the knees and pitched into the turbulent labour market. The choices were few and gruesome. I could boil a glue pot and sweep up wood shavings, carry a tailor's sack from workshop to retailer, learn to baste a hem, press out a seam, nail a fur, lather a chin, weigh sugar into one-pound bags, or diss a stick of lead type with average competence. During my first week I'd be sent on errands for pigeon's milk, rubber nails and elbow grease, be ordered to take my hands out of my pockets and stop playing pocket billiards and might well be held down while boot-blacking was smeared on my penis. At the end of the week I'd buy my first packet of fags and have nothing to hope for but the Revolution.

In contrast, college was Greyfriars, Harry Wharton, the jolly heroes of the Remove and comic masters in tasselled mortar-boards. Then I discovered that a cordwainer was someone who made boots and shoes. *A boot and shoe college yet*. But somehow, in a manner unforeseen, I retained a desperate hope that Cord-wainers' might still lead to the cloisters of the elect.

The Headmaster adjusted his glasses to peer more closely at the register. He was having trouble in pronouncing the next name. 'Lit – in – totinoff?' His head rotated in its starched collar as he surveyed the class. 'Did I get it wrong?' He tried once more. 'Lit – pot – sky – off, E.'

No one answered.

'Well,' he said in a tone of surprise, examining the register yet again. 'We are 'aving difficulties. Hi wonder, now, could it be that fine old Hanglo-Saxon name Levinskinoff?'

I had the sensation of taking up a role I'd long rehearsed,

a disagreeable but not unrewarding feeling. It happened to all of us. I was thirteen years and ten months old: time already. My brother Abie once refused to read the part of Shylock, explaining that it insulted his people. Six times he was caned on the palms of his hands, six times he refused. And Abie, then only twelve, became the hero of the neighbourhood for a week. Here I was, facing my own test, surrounded by strangers and a long way from home. It was a stern and lonely prospect. With what seemed extraordinary patience, everybody watched and waited. My bladder suddenly filled with the strain of it.

'Please, sir,' I blurted out, 'can I leave the room?'

Mr James coughed disapprovingly and glanced at his superior. 'What's *your* name, lad?' the latter asked with an innocent stare.

'Me, sir?' I had to swallow to get it out. 'Litvinoff, sir.'

'You're not 'ard of 'earing, har you?'

'No, sir.'

'Then why didn't you speak hup when you were called?'

'Hi – I . . . wasn't, sir. Called.'

The Headmaster looked round the class in a puzzled way. 'Did the rest of you 'ear his name read hout?' They said they had. 'Did you, Mr James?'

'I did, sir. Very plainly.'

'There, lad, you must a been daydreaming. Hit won't do, you know. Not in Cordwainers'.' The tone was mild, tolerant and amused. 'Hand another thing. Any boy worth 'is salt hought ter be able ter control 'is hanimal functions till break. Ain't that so?'

What defeated me was not so much timidity as bad timing. The mutilation of my name could hardly be made an issue now that the subject had been changed to one so embarrassing and unheroic. Besides, I wasn't going to be able to hold it in much longer. 'Yessir,' I groaned. *For Christ's sake, hurry up!*

Two dimples appeared in the Headmaster's fat, red-veined cheeks and his eyes had a pigly twinkle.

'Righto, young fellow,' he said cheerily. 'Lavatoryoffsky.'

The laughter erupted like a great fart, and an extraordinary thing happened. The Lord stood at my right hand. He anointeth my head with oil and the need to pee miraculously vanished. I stood up slowly and searched for the annihilating phrase as David must have searched for the pebble that struck down Goliath. Pow!!!

... But nothing came; not a single coherent word, except balls.

'Balls!' I yelled, and made a dash for the door.

'Grab 'im, Mr James!' the Headmaster ejaculated.

He caught me with a flying tackle as I sprinted down the hall and marched me to a room. The walls were lined with cryptic trophies. A glassed mahogany case held a display of slender-ankled boots and the place smelled punishingly of greased leather. 'You got off to a good start, old son,' Mr James remarked, sitting on the edge of the desk and swinging his leg. He jumped up hurriedly when the Headmaster entered and eagerly offered to return to the class, as if to show how much he loved his work.

The Head rubbed his palms together. 'You do that. They're all sitting nice and quiet.' When we were alone, he said: 'Do you suffer from a weak 'eart or any hother physical weakness that could be hacerbated by corporal punishment?'

'N-no, sir.'

'Very good, stand over 'ere.' He pointed to a spot on the carpet well worn by the feet of the guilty.

The lecture was severe and brief. I'd behaved shocking. Insubordination wouldn't be stood for. In his school things had got to be done the British way. It was either make or break and the choice was up to me.

'Hi don't enjoy this, yer know,' Mr Sloper concluded. 'Hit don't gimme no pleasure to chastise a lad.'

Several canes stood in an umbrella stand. He selected one of suitable thickness and flicked it a few times to test its flexibility – wheesh! ... wheesh! ... wheesh! ... Satisfied, he ordered me to bend down, keep my knees straight and touch my toes.

His face glistened rosily from exertion. With every stroke our grunts mingled. It really did sound as if it hurt him more than me.

It was over at last and I limped to the bog. I did a long pee high up on the wall. My rear felt as if it had been seared with a red-hot poker. Locking the door of a lavatory stall, I pulled down my trousers and fanned the inflammation, swearing a secret revenge. Then I washed the tears from my face under the cold tap.

And back to the battlefield.

Cordwainers' taught me the painful lesson that whenever they start separating sheep from goats they're searching the flock for the scapegoat. I bent to touch my toes on average about twice a week. Mr James beat me for having filthy habits (a squashed sardine was found on the floor under my desk), for losing tools (a one-and-sixpenny clicking knife), for dumb insolence, talking back, sucking bull's eyes in class, creating a disturbance by getting my ear in the way of an ink pellet, and for other cardinal infractions.

A Headmaster's flogging was an occasion as ceremonious as Trooping the Colour and hence less frequent. To achieve one on the very first day was something of a record. But I most resented the punishment he gave me for cheating from a dim-witted chap named Sagger. Specifically it was for copying Sagger's composition on 'Footwear in Work and Play'. Protesting my innocence apparently made it worse: it wasn't True Blue.

Retribution included segregation at the back of the class as well as the stick. Leper Litvinoff.

Venturing into the playground was a fearful undertaking. It was a lucky day if I escaped without being tripped, shoved, pummelled or having itching powder forced down my neck. During games, Grindle, a fast bowler, pitched yorkers at my head and once raised an iridescent lump as big as a pigeon's egg. When I dropped the bat to mop my streaming eyes, Mr James cast doubts on my sex. But the crowning humiliation, the thing that injected hatred drop by drop into my soul, was the odious nickname they fastened on me. Pissoffsky.

It was raining one day. An oily suck of viscous liquids sounded in gutters as if London was bleeding into the sewers. Everyone huddled under the inadequate roof of an open shed, but I stood in an exposed doorway alone, moisture trickling under my collar. It was sodding cold! As unobtrusively as possible, I squeezed into the crowd under the shed. 'Pissoffsky – out!' someone said. The cry was taken up: it was a chance for a bit of fun.

My temper went off like a bomb. In a rapture of kicking, punching, screaming violence, I exploded into the soft mass of bodies. The surprise and momentum of this attack caused a stampede and boys fell over each other in a wriggling heap on the ground, hitting out in aimless panic. One of the masters came on the scene and seized four of us at random. With my luck, it was inevitable I would be included. So was Grindle. We were all caned. Grindle rubbed his smarting backside and said in a low voice: 'I'll getcha for this, Ikey boy! I'll nail you to the bloody wall, God 'elp me!'

I would not like to suggest that every single boy – or even master – joined in this persecution. Some of the lads went out of their way to be discreetly friendly. But the school was a frightening place. One passed through the gates and entered a zone of danger. Classrooms were unnaturally quiet and orderly. In the workshop too no unnecessary words were spoken, partly because you couldn't talk with a mouthful of tacks. Instruction was given in the cold level tones prison warders might use to read regulations to convicts, and the work seemed no more useful than oakum picking. In the short while I was there, I never did more than practise skiving scraps of waste leather, and nobody ever made a real shoe. Each day was a curious disconnected experience. I would escape from the pervading misery into a grey stupor, returning as if from a long journey. In fact, being a vivid dreamer, there were times when I had the ghostly feeling that the place only existed in my perverse imagination.

Another lonely boy was 'Okey-Pokey' Leoni. The nickname came from an old street cry of Italian ice-cream vendors: 'Okey-Pokey, penny a lump!' No one associated with him, but neither did anyone molest him. He owed this immunity to the popular idea that Eyeties were quick to stick a knife in your gizzard when aroused, being very hot-blooded. It was the period of cigar-chewing Chicago gangsters with enormous padded shoulders who made love to the broads with a wisecrack and buried their massacred rivals in sumptuous wreaths of flowers. Some of that romantic violence rubbed off on all the spaghetti fraternity, although no one could be less like Al Capone than skinny four-eyed Leoni, who was quiet and rather old for his age, the sort of boy who looks as if he's worked out his whole life in advance.

During the first couple of weeks, Leoni and I passed each other as if we lived on different planets. Then one lunchtime I went into a café to get a cup of tea to drink with my sandwiches and he was sitting at the only table with a vacant chair. Between us, a meat porter in a bloody smock hacked away at a plateful of steak and chips. Leoni unwrapped a piece of salami, cut it into slices with a penknife, unscrewed a small jar of olives and proceeded to eat with neat composure. After finishing this meal, he lit up a fag and inhaled expertly.

'Do you smoke already?' I asked, highly impressed.

He flicked some ash in my direction and said, lifting the corner of his mouth in a cynical smile: "Course I do. I'm over fourteen.'

The meat porter grinned. 'What about wimmin? 'Ad your under yet?' Leoni's sallow face reddened but he kept silent. 'I 'ad my 'and on it all night,' the man said. 'Wanna smell?'

Still silent, Leoni carefully nipped the glowing end off his cigarette and left. So did I. We walked side by side along Farringdon Road. Lunchtime crowds browsed at the second-hand bookstalls. A group of factory girls with plucked eyebrows and broad scarlet mouths sat on a low wall, pretending not to hear the coarse flatteries of their unshaven fellow workmen. There was the cheerful rattle of trains shunting in the nearby railway. Soprano noises came from a junk-stall gramophone, giving a lilt to the sunny afternoon. It was spring: there was companionship: I felt pretty good.

'Do you like the English?' Leoni asked, frowning.

I looked up in surprise. 'I am English.'

'Then why you got a Polish name?'

'It's not Polish. It's a world-famous Russian name. Everybody knows that.'

Leoni walked in silence for several paces, hands thrust deep into his pockets and shoulders hunched, thinking it over.

'You don't look English to me,' he said. 'Old Grindle was telling everyone you're a Jew from Whitechapel.'

'Sod Grindle!' My ears began to roar. 'Whitechapel's not in a foreign country, is it? It's in London, the capital of England. And plenty of Jews are English.' A superior kind of English, I could have added. Cleaner, cleverer, soberer, harder-working, friendlier, nicer to live with – altogether better class. 'Some of the leading English people are Jewish people,' I added heatedly, trying to think of a suitable example. 'Did you ever hear of Colonel Kisch?'

'Colonel who?'

'He was only one of the biggest heroes of the war!'

'OK, no need to shout,' Leoni protested mildly, and dropped the subject.

When we got to know one another better I discovered that although Leoni was born in London, in the Italian colony of Saffron Hill, he thought of Florence – where his family originated – as his native city. He despised the English because Italians were cleaner, cleverer, more sober, harder-working, friendlier and more religious. Until the Roman Italians came under Caesar, the English couldn't read or write, had no laws and roamed about in animal skins slaughtering one another. As soon as Leoni was old enough he intended to return to the Firenze he'd never seen and set up as a high-class shoemaker. The Italians made better shoes.

Once he took me to his home, a dark and airless apartment in an ugly block of flats on the main Clerkenwell Road, muffled from the din of traffic by dusty curtains. His father, who worked late, was asleep in a screened alcove. The place was full of swarthy moustached women with black braided hair and big hanging breasts who gabbled fiercely in their strange language as if engaged in an interminable quarrel. Although there was a tribal resemblance to my own world, this was distanced by pictures of saints and crucifixes and, most of all, by the pervading smell of foreign cooking. It made it easier to understand why Leoni was not English like me.

So now I had a friend and, in a way, it meant I'd begun to settle in. Every morning I left home and stole rides to school on the backs of lorries. I'd learned to smoke and money saved on bus fares went to buy Woodbines. The smell of the meat market no longer bothered me. An inner toughening had taken place. I walked into class like the Lone Ranger entering a hostile barroom, eyes narrowed, hands resting loosely on the holsters of my invisible six-shooters. There was even something flattering about my notoriety and I played up to it. Whenever Mr James asked some simple question I gave an insolent display of knowledge, having acquired a fund of curious information from Bethnal Green Public Library.

'Let's ask old Clever Dick,' he would say, and the boys grinned in pleasant anticipation. 'You up there at the back, why did Lancashire become the centre of the cotton industry?'

'The problem with cotton-spinning,' I'd reply with relish, 'is it's hard to stop the fibres breaking except in a very humid atmosphere. Lancashire has a high rainfall, and is therefore an ideal place for cotton-weaving. Besides, sir, in the Industrial Revolution much use was made of child labour. Now, according to Karl Marx –'

'All right, we'll have none of that,' Mr James would growl, and I'd sit down, smirking.

So the weeks passed and it looked as if I'd get through term alive and chipper. But on the grave occasion of my fourteenth birthday I tried to look beyond this limited horizon. No anniversary could be more momentous. If the Headmaster should pick on me again I could, with glorious impunity, snap my fingers in his face and exit from Cordwainers' for ever with a careless laugh. And then – what? Although I had an inner conviction that an exceptional destiny awaited me somewhere out there like a made-to-measure suit, as a class-conscious boy who read the *Daily Worker* I also knew that fourteen-year-olds were glutting the labour market and being ruthlessly thrown on the scrapheap. On the other hand, if I sold out to the system by staying on after the term was over I'd qualify for a modest grant. And, perhaps – who knew? – an influential school inspector would enter the room just as I was skilfully expounding Einstein's Theory of Relativity and, summoning the Headmaster, declare: 'Who is this erudite scholar? I demand to know why he is wasting his time here instead of being prepared for a brilliant future at Oxford University.'

The importance of becoming fourteen led me to scrutinize myself more closely than usual in my mother's full-length fitting mirror. It showed a tallish boy at an unfair disadvantage because he'd outgrown the sleeves of his threadbare jacket and his skimpy trousers exposed more shank than was dignified. Seen from the front the nose was not too long and roughly in the right place, but he had thick negroid lips, big square teeth with a gap in the middle, and one hinge of his nickel-framed glasses was tied with cotton. Discouraged, I retreated a few paces and turned swiftly to catch the reflection by surprise, the way it might be seen by a stranger. It hesitated and shambled towards me with an agonized look. It didn't have the appearance of a successful boy.

'I think I ought to leave school and make a career,' I said despondently that evening over supper.

My stepfather stretched his pale eyes in mocking amazement. 'Career?' Laughter gurgled in his throat like phlegm. 'What in, banking?'

When the usual recriminations subsided, he said he might be able to get me a job in the tailoring. My mother handed me an extra-thick slice of cheese with an expression of moist tenderness that said she wished it could be everything – health, wealth and happiness. Abie had seen an advert in a Brick Lane grocer's window for a tricycle delivery boy and, with his usual crude humour, suggested I'd soon work my way down to chief floor-sweeper. We kicked one another under the table and started another row. Grimly rolling a shag cigarette, Solly announced that I'd soon find life was no bed of roses.

'Must you put a curse on the child?' my mother shouted, cutting furiously into a loaf of bread.

But my real curse is indecision, and when I act at all it is impulsively, in most cases at the wrong moment. I started behaving recklessly in school in the hope that the consequences would be so nasty as to force me to leave, but nothing worse than the odd caning befell me. The Head himself stopped giving me special attention and no longer had any difficulty with my name. In fact, he addressed me only when it was unavoidable, averting his face as if my proximity was too disgusting to bear. If only they would torture me to become a Christian, or force me to eat pork . . .

But the end, when it came, did involve principle. It was during break one Monday morning. Leoni and I were segregated as always in a corner of the schoolyard and began an argument over Italian Fascists pouring castor oil down the throats of Communists. Leoni paced around with his hands in his pockets, scowling. It served the Communists right, he said ferociously. 'Look what they did in your country. They killed all the priests.'

A ball bounced across the yard. I fielded it and sent it back to the players with a drop kick before turning to deal with this unexpected statement.

'Whaddya mean, my country?'

'Russia. Your fatherland. You say "I'm English, I'm English", but even a Chinaman can be born in London.'

'Then he's an English Chinaman,' I said. Leoni pulled out a crumpled handkerchief and blew his nose in a highly contemptuous manner. His drawn-out shadow made a grotesque shape on the brick wall. 'Are you a Fascist?' I asked, raising an eyebrow. Bash! right in the solar plexus.

'All Italians are proud to be Fascists. *Dei et Patria*. Good on Mussolini! I hope he shoots all Communists!'

93

I'd never met a Fascist before and would certainly have expected visible signs of brutishness and depravity. Leoni didn't even have pimples.

'You like Mussolini?' I gasped. 'Even if he sucks the blood of the workers?' A distant fire glowed in his sooty eyes. Then he thrust two fingers in front of my face and began to walk away. 'Mussolini's a bastard!' I yelled after him.

He whipped round, tense and glaring, and pushed me clumsily against the wall. I pushed him back. We both took off our glasses carefully to show we meant business. Grindle, my chief enemy, strolled over with a group of his cronies.

'What's a marrer, Okey-Pokey?' he drawled solicitously. 'You and your pal 'aving trouble?'

'He – he insulted my country,' Leoni panted.

'Fucking Jewboy,' Grindle said. 'Why don't he go back to Palestine?'

I shuffled forward, fists up and chin tucked in, hoping to scare them off. It sometimes worked: but not this time.

'Look at 'im, Ted "Kid" Lewis,'[36] jeered Grindle, and Leoni laughed gratefully. 'Muscles like sparrer's kneecaps and a cock like a peeled banana.' Encouraged by the applause this witticism aroused, he danced towards me, feinted, and flicked a light left at my jaw. I backed away with a belligerent scowl.

'Needle fight! Needle fight!' somebody yelled.

'Aah, not werf it,' he said.

'Gawn, Tom! You can 'andle 'im.'

Grindle still hesitated. Half lowering my fists, I tried to maintain an appearance of confident indifference. He had the knobbly face of a good fighter and shaved already. My irresolution must have got through. Grinning evilly, he said: 'OK, then, yeah! I'll see you after school, Pissoffsky.'

They all began a frantic yelling. 'Now! Now!'

With unnerving calm, Grindle took a large watch out of his

waistcoat pocket, consulted it in frowning concentration, then remarked: 'We got eight minutes. Awright.' I made the mistake of waiting. He put the watch away and hit me almost at the same moment. As my head jolted back, I caught a fleeting glimpse of Leoni, miserable and contrite. Grindle hit me again. I grabbed hold of his coat to restrain him and by some miracle he spun round, overbalanced and fell on his back. We were both astonished, but he was also alarmed.

'Cor! 'E knows Jujitsu,' someone exclaimed in awe, and I was flooded by a premature feeling of victory.

Mr James came sprinting across the yard, the forelock of his blond, curly hair blowing in the wind, and pushed energetic-ally into the centre of the crowd. He glanced from me to my reclining adversary in surprise.

'Get up, Grindle!' he commanded tersely. 'What's it all about?'

Like the true sportsman he was, Tom Grindle kept mum, but several other boys eagerly volunteered the information that the two of us were having a needle fight.

'A needle fight? Well, well, well!' Mr James made no attempt to conceal his satisfaction. For the first time ever, he gazed at me with approval. 'Good!' he said. 'That's the sporting way to get rid of bad blood. But it's got to be according to the rules. I'll speak to the Headmaster and we'll have it made official.' He gave us a chummy grin. 'You can bash each other's brains out in the gym at 4.30. If you got any. I'll be ref.'

All the rest of the day I was rocked by alternate waves of hope and panic, mainly the latter. I developed distressing physical symptoms. There didn't seem enough air to breathe; there was a hole in my stomach like a hundred-foot drop; I couldn't concentrate; my heart was pumping its heavy reluctant blood from somewhere outside my body; I felt faintly sick and kept wanting to pee all the time. At half past four Mr James smiled and nodded at me: 'Feeling in good shape, lad?' I grinned weakly and said yes in a shivering voice. It seemed to have got very cold for the time of the year.

The whole school tramped to the gym and formed up around the walls while Grindle and I stripped down to shorts and undervests. A hitch occurred when Mr James asked for someone to act as my second. Everyone became terribly quiet. Mr James repeated the request. There was a stir behind me as someone pushed his way forward.

'I'll do it,' said Leoni in a low voice. I don't know why he volunteered but he laced on the padded boxing gloves without once looking at my face, as if to make it clear it didn't mean friendship.

All I wanted now was to end the suspense for better or worse, but we had to wait for the Headmaster. He trotted in at a brisk pace, a busy man attending to essential duty, and sat down in a chair placed deferentially at the ringside by Mr James.

'Right, lads,' said the latter, having called us into the centre of the ring. 'Two-minute rounds, needle-fight rules. That means,' he added alarmingly, 'fight to the finish or till someone gives in. Unless, in my opinion, one of you is too badly beaten up to carry on.' He slapped us on our backs encouragingly and the battle began.

As we advanced cautiously towards one another I noticed that Grindle seemed nervous. The hard muscles in his cheeks twitched and his eyes were screwed up uncertainly. Heartened, I rushed in, flailing my arms. He went back on the ropes and cowered behind his forearms. Except for the slap of leather gloves, there was a dismayed silence in the gym at the unpromising performance of the favourite. I knew a sweet surge of confidence. Grindle put his arms about my neck, his breath warm and close. Mr Sloper's mouth twisted in displeasure as I hammered my opponent's body.

'Break,' he said, looking peevishly over at Mr James. 'Break!' shouted the latter at the top of his voice.

We did so and Grindle swiped me smack in the nose. He was a strong boy. Blood and snot gushed out. As I staggered back, there were yells of excitement and all the bells of Christendom rang in my head. Grindle hit me again and again, a look of ecstasy on his blurred face.

In the midst of confusion, noise, helplessness, I felt disconnected and, somehow, resigned. There was so much shouting going on and some of it may have been meant as encouragement for me. But I couldn't believe it. Grindle was punching me, but I was fighting them all. Somewhere, in some deep recess of my being, I knew this was not for me: it was not my way.

Leoni mopped my bleeding nose with his own handkerchief. 'You better give in,' he muttered. 'He's murdering you.'

I went in throwing my arms about wildly, desperate to keep Grindle off. One lucky blow caught his eye. Or unlucky. Blotched and livid, he rushed past my pounding fists and drove me into a corner. In his reddened eyes I glimpsed something terrifying. Grindle really did want to kill me! Even if I could smash every bone in his face, the look of hatred would remain.

An excruciating pain sliced through me as he punched me in the stomach. I was clubbed on the face, the body, the head.

'That'll do,' Mr James said, forcing Grindle away. Through bloodshot darkness, I discerned a wryness in his expression which could have been pity, but the Headmaster was smiling.

There was no school for me the following day, nor ever again. I was fourteen years and three weeks old. Walking along Barbican, in the Clerkenwell district, one sunny morning, I saw a notice on a factory door. 'Strong boy wanted to learn the trade. Third floor.'

Summer was beginning, the height of the fur-trade season.

9

The God I Failed

I drifted into Communism when I was about eleven under the influence of a militant boy named Mickey Lerner.[37] He was thin and undersized, with a chronic cough, and suffered many indignities at the hands of bullying masters and pupils. His father, a presser, also coughed because his lungs had been rotted by the steaming cloth he pressed ten hours a day. In fact, the whole family coughed. They lived in the sooty air of a Brick Lane alley overhung by a railway bridge and had a habit of blinking like troglodytes in full daylight. This made them seem puzzled and defenceless when, in reality, they were a tough and stiff-necked tribe. I was led into Communism more by the misery and toughness of the Lerner family than by anything in my own predicament.

At school, Mickey was often caned for acts of ideological insubordination, like refusing to sing 'Land of Hope and Glory'. When the stick cracked across his open palm a hissing noise came from his pursed blue lips and the tendons of his skinny neck went rigid, but nothing they did could make him sing that song. Every time it happened I became more of a Communist. Too scared to emulate Mickey entirely, I sang the well-known scurrilous version, 'Land of Soap and Water, Mother Wash My Feet', switching guiltily to the proper words when the master looked in my direction. It was a poor gesture of rebellion so I tried to be militant in other ways, like scribbling 'Down with the Boss Class' on the inside covers of library books and joining the Pioneers.

We used to get together once a week near Whitechapel Road at the back of a second-hand furniture store that reeked of dust, mildew and decaying leather, and those smells became part of my Communism too. Our leader, Comrade Bill, was a ginger-headed man in a boiler suit who spoke with a refined accent, like a scout master. He taught us simple facts about the class struggle – that capitalists burned coffee in Brazil to keep up the market price, wars were engineered for profit by international arms manufacturers, religion was the opium of the masses, and so on. Once he asked the Jewish children to put up their hands. Nearly all of us did so. 'In the Soviet Union,' Comrade Bill remarked with a kindly smile, 'anti-Semitism has been abolished.' He went on to explain that the toiling Jewish masses were being exploited by rich Jewish capitalists who would sell their grandmothers for gold. But not to worry. After the Revolution there would be no Jews left, only workers. In shrill unison, we sang 'The Red Flag'.

So the seeds of faith were sown and grew like the green bay tree. One of my jobs at fourteen was as an apprentice in the ladies' garment trade, a hotbed of industrial unrest. In the workshop, elderly tailors sat cross-legged on their benches glumly stitching away, or chewing garlic sausage sandwiches, waiting – according to their predilection – for the Messiah or the red day of reckoning. I held myself ready for a similar apocalypse.

When I look back at that time, I realize that my Communism was not truly of Marx and Lenin. I tried to read the *Communist Manifesto*, but the words buzzed around in my brain like a cloud of gnats bringing discomfort, not profit. In my fifteenth year, I grew five inches with psychic growing pains and glands discharging like mad. Most sensitive of all, my tear ducts overflowed at any slight stimulus – the sight of a scabby cat, a full moon, my own melancholy face in a mirror, the croon of Bing Crosby hymning unrequited love. So Communism was the cure of all these things, the gin-soaked tramp made handsome as a Prince of Wales, bugs crawling out of cracks and turning into butterflies, as much tinned pineapple as the belly could take, death at the barricades and resurrection in the pure and loving embrace of that golden girl who waited somewhere in the world for me alone.

In the meantime, I'd graduated to the Young Communist League and there met Hannah Fishbein, long brown hair, sweet smile, schoolgirl freckles and plump young breasts I blushed to notice. At branch meetings her electric presence stung me to strident self-advertisement. I volunteered for everything, selling the *Worker* on street corners six bitter January nights in a row, going on strike pickets, carting platforms around for other comrades to speak from, carrying banners to Trafalgar Square. Even Mickey Lerner, who was, of course, our branch secretary, held me up as an example to less militant members. Now at grammar school, he was still single-minded and weighed down with a gravity beyond his years. When Mickey spoke, we listened. He was our Stalin and could say no wrong. His praise warmed me almost as much as Hannah's thrilling smile.

One evening I volunteered to paint slogans in the streets and, after mixing a bucket of whitewash, began the solitary task, nervously alert for a patrolling policeman. I was scrawling 'Stop Fascism Now' on the brick wall of a brewery when a girl cycled slowly along. As she passed under a street lamp, I saw it was Hannah. She wore blue shorts and a tight red jacket. I was shaken by a sweet and terrible violence.

'Hullo!' she said. 'How are you getting on?'

'Fine!' I replied.

'You've got nice handwriting,' she said with a giggle.

The whitewash was dripping on my shoes, but I dared not move and tried desperately to think of some debonair remark.

Hannah spun the pedals of her bike aimlessly until the silence became too embarrassing.

'Well, see you at the YCL,' she said at last, and cycled away.

Solid, policeman-like footsteps sounded nearby, so I picked up the bucket and fled, ignominiously. I didn't even stop to finish painting the slogan. The sign was left to read 'Stop Fascism No'. All I could think of as I ran was how terrific Hannah looked in her little red jacket, and what an idiot she must have thought me, not being able to carry on a decent conversation.

For a few days I felt terrible – surly at home, in the workshop absent-minded, haunting empty streets at night for the melancholy satisfaction it gave. That Sunday we all went rambling in Epping Forest. It was a clear, cold February afternoon. Trees stood in petrified silence, branches brittle with frost, and the forest was hollow and mysterious like an empty cathedral. I went off alone and began to run, the bitter air stinging my face. 'Hooray!' I yelled suddenly. 'Hooray!' Then, at a safe distance, loud enough to burst the sky: 'Han-nah Fish-bein! I – love – you!' My voice stopped abruptly and stillness resumed more intensely than ever. I sat down on a tree trunk to catch my breath, and then – unbelievably – she was there.

'I've lost the others,' she said, pink-cheeked and shy.

We walked side by side, saying little. For me it was miraculous that even the two clouds of our breath mingled. Climbing over a stile, her lithe weight pressed against my shoulder and stayed a moment longer than necessary. In the cinema that evening the dark made us bold. Our hands touched, then our knees and Hannah's long hair brushed my cheek. The buds of manhood swelled in my thin boy's body and I burned for the first time in the phoenix fire.

So I began to see a lot of Hannah. She was a grocer's assistant and we'd meet two or three times a week when the store shut, mostly to walk around looking in shop windows. It was too cold to sit in the park and we couldn't afford the pictures more than once in a while. When we got tired of walking we'd sit in a café talking desperately about life and the hopes we had in it. Hannah was the first person who didn't laugh when I said I wanted to be a writer. We discussed free love, with only a little embarrassment, and agreed, in theory, why not? Grown-ups were hypocrites about sex. Hannah's older brother married a non-Jewish girl at eighteen and her father refused to attend the wedding, even though he was a member of the Communist Party. One day she was going to live in Russia and help build the Revolution. I wanted to make the Revolution here so that my mother wouldn't need to work like a dog and there'd be a private WC for every family living in our buildings. We were sure life was going to be very, very beautiful and worth waiting for. It was so interesting talking like this, we didn't go to YCL for weeks.

One evening I'd just got back from work when Mickey Lerner called. He looked hot-eyed and sick and my mother made him drink some lemon tea. It was embarrassing the way she kept asking him about school and about his family, because I knew he'd come to tell me off for not attending branch meetings.

When we left the flat, he said in a challenging, unfriendly way: 'Why don't we see you any more?'

'I've been working overtime, Mickey,' I said, uneasy at the lie.

He kept looking away with that bleak, determined expression he used to have when they caned him in class.

'Hannah Fishbein also doesn't come, not since that ramble in Epping Forest. She's also working overtime, I suppose.'

I didn't say anything. At that age I could be made to feel

guilty very easily, just as easily as I was made to cry. And I was especially guilty about Hannah because of the way I sometimes thought about her when I couldn't get to sleep.

'If you want to be apathetic, please yourself,' Mickey went on in a miserable voice. 'But you're leading one of our best comrades astray. I saw you the other night, kissing.'

'We weren't kissing,' I said indignantly. 'We-we have a platonic relationship.'

'You were smooching like mad,' he insisted. 'It was disgusting! I wasn't the only one who saw.'

The more I protested my platonic relationship with Hannah, the more insistent Mickey became that I was practically a sex maniac, and there was little I could say because I did think about sex most of the time and was worried that I might be. A sex maniac, I mean.

'Are you in love with Hannah Fishbein?' he demanded.

I admitted to liking her and, when he pressed me further, to liking her a great deal, more than any other girl I knew.

Mickey stared at me with savage contempt. 'Don't you realize that love is only a biological necessity? Every lumpen proletariat goes around slobbering about love. You're supposed to be a militant comrade!'

I protested that I was a militant comrade.

'You don't even know what the word means,' Mickey said. 'No militant comrade would take a girl member of the YCL and try to keep her all for himself.' That was the kind of thing you'd expect from a bourgeois opportunist. After all, what had Lenin himself said? Sex was not like a drink of cold water.

He hurried away with shoulders hunched, leaving me in a rather confused state of mind.

The next time I saw Hannah she was very quiet and looked at me rather oddly. I guessed that Mickey Lerner had spoken to her and was afraid he might have said that about me being a sex maniac. She had on a short skirt and a red woollen jumper belted in tight at the waist. All the way down Whitechapel Road she kept her thoughts to herself until we went to a milk bar in Aldgate. We sat side by side on two high stools and I did my best not to look at her legs, which got rather exposed because she kept crossing and uncrossing them.

'Are you fifteen yet?' she asked unexpectedly.

I said yes, I was fifteen, but that lots of people took me for seventeen because I was old for my age. Actually, it wasn't quite true. I wouldn't be fifteen for another six weeks.

'I'm sixteen in June,' Hannah announced, and managed to say it in a manner that was very annoying.

I lit up a Woodbine, flicking the spent match away like George Raft in *Little Caesar*. 'Some people of sixteen are about thirteen mentally,' I remarked coolly.

Hannah smiled so that everybody around could see her marvellous teeth and, speaking in a very distinct voice, asked: 'Aren't you too young to smoke? It might stop you growing.' I wouldn't deign to answer. 'Are you feeling hot? You're face has gone all red,' she said.

Just as I was about to walk out in disgust, she nudged my leg with her knee. 'Silly,' she smiled. 'I'm only kidding.'

The Aldgate pavements were swarming with raucous crowds rolling beerily out of pubs. Hannah clutched my arm and urged me into a side street. The pressure of her shoulder against mine and the touch of her hand made my heart bump inside my ribs. Someone somewhere was playing a mouth organ, a coarse, honey-sweetness of sound. The drifting tang of jellied eels made me think of Southend pier on a summer night. We began to walk slowly and, as we approached a factory door, our footsteps stopped.

In a small, husky voice, Hannah said: 'Do you believe in platonic love between a boy and a girl? I mean, as a Communist and a member of the YCL.'

Until then I was sure she wanted me to kiss her. I'd been thinking about it and all the signs seemed marvellously right. Now she'd confused me. It wasn't clear what she wanted. It was difficult to cope with an intellectual question like that when you were in the middle of having an emotional feeling.

'What do you mean, Hannah?'

'Do you believe in platonic love?' she repeated, as if addressing an idiot.

I withdrew my arm from her. 'Well . . . that's a hypothetical question.'

'Yes or no?' she insisted.

Had Lenin said anything about platonic love? Mickey Lerner, as a dialectical expert, would have known for sure. I gave up the struggle.

'I – I suppose so.'

'You won't when you're older,' Hannah said coldly, and walked on.

She didn't turn up for our next date, so I spent the evening playing the pin-tables. A couple of days later I called at the grocer's where she worked and bought a doughnut. Hannah pretended to be busy. I hung around near her house several times, waiting for her to come out, but if she did appear I hid until she'd gone. The fact was I'd got the sack from my job and had plenty of time on my hands. All day I sat in the public library reading detective stories, and night after night dreamed about girls – not only Hannah – in ways that convinced me my sex condition was becoming more alarming.

After a couple of weeks like that, I developed a craving to go back to the YCL and hear a human voice other than my own family's. Shivery and nervous, I had to force myself to go inside. Mickey Lerner wasn't friendly. The first thing he did was ask for my dues, which took the last sixpence from my pocket. Hannah Fishbein gave me a distant look as though she stood a mile off and started a vivacious conversation with one of the boys. Mickey strutted across the room and joined them, making some comic remark that set them laughing like maniacs. It was obvious to the world that they were laughing at me. For the first time I noticed that Hannah had rather a big nose for a girl.

The meeting started. Mickey went on to the platform and was introduced by the chairman. Everybody knew him, of course, but he insisted on doing things the correct way. 'Comrades!' he began. Mickey was a very good speaker and usually I agreed with everything he said. But that night it became obvious to me that he was a show-off. He kept looking at Hannah every time he made some little joke and she laughed and laughed as if he was the greatest comedian.

When the discussion opened, they all agreed with each other, as usual, and especially with Mickey, at the same time pretending there were fine points of difference.

'Comrade,' Mickey said, looking at me, 'from the expression on your face you seem to have a problem.'

The trouble was that as soon as I got on my feet everything I wanted to say rushed out of my head. He was right, I did have a problem. And I couldn't even explain it to myself. I tried to say something about it. Sometimes people wanted to be alone and sometimes they didn't want to be alone. The idea wasn't clear. It was hard to get it out without stammering. I looked at Hannah, but she stared straight ahead. Unable to think of anything else, I sat down abruptly.

Mickey nodded gravely. He said of course people had problems under capitalism, Comrade, and any time I wanted to discuss my personal problems they'd be glad to listen. But if I thought about it dialectically, I'd know that Communism cured every problem. Standing on the platform, he didn't look short and skinny at all. He had a wonderful vocabulary for his age.

'If Communism cures everything,' I called out defiantly, 'tell us how it cures a corn on your foot?'

Most of them laughed, but Mickey didn't even smile, he just jerked his head as if his collar was tight.

'All right, Comrade,' he said in a cold, hard voice, 'I'll give you the Party line. Why do people get corns on their feet? Because they have to wear cheap, mass-produced shoes. You'll never find a capitalist suffering from corns. He can afford to have his shoes specially made. Under Communism every worker who needs special shoes will have them provided free by the state and corns will be a thing of the past.'

It was, of course, a brilliant answer, and it left me crushed.

They expelled me from the YCL soon afterwards. They said it was because I was a Trotskyist. The decision was unanimous and Hannah voted with the rest. I didn't know what Trotskyism was exactly, but someone said they were shooting people in Russia for it.

A View from the Seventh Floor

That summer I was sixteen there were no sparrows in the streets, and the sun never shone, and the laughter of distant voices mocked my despair. All day I inhaled the hairs of dead foxes, skunks and rabbits in Dorfmann's rat-infested fur workshop, and would do so, it seemed, until my lungs were stuffed full as a feather pillow. At night I slept amid the debris of failure – God had torn up my dreams like an impatient schoolmaster.

In Dorfmann's, I was the only one who didn't belong to the family. His wife, the machinist, had big muscular arms and shaved every day, a misfortune she could not conceal by powdering her jaws. Luba, the finisher, an old-fashioned girl, was his niece. Braided plaits of jet-black hair were wound around her delicate ears and her high plump breasts were like two nestling pigeons. She stitched away industriously and blushed when our glances collided. In that place I was her prisoner, thinking of her hotly, with shame, as I stroked the silken pelts spread out on the bench. So even though the pay was meagre and the work hard, I counted these the wages of lust and did not rebel.

'Don't you want to improve yourself any more?' my mother said in her suffering voice.

She stood at the stove ladling soup into my plate, the latest baby squirming in the crook of her arm. A man's cardigan hung shapelessly on her body, but her belly was seen to be big again.

We were ten already, the largest family in the buildings, and nothing helped – not whispered conferences with neighbours, nor the tubes and syringes concealed among the underwear at the bottom of the wardrobe, and certainly not Fat Yetta, who sometimes lifted the curse of fertility from other women but only left my mother haggard with pain and exhaustion.

'Manny,' she said, 'I'm talking to you!'

My hands reeked of the corpses of small animals and there was no redemption. 'Leave me alone,' I cried. 'I don't want to improve myself.'

'*Boobele*, take a little soup, it's good for you,' she crooned, forcing the spoon into little Frankie's reluctant mouth. 'And Jacky, stop playing with the sewing machine! Where's Davey! Where's Sonia! Close the door, somebody, there's a terrible draught!' She would have gathered us back into the womb had God's housing inspector permitted such overcrowding.

Solly, my stepfather, had the gift of detachment. He stirred his vermicelli and read *The Freethinker* with the credulous fascination of a believer. My brothers came in one by one to quarrel, eat ravenously, and depart unsatisfied. Food could not appease our hunger.

'God made the world in six days, but who made God?' Solly said with a dry chuckle.

'Better to think of shoes for the *kinder*,' my mother replied sombrely. She turned back to me. 'Maybe in night school you could learn to be a typewriter.'

'Don't speak in Peruvian,' Solly said. 'You're wasting your breath. That boy's got no ambition, can't you see?'

My ears began to pound like kettledrums. Tyrants would tremble if they knew my power. I'd blow up banks and start a revolution, invent a miracle, make Rothschild look a pauper. A thousand years would remember my name. I was a bomb waiting to explode the world ...

'I'll join the army!' I said in a choking voice. 'I'll go to Australia! Maybe I'll be an all-in wrestler.'

'With your physique?' Solly said. 'Don't make me laugh!'

He laughed. I poured my soup into the sink. Solly rolled up *The Freethinker* and chased me out of the house. That night I didn't go home at all. I hung around in the shadow of a factory doorway until darkness annihilated the street, then slouched to Westminster Bridge and sent my spit flying into the royal Thames.

After thinking it over carefully, I asked Dorfmann for a rise.

'You gone out of your head?' he demanded indignantly. 'With me you got a future, a golden future. For why should you spoil it? In the middle of the busy!' His breath stank of herring and Turkish cigarettes and when I looked away he mistook it for insolence. 'Pay a little respect!' he shouted. Luba came by carrying an armful of furs and brushed against me, weakening my resolution. 'I've got to improve myself!' I insisted doggedly.

He went to confer with Mrs Dorfmann. She turned her bearded face and gazed balefully in my direction, then began to talk back at her husband, beating the air with her hands until he cringed. Dorfmann nodded subserviently and came back.

'Money we don't give for nothing,' he shrugged, his mouth twisted as if by a lemon. 'You work hard another month, maybe yes.' His wife nodded severely from across the room. All that day she tried to catch me slacking. 'Max! The boy! Look at him, the dreamer! Give him something to do!' she said, heaving herself off the machine stool and plodding on thick legs to the toilet. Dorfmann went out to discuss business over a glass of tea with a skin merchant. I was left alone with Luba. It was so quiet, you could hear the scrape of the needle on her metal thimble.

'What do you do on weekends?' I stammered.

'On Saturday,' she whispered without lifting her head, 'I go to the synagogue with my aunt.'

Soft black hair curled on the nape of her slender neck and I was tormented by her narrow, sleepy Russian eyes. I wanted to say something miraculous and unforgettable, or so sharp, cruel and eloquent it would remain a fresh wound all of her life. But instead I said: 'Does your aunt shave on Shabbos?'[38]

I looked at her horrified. She stared back in disbelief.

'Well, it's against the religion, isn't it?' I blustered just as Mrs Dorfmann returned. 'What's going on?' she said sharply. I was already halfway to the door.

The street was full of furriers. There was a sign on Bloom's in the next building. 'Cutters, Nailers, Machinists Wanted', it said. Mr Bloom was a small brisk man who talked very fast.

'What did Dorfmann pay you?' he demanded.

'I had a future with Dorfmann. He paid me thirty bob.'

Mr Bloom cackled. 'A future? With that *shmock*?[39] He'll be bankrupt before next season. Do yourself a favour! Here, we got scientific methods – powered machines, refrigeration, the lot. I'll put you on piecework. As good as being your own master. You can take home two–three pound every week.'

I accepted, of course. There was a pain in my chest as if a lump of living flesh had been torn from me and I wished I was eighteen already, and there was a war. In those days I had the shadowy premonition that unless my life was shattered to pieces and I could put it together differently, I'd never, never be myself.

Working in Bloom's cauterized these raw feelings. Everyone was on piecework and they grudged time lost in factory gossip and laughter. The machines purred like metal cats; great piles of skins were hurled on cutters' benches, to be stretched, matched and sliced under the quick knives. I hammered nails until my fingers blistered, wilting in the heat of the great coke ovens. Dinnertimes, I climbed on to the flat roof above the sixth floor to eat my sandwiches, leaning against the brick coping with torpid indifference as chimney stacks discharging dense clouds of smoke poisoned the city. I went to the cinema as often as I could. It was the era of Mae West and, slumped in the masturbating dark, I longed hopelessly for a love that would be both sacred and profane. At home, everybody was squabbling. The infants crawled about the floor and pestered my mother at her dressmaking. My stepfather would come back from work, sleep for a while, then make himself debonair for a night at the dog track. Hurricanes of rage would blow up suddenly and sweep through us all. The house resounded with threats and defiance; plates were thrown, doors were slammed, screams thrilled the neighbours. But there was only inward bleeding, and that was too common to make more than a routine drama.

No, Mr Bloom was wrong. I had done myself no favour at all. What good was the money I was making, anyway? I bought a few things – a Japanese cigarette case, a racing saddle for my bike, some steel chest expanders, a six-bladed pocket knife. On my sixteenth birthday, rattling shillings in my pocket, I went with big-nosed Izzy Birnbaum to a temperance dance in Hoxton, hoping to find a couple of older girls with experience enough to be more than friendly. Of course, nothing came of that and we ended up drinking bitter beer somewhere, pretending not to care.

More often I used to hang around near Spitalfields Market, where Luba lived with the Dorfmanns, scrutinizing the small windows of their tenement in the hope of seeing her shadow on a curtain. Time passed with excruciating slowness. People stared out at the street, or moved aimlessly in drab, overstuffed rooms, their mouths opening or closing as if gasping for air. Sometimes I saw, or thought I saw, the grapplings of lust, and once a man was brought out on a stretcher with his throat cut. The main diversion came when pubs closed, especially on Saturday nights when professional strongmen and other motley performers were drawn away from their West End pitches by tipsy Cockney generosity.

The one place I never looked for Luba was on the factory roof, but that was where I saw her. It was hot enough to fry a bug and people crowded on top of the buildings as if the Lord Mayor's Show was about to begin at any minute. Workers lay around with unbuttoned shirts playing cards, or luring pigeons on to their shoulders with crumbs. A crowd of men at a window across the street whistled shrilly. I glanced up and there she was on Dorfmann's roof, just a few feet off. We stared at one another, then looked away quickly.

There was a gust of hot wind and a sheet of somebody's newspaper took off, swooping over the chimneys like a clumsy bird. Luba arched her soft-skinned throat to watch it soar towards the dome of St Paul's, and I watched her. We both laughed. Some workmen began to chaff her coarsely. She blushed and edged towards the concealment of a chimney stack. Seizing the excuse for chivalry, I climbed the iron railing, gazed dizzily into the pit of the street sixty feet below, and leaped across. The men set up an ironic cheer.

'I hope my uncle doesn't see you,' Luba said discouragingly. 'He thinks you're a Communist.'

In those days there were still people who believed Bolsheviks ate babies and Soviet girls belonged to everybody, like the means of production. But I'd already been expelled from the Young Communist League because I shared the taint of Trotsky, whatever that was. (I never found out exactly.) My mother's family had starved to death in the Ukraine and when

I mentioned it to Mickey Lerner, the ideological leader of Bethnal Green Young Communists, he told me you couldn't make an omelette without breaking eggs. I was against making an omelette with people, so I was no longer a Communist, only a revolutionary.

When I explained all this to Luba, her soft mouth trembled and she sighed with that rich Jewish sadness that is easily aroused at the mention of tragedy. It brought us closer to one another. Her glowing dark eyes and full soft bosom belonged to me a little by reason of that kinship.

'I thought you were an idealist when I first saw you,' Luba said intensely.

The sun blazed up and lit the world from here to China.

She was there again the next day, and the next. It became our routine. As soon as she appeared I climbed over the railings and we sat together, sharing our sandwiches. It was amazing how quickly we felt at ease with one another. Once she asked abruptly: 'Do you believe in God?'

'In God?' I laughed, not because I was amused but because we were there, together, far away from everything.

'Don't laugh,' she said gravely.

Thinking about it for a moment, I had to give God the benefit of the doubt.

'Then how can you believe in the Revolution?' Luba said.

'God believes in the Revolution,' I said.

She told me she was born in the Russian town of Podolsk and was brought to England when her mother died. She would like to be a singer and hummed Yiddish songs remembered from childhood in a sweet, thin voice that trembled with shyness. When I spoke facetiously of the Dorfmanns, she was upset because they were good people and she loved them. I was not to make fun of her aunt's beard. Mrs Dorfmann had been a beautiful girl, but at fifteen she was attacked by a *pogromchik*.[40]

Not only did the hair then grow where it shouldn't, but it stopped her aunt from having children, and that was why she could never be a happy woman.

We talked about other people with the grave sympathy of those who feel themselves immune from misfortune. The only trouble was, Luba wouldn't meet me after work because her uncle was very strict. I wanted more time. It wasn't enough, this brief interlude in the middle of the day when the machines fell silent for an hour and we came together under the open eye of the sky.

I hadn't time enough to tell her a hundredth part of my raw yearnings, and I believe Luba felt the same. Her mouth was moist and full; a sad sensuality smouldered in her indolent brown eyes as we talked of going to the country for a day, of visits we would make to the cinema, of rowing boats on the Serpentine and river steamers floating at night past the lighted city. But she wouldn't change her mind because of the hated Dorfmann.

Birds flying from roof to street and back again gave me an idea. Hazardously, I said: 'We could meet here after work?'

'On the roof?'

'Yes . . . we'd be all alone.'

The idea amused and embarrassed her. 'They'd send the fire engine to bring us down,' she said.

'Let's try it and see what happens.'

Luba didn't know: she wasn't sure: supposing her aunt should see her? Eventually, however, she came to an adventurous resolve. When the Dorfmanns left she'd make an excuse to go home separately and slip upstairs. But only for a few minutes. A few minutes could be prolonged for an hour, perhaps more. Darkness and silence would rise out of the deserted factories, stars would hang in clusters above our heads, and our pale faces would meet and kiss.

That afternoon I tried to kill time with work, hammering nails into the furs as if each moment was made of metal. The clock on the workshop wall was frozen for hours on end. Then machines ground to a stop, benches were cleared and everyone began to leave. It was six o'clock. I climbed out of the catacombs. At the level of the seventh floor, London was a ghost city at this time. I stood alone among the petrified chimneys, watching the gold medallion of the sun and waiting for Luba.

Footsteps climbed the iron rungs of the skylight. I turned eagerly. Dorfmann's tousled grey head emerged and he stared at me, eyes red-rimmed with fatigue.

'*Nu*, you didn't expect it would be me?' he said in a sunken voice. 'Low-life! Cumminist! Hasking a young gel to come up on the roof.' He began to screech. 'It's dangerous! You want to break your own neck? Please! It's a free country . . .'

I arrived home to find my brother Abie in a nasty temper. 'Where's my shirt?' he demanded. 'You took my shirt!' I'd dressed myself up in the morning to look decent and it was the only clean shirt my size in the drawer. We started to fight. My stepfather tried to separate us and my mother screamed at us all. The younger boys complained that they couldn't do their homework in all the noise. It was a fairly normal evening. After supper I went out. The moon rode in an empty sky. It looked down at the street as if it was a stranger.

II

A Charity Pair of Boots

Middlesex Street, Whitechapel. The heat of a famished July. Starved pigeons scavenged in trampled horse dung and all over the city optimists were lifting dustbin lids as they trudged aimlessly through the afternoon sunshine. I was drowsing on the pavement outside the Salvation Army, sitting on a newspaper headline which reported three million unemployed. Trevor, a black-haired boy from the Rhondda, dejectedly read the situations vacant on another page.

'What I'm looking for is a career, bach,' he said. 'Respectable employment, not this bloody in today, out tomorrow, tanner-an-hour and kiss-my-arse stuff.'

I leaned my head against the brick wall, staring with closed eyelids at the sun. Something bit me in the left armpit and disturbed my orange-coloured reverie. Six weeks since they'd chucked me out of the house and I'd not had a hot bath once. If only my mother could see me now. She'd murder me, but maybe forgive. *Save me, Mum. I'm going down the drain.*

'All they want is a few bloody clerks,' Trevor went on in disgust. He folded the paper and put it carefully into his pocket. 'Did you eat yet?'

I worked my flea-bitten back against the wall, up, down and sideways. What a question! The last solid grub I'd eaten was when Pinny sneaked me a cheese sandwich while I hid in the yard. The day before yesterday, was it? 'Trevor,' I said faintly, 'how long does it take to die of starvation?'

'I have the cure for that,' he answered. 'How'd you fancy' – he swallowed a gobbet of saliva and stared upwards with a love-sick expression – 'some nice roast beef, fat all crisp from the oven, a load of well-browned roast potatoes with some of them juicy big Brussels sprouts and a great knob of yeller butter melting on top, two whacking great slices of bread and a steaming mug of tea to top the lot? Marvellous, boyo, eh?'

We joined the queue in the Salvation Army canteen. 'Leave orf shoving!' grumbled an old man, glaring with watery eyes. A mouth organ sticking out of his breast pocket gave his trade away. There were quite a few beggars with tin whistles, concertinas and other musical instruments. Some were wearing war medals and leaning on crutches. They exuded a sour misery and carried their threepenny bowls of soup as if every drop was bought with their life's blood.

A girl in uniform dished up tea and bread-and-dripping, smiling charitably as she collected our coppers. Randy as most Welshmen, Trevor slopped half his tea looking at her.

'I don't fancy the easy sort. It's them that are rosy with religion gives me dirty ideas,' he was explaining, but I was distracted by the appearance of a fellow with the broad-brimmed black hat and glossy coat of a Polish Chassid. Blond curls hung on his pale cheeks and fine gold hairs straggled sparsely across his upper lip. He came in dreamily, with the fragile mincing movements of a girl, as if a synagogal meditation isolated him from the sour charity of Christ. A lamb among the *goyim*: his coming rocked my heart like a dark ancestral wind.

'Religious women are very hot-blooded, bach,' Trevor went on. 'It's wicked really. I mean, they only go to chapel to pray the sex away, don't they?'

The boy washed his hands in a fire bucket and opened a
tin of sardines, all the while muttering a Hebrew blessing. He
glanced gravely into my eyes and a spark of recognition flew
between us. The Salvation Army girl came over and placed
a religious tract beside him on the table. 'You're welcome to
join us in prayer,' she said reverently. All he did was move his
sardines a fraction away, but rejection was absolute. The spark
ignited a small flame. I extinguished it with a cold, definitive
stare. We were not going in the same direction.

The Chassid lurked in the ghetto of my mind. It was hotter
than ever outside. Enormous flies grazed on my greasy hair
and I was disgusted by myself; by my filth, my failures, my
terror that I was being drawn into some useless and predes-
tined martyrdom. Life was loitering yet passing quickly away.
And although I had no idea where to go, restlessness churned
inside me and made flight imperative. I took off my shoes and
began to stuff the soles with fresh newspaper. They had been a
fancy pair of ox-bloods borrowed from my stepfather the day I
left home. His best shoes: he must have been furious when he
found out but they'd be no good to him now. 'Going? Where?'
Trevor asked, surprised.

'Brighton,' I said. It was the first place to come to mind.
'Might be a job there selling ice cream.'

'Listen, are you not a Hebrew, boyo?' said Trevor. He
pointed at a door on the other side of Middlesex Street. 'Go
and ask for a pair of boots. Them shoes won't get you to
Brighton.'

A brass plate on the door read 'Board of Guardians for
the Relief of the Jewish Poor'. Passover matzos, free kosher
food, paupers' burials. 'I don't want no bloody charity,' I said
in disgust.

Trevor frowned at such obtuseness. 'Boots is not charity,' he
pointed out. 'You're entitled to boots.' He gave me a friendly

push and winked. 'See if they got a spare pair of socks for a Welsh *goy*. I'll be waiting.'

I crossed the road and never saw him again.

The moment I stepped into the Welfare Officer's room we recognized one another, the Captain and I. In six years he hadn't changed at all. He still had the appearance of a man who'd look good on a horse. Handsome, virile, the remote gaze of one accustomed to stare at the horizon. I was bigger, of course, and dirtier but must have changed less than I'd imagined. He scrutinized me briefly, then smiled with satisfaction. I'd been placed exactly.

'You're Litvinoff,' he said. 'Never forget a boy's face. Abraham, yes?'

'No, sir.' I could hardly trust my voice. 'Emanuel.'

When I was ten, a raw recruit in the Jewish Lads' Brigade, Captain Diamond had sought to drill me in military virtues. Whatever I did seemed insubordinate, slouching instead of standing properly to attention, losing step, mistaking left for right, parading in dingy brasses. At the annual summer camp I narrowly escaped being drummed out of the Brigade for stealing the Captain's chocolates, although I'd taken only one – or maybe two. He had me polishing his leathers as punishment until the day we returned to London.

Panic filled my hungry belly. The Captain would surely place me under escort and march me home in disgrace. My mother would recite my sins. An out-of-work boy, doesn't bring home a penny. But his suit from the Fifty Shilling Tailors he takes to the pawnbroker. To help pay the rent maybe? To buy food to put in the children's hungry mouths? (A bitter laugh.) Absolutely not! A tent he takes and goes to the seaside with girls, boys, Communists – who knows? People are walking the streets starving, he spends money on a luxury holiday. Speak to him like a human being, explain, beg for a reason – it's worse than talking to a deaf person. (She'd try not to cry and fail.) To say such things about your own child, your flesh and blood, it's not easy, believe me . . .

I lifted my feet to show the Captain the holes in Uncle Solly's shoes and asked if they happened to have a spare pair of boots. Instead of a direct reply he began to ask embarrassing questions.

'No, sir,' I said, avoiding his eyes. 'I've got no home.' My mother? She was – she was . . . dead. The awful lie stuck in my throat and the taste was foul. It was going to take a long time to forgive that act of matricide. Bad enough swearing on the life of your mother, never mind pretending she was, actually, just for a mouldy pair of boots, dead.

Captain Diamond was gruffly compassionate. 'Sorry about that, Litvinoff.' He observed a brief and mournful silence as if the guns had sounded the Armistice Day remembrance. 'You had a stepfather, didn't you?'

That was easier. 'My stepfather went off with another woman.' I waited for his reaction. It was stern, disapproving. 'A Christian lady,' I added recklessly.

This left him briefly speechless. He merely nodded, then enquired about my brother, Abie. The last time I'd seen Abie we had to be forcibly separated to prevent us maiming one another but, though it would cause me no crisis of conscience, to pretend he was also dead would be unconvincing.

'Gone to Canada, sir. The Empire Farm Training scheme.' God help me if he asked about the other kids, but luckily he didn't seem to know we were a large family. Instead he asked what jobs I'd had, if I'd learned a trade and how I'd been living since becoming orphaned. It was alarming to see all the lies carefully written down for posterity.

'You should have come to us before,' the Captain said, placing his notes inside a blue folder. 'I remember your mother well. A decent, hard-working woman. Gave you a good Jewish upbringing.'

'Yessir,' I replied remorsefully. If only he'd let me take the boots and get the hell out.

'Now go and wait outside. I want to make some telephone calls. We can't let a boy from the Jewish Lads' Brigade live like a tramp. That won't do at all. Have to get you shipshape.'

'But, sir,' I protested, 'all I want is a pair of boots.'

'Nonsense, laddie! Unthinkable! From now on you are to look on the Board as your father and mother. And the first thing to do is get a roof over your head.'

There was a stern, if kindly, Victorian ring in his voice that made an Oliver Twist out of me. Fallen into the toils of the workhouse! According to our folk, the worst thing that could ever happen to a human being was to become the recipient of charity. Justice had indeed been swift.

In the next couple of hours I was stripped of my rags, bathed in hot water and carbolic soap and issued with two sets of underclothes, a couple of neat flannel shirts, four pairs of woollen socks, two sets of striped pyjamas, a second-hand suit with a Savile Row label – slightly too large in the chest, but freshly cleaned and pressed – and a pair of strong new boots reinforced by metal studs.

Captain Diamond inspected me back and front. He pulled the jacket straight and made a geometrical adjustment of the tie, pleased at the transformation. 'Handkerchief?' I didn't have one. Someone was sent to the store and returned with half a dozen, quite new. The Captain arranged one in my breast pocket. 'Makes a good impression,' he advised.

My life, meanwhile, had been mapped out completely. Come eight o'clock Monday morning, report to Mr Cecil Zolofsky at the Zolofsky Furniture Factory in Wembley. Wages fifteen shillings a week, less insurance, all but half-a-crown pocket money being repaid to my foster mother. Saturdays and Jewish holidays would, of course, be free. I was expected to go to synagogue. Thrift was also recommended. A shilling a week invested in a post-office savings account would safeguard the future.

A further disagreeable surprise awaited. The Welfare Officer chose to deliver me to my new lodgings in person. Even blind-folded, I'd have known where we were by the smell of the different streets – reek of rotten fruit: Spitalfields; scent of tobacco warehouses: Commercial Street; the suffocating airless stench of the Cambridge Picture Palace; Hanbury Street and the pungency of beer from Charrington's brewery. Then Brick Lane, with half the women from our street jostling among the market stalls. At any moment, the Captain and me were likely to be confronted by an accusing ghost who'd swipe me round the ear with her shopping basket for causing her more aggrava-tion. It was getting unbearably warm. Should I drop the parcel of charity clothes and run?

'Why are you lagging behind, lad?' the Captain demanded testily. 'Are those boots too tight?'

'They're killing me, sir.' Those bloody boots!

He grabbed my arm and forcibly led me into Bacon Street. Oh, God! Except for Fuller Street itself, only a couple of hundred yards down, nothing could be worse. This was the pet-market end. Sad monkeys, parrots, mongrel puppies, neutered kittens, canaries doctored to make them sing sweeter were all on sale here every Sunday. In cages. And goldfish in bowls. Unlike Regent's Park zoo, the animals were on view for nothing, so every kid in the neighbourhood came.

'Well, here we are,' the Captain said cheerfully, stopping at the side door of a bird shop. 'Home, sweet home.' He brought the knocker down hard.

I was trapped.

Mrs Schiller, my appointed foster mother, was a big-chested lady as mellow as a full moon. Her cheeks shone rosily and she smelled of newly baked bread. The Captain drank tea with her in a parlour lustrous with polished mahogany and discussed my case. Orchards of fruit filled a large silver bowl on the sideboard, not a wax apple among them. It needed an effort to realize that beyond the velvet-curtained windows was the hungry city and its depressed multitudes.

When we were alone, Mrs Schiller showed me my room. It was to be shared with Sammy Feigelbaum, an upholsterer's apprentice and, she said with a smile of heartbreak, an orphan since he was four. Blankets of soft lambswool were spread on the beds and the walls were papered with roses. It had been her daughter's room but now, thank God, the girl was married to a bookbinder in Stoke Newington with a self-contained flat. Here I could do whatever a boy liked to do, only not like the boy who smoked in bed and caused a terrible fire, which was strictly against the Board of Guardians' rules. If I was also a smoker, please I should do it in the yard. The toilet was also in the yard and please I should lift the seat. You should excuse me, she added delicately.

For supper there was lockshen soup, a quarter of tenderly boiled fowl garnished with carrots, floury potatoes and pickled cucumber, followed by plump black prunes in syrup with thin slices of lemon. Mrs Schiller was a wonderful cook. 'Thank God, you got a lovely appetite,' she remarked approvingly. Her chest rested comfortably on the table as she examined me with curiosity. 'I'm sure I know you from somewhere.' Feigelbaum came in from work and distracted her, but as she served up his food she kept glancing at me in a puzzled way.

Ten o'clock was lights-out. Feigelbaum, not very talkative, folded his clothes neatly as he prepared for sleep and was soon softly snoring. I unlaced my boots, put them under the bed. A crow flapped its black wings in the darkness. The boy Chassid stared at me with huge eyes of sorrowful innocence. I had a terrible dream that my mother gave birth to a litter of malevolent cats.

Mr Cecil Zolofsky was a brisk young man with soft hands and gold-rimmed glasses. His suit had wide lapels like a gangster's and he wore a black pencil-slim Ronald Colman moustache. 'Dad,' he shouted, 'it's the Board of Guardians' boy!' He had to shout because the noise from the factory floor below was deafening.

'Wait a minute!' he yelled at me irritably, and went into the next office. The elder Mr Zolofsky came to look me over. His vast paunch almost blocked the doorway and a flat, grease-stained workman's cap rested on his bald head. Small eyes travelled over me from head to toe while he nodded cryptically in a way that made his pendulous lower lip tremble.

'*Nu*,' he said. 'Put him on the French polishing.'

'I already got two boys on the polishing, Dad,' Cecil shouted furiously.

The elder Zolofsky waved his hand in a dismissive gesture. 'So let him learn the veneering machine.'

Cecil seemed in a terrible temper. He took me downstairs amidst the racketing machinery and yelled into the foreman's ear. The foreman, in turn, put his mouth against Cecil's ear and yelled back. I got the impression that my arrival was unwelcome.

'What d'they call yer?' the foreman asked. He was a small tense man with a rasping voice like a saw biting into wood.

I told him.

'Not yer fucking surname, sonny.'

'That's ridiculous!' he grumbled, when I gave him my first

name. 'I'll call yer Jack. 'Ere, Jack, take this fucking broom and start sweeping from the top of the shop. By the time you get this end you can go back and start again.'

'Mr Zolofsky said I should learn the veneering machine.' I hadn't come there to do a dead-end job but to be a properly certified apprentice.

'Sweep the fucking floor, boy, and stop arguing.'

I'd hardly finished sweeping the fucking floor the second time when it was tea break. Silence clanged like a steel shutter and workers congregated in small groups, or wandered out to the yard to smoke, stirring cans of tea with glue-encrusted sticks. By the time I'd found a spare cocoa tin and filled it at the urn, the foreman was blowing his whistle. In slow motion, the men nipped out cigarettes and tucked them behind their ears before shuffling off reluctantly to their benches.

'You, Jack, look lively!' the foreman yelled as he ran around getting everybody back into production.

After dinner break he put me on glue-making. It consisted of keeping the fire trimmed and stirring brown slabs of glue into pots of hot water until the viscous mixture gave off its clean and resinated stench. The smell of fresh glue and the heat of the fire sent me into a nostalgic reverie of schooldays. Chalk dust floating in afternoon sunshine, the sour sarcasm of bored masters, boys crimson with the effort of producing their rebellious farts. Dreams of the past, smoothed of its rough texture. Top-of-the-class days. Days when a brilliant future awaited for sure, sweet Hannah Fishbein still to be met and, who knows, triumphantly loved.

'Asleep again?' the foreman rasped in my ear, and the ache began again under my ribs. He sent me out to unload planks of timber. I carried dining-table tops into the carpenter's shop to be fitted with claw legs. I swept the workshop floor again and yet again. The bastard kept me running until the blast of the six o'clock hooter.

It was usually half past seven before I got back to my lodgings. The train from Wembley was crowded with sweaty workers dropping in fatigue. Some fell asleep on their feet. I was too tired to live. After supper and a couple of games of draughts with Sammy Feigelbaum, I'd go to the pictures or hang around Whitechapel Road, watching the girls parade in silver foxes hoarded from prosperity. Things ought to have been looking up for me, but a full stomach and the jingle of pennies in my pocket gave no joy. In spirit, I was down-and-out and still sinking. *Mother, save me. I'm going down the drain.*

Mrs Schiller thought I was alone too much for my own good. 'This evening I'm inviting you,' she said one morning, handing me my egg sandwiches as I left for the factory. She nudged me playfully. 'A nice party, you'll see.'

Her daughter came, big tits pushed up to her neck, together with the son-in-law who wore check plus-fours and didn't look at all like a bookbinder. Apart from Sammy and me, the only other guest was an old man who spoke nothing but Yiddish and smoked Russian *papirosa*, dropping the ash carefully into a brass tray our hostess hurriedly produced.

We had lemon tea, halva and home-baked macaroons. Mrs Schiller wound up the gramophone and played cantorial music by Goldfarb, a famous synagogue tenor. The bookbinder imitated Goldfarb's wailing vibrato which was supposed to be funny. Hunger marchers were on the move everywhere, but in Mrs Schiller's the clock had stopped at 1911. It was more depressing than ever. I went out to the yard to smoke my fag, wishing I had the nerve to walk down the street and go home.

The bad luck continued. A few days later one of Zolofsky's cabinet-makers drew me aside. 'Had a meeting about you,' he began in an unfriendly voice.

'About me? What have I done?'

'You're taking home fifteen bob a week. Right?'

'Less insurance,' I said.

'The rate for the job is seventeen and six,' he remarked nastily. 'As you very well know.' Producing a Party card from his overall pocket, he announced: 'Feldman. Unofficial Shop Steward. I can 'ave you sent to Coventry.' The foreman came hurrying over. 'I'll see you afterwards,' Feldman said, going back to his bench.

At dinnertime there were three of them, the factory cell, more militant than the Red Army. Feldman did most of the talking. Where was my class solidarity? I disgraced the memory of the Tolpuddle Martyrs. Undermined the hard-won gains of the trade union movement. Who did I think I was, Comrade, if I was a comrade? A capitalist stooge, a Trotskyite wrecker, a stabber-in-the-back of Soviet workers?

The injustice of it made me too incoherent to defend myself properly. But if Feldman was right about the rate for the job then, objectively, from the dialectical point of view, he had a valid point.

After worrying about it all afternoon, I opted for class solidarity. Cecil Zolofsky took off his gold glasses, swivelled towards the window and gazed in disbelief at the sky. 'Been here a couple of weeks and wants a rise already! You ever hear anything like it?' He began to tell me how he'd started in the business at six bob a week. It was a year before his father raised it to seven. Old man Zolofsky came panting into the office from a routine inspection of the workshop, the stump of a cigarette stuck in the corner of his mouth. 'Guess what?' Cecil said, grinning wryly. 'He's asking for a rise already.'

The old man stroked his monstrous paunch. 'Take on a Yiddisher boy,' he groaned, 'a *pisherle*. In no time he's opening up a business for himself. Give him another five shillings.'

Cecil waved his hands in his father's face. 'Whad'ya mean?

It's a liberty! We got a whole bloody orphanage here! You and your Board of Guardians! Are we a public charity?'

'Ach, Cecil!' The old man lifted up his hand and flung it away. 'A few shillings. What's the difference? Give!' He closed the door against further argument.

'I break my head to introduce modern business methods, scientific costing,' the younger Zolofsky shouted. There were tears in his eyes.

Later I saw him in conference with the foreman. They kept looking in my direction. On Friday my pay packet contained eighteen shillings, equivalent to one pound less insurance and tea money. It also contained a typed notice of dismissal. I told Feldman, thinking he'd at least call an unofficial strike. 'Good lad,' he said. 'You struck a blow against the boss class.' It wasn't much consolation.

'Wait here,' the Welfare Officer's secretary ordered coldly. She left me in a room dominated by a severe patrician portrait of the benefactor, Sir Moses Montefiore. There was nothing to read except for a copy of the *Jewish Chronicle* filled with parochial reports and hatch-match dispatch announcements. I stood at the window and looked across the street at the Salvation Army. The usual derelicts were squatting on the pavement. One man had his arm through the neck of his tattered shirt, trying to trap the lice on his body. Somebody else was scraping a pair of Japanese socks from the horny soles of his feet with a penknife blade. An old fellow in an army greatcoat that reached to his ankles was shredding cigarette ends into the clay bowl of his pipe.

As I was about to turn away, depressed by the prospect of rejoining this brotherhood, the young Chassid came round the corner and sealed the moment into my memory for ever. Thinner, shabbier and even younger than I'd thought, he glanced up at the window where I stood, holiness blazing from gentle eyes. I was reminded of Pinny, the most silent and long-suffering of us all. His gentleness, too, carried spores of martyrdom. I gazed at the Chassid until the secretary came to lead me to the conference room. He was still there, looking up, as we left.

Five men sat aristocratically along the side of a long table, one of them Captain Diamond. They stared with grave deliberation and did not ask me to sit. An elderly, upright gentleman, narrow face dominated by a large authoritative nose, seemed to perform the function of chairman.

'Shall we start, Sir Abraham?'[41] the Captain enquired respectfully, and proceedings began.

The members of the committee took out expensive fountain pens and made notes as my case was outlined. 'Orphan,' I saw one of them write. 'Destitute. Put into care.' They nodded in agreement when Captain Diamond pointed out in his Welfare Officer's manner that I'd been given every opportunity to make good. However, he went on in curt military tones, my employer was reluctantly compelled –

'Just a moment,' the chairman intervened. 'We'll ask the young man to explain that, I think.' He bent upon me the severe gaze of a hanging judge. 'Why did your employer dismiss you?'

'W-well, s-s-sir –'

Sir Abraham turned to the Welfare Officer. 'Has he got a speech impediment?'

'Certainly not!'

'Carry on, boy,' one of the other gentlemen said encouragingly. 'Start from the beginning. There's no need to be nervous.'

It all started outside the Salvation Army, I said. 'The Salvation Army?' The chairman glanced up sharply. 'You haven't changed your religion, have you?'

'Me, sir?' It was a shocking suggestion. 'I would never do a thing like that.'

'Splendid!' somebody said, with considerable satisfaction. 'An ancestor of Sir Abraham Mendoza was burned at the stake because he insisted on remaining steadfast to Judaism. Isn't that so, Sir Abraham?'

'Indeed yes.' The chairman smiled. 'Don Israel Lopez Mendoza. It was in Toledo in 1492. In the presence of the Grand Inquisitor himself.'

This seemed to put everyone in a friendly mood, and, losing my shyness, I told them exactly what had happened and that I'd only demanded a rise on the principle of working-class solidarity. Sir Abraham hurriedly scribbled a remark on a sheet of paper and shoved it across the table to Captain Diamond. The Captain scribbled a reply. They frowned at me and I was struck down in mid-sentence by their high-velocity disapproval.

'Are you saying you were led astray by a political agitator?' Sir Abraham demanded peevishly.

Even with my rudimentary ideological experience, I knew the gulf between us was unbridgeable. Their class and mine occupied opposite sides of the barricades. My case was lost.

'Someone in your position can't afford to have these – er – political principles,' Sir Abraham commented with fastidious distaste. 'You'd better let us hear that letter, Captain Diamond.'

A file was produced with my name on the cover. It was of formidable thickness. The Welfare Officer extracted a sheet of embossed stationery, cleared his throat, and read out the following indictment:

'Dear Sir, re Jack Litvinoff. We regret to inform you that the above-mentioned was dismissed by myself for being an idle troublemaker unsuitable for apprenticeship training in the Furniture Trade. Signed Cecil B. Zolofsky, Director.'

Sir Abraham glanced at his fellow magistrates. There was, of course, no counsel for the defence. 'What have you to say about that, boy?'

It was the kind of scene I'd rehearse in front of the mirror brilliantly. Now it went badly.

Me: I never made no trouble. He's – he's a liar!

Sir Abraham Mendoza: (Severely) That language is quite uncalled for, young man!

Me: I only asked for my rights. Fifteen bob is sweated labour! It's not the rate for the job. On my mother's life – I mean, memory!

(The blunder so narrowly averted left me feeling weak. Had they noticed? The Captain looked disgusted.)

Captain Diamond: You will observe, gentlemen, that nothing is mentioned in the letter about a dispute over wages. I need hardly say that Mr Cecil Zolofsky has been connected with our welfare work for many years. He is a public-spirited personality of the highest character.

Sir Abraham Mendoza: Certainly. Of the highest character! (Scrutinizing me with growing irritation.) What's the matter with the boy, Captain Diamond? Why does he keep wriggling about? Does he need to empty his bladder?

Captain Diamond: You'll find the place at the end of the corridor, Litvinoff.

Sir Abraham Mendoza: When you've relieved yourself, wait outside until you're called.

'We've considered your case very carefully,' Sir Abraham said when I'd returned, 'and frankly we take a poor view of it. You seem a very insubordinate sort of a lad. I understand you were a bad cadet in the Brigade. Indisciplined. That sort of thing gets you nowhere.' He took a handkerchief from his sleeve and deftly blew his nose. He seemed uncertain how to proceed. 'Politics!' he muttered. 'Yes, politics . . . Now, there are a lot of things in the world you're not old enough to understand. Nothing is more intolerable than presumptuous ignorance. That's one thing you've got to get into your head. If it was not for your – um – unfortunate situation, we'd wash our hands of you altogether. But we are prepared to give you a choice of pulling yourself together and trying to become a decent citizen, or sinking into a life of uselessness and depravity. Now,' he added more kindly, 'I'm sure you don't want that to happen.'

When he'd satisfied himself that I didn't, Sir Abraham rotated his head and addressed one of the five committee men. 'Mr Green, I believe you have a suggestion to make.'

Mr Green was brisk and stout. 'I'm in the meat business,' he informed me. 'Smithfield Market. You look a strong boy. Would you take a job as a meat porter? Carrying carcasses? Thirty shillings a week to start.'

Smithfield again? Oh, no! . . . But on the other hand thirty bob! Every week! A fortune! I deepened my voice, a strong boy's voice. 'Yes, sir, I'd like to work as a meat porter.'

'It's hard graft,' he warned with grim relish, 'filthy and back-breaking. Hours are from four till eleven in the morning. No joke in winter when it's freezing cold, I'll tell you. But it's a healthy life and if you put your heart and soul into it I can promise you a good future.'

The reference to heart and soul stirred a vague misgiving. Was Mr Green a kosher butcher? Without being at all religious, I had not yet tasted unclean meat, and the severed pigs' heads in Christian butcher shops, a popular delicacy among workers, always filled me with disgust. The matter had to be clarified.

'Would I be asked to carry pork? I could never do that, sir.'

I knew it would be a mark in my favour, and the way they all looked and nodded it seemed I was no longer regarded as beyond redemption.

Smithfield at four in the morning. The nightmare of the human gut. Cold lights shone in refrigerated trucks as blue-coated porters unloaded slaughtered beasts and wheeled them on trolleys into the high-domed market halls, where they were hoisted on to heavy iron hooks. Their heads hung down in serried rows, mucus frozen on their rigid muzzles. Everything was penetrated by the stench of neighbouring offal yards, the shithouse of Smithfield's stomach, where hoofs, bones, hair and intestines were boiled to glue or rendered to fertilizer.

None of this appeared to affect the Smithfield tradesmen – known the world over for their cheerfulness – but I waited in a numbness of spirit until my own hands would have to grasp dead flesh. They said you got used to it. It was, after all, no more repulsive than handling skins ripped from the bodies of animals bred and destroyed for the beauty of their fur. The foreman approached with a broad smile and the fresh open face of a countryman.

'Are you the new lad?' he asked. 'I'll start you off the right way – with a cup of char.'

We sat in a small office, the tea was brown, sweet and scalding and he spoke enthusiastically of the Smithfield fraternity. 'Won't find no better blokes anywhere. No Smithfield man ever let a mate down.' Meat porters lived like lords. Their own licensing laws – market pub open five in the morning – sleep all afternoon if they liked or do two jobs and pick up extra money. He himself ran a tobacco kiosk near the Arsenal football ground helped by the missus. Never spent a day on the dole in his life.

A line of butchers' vans were being loaded. The foreman selected a decapitated carcass and lifted it on to his back by its hind legs. 'See, it's a piece of cake,' he remarked. 'Here, try this one for size.'

It was a pig.

'No, son, it ain't. The gaffer said you wasn't to be put on the pork. It's lamb. New Zealand.'

'It looks like pig,' I said.

The foreman laughed. 'Charlie,' he called out to a passing porter, 'what's this? Tell the kid.'

Charlie was smoking a pipe. 'It's not a fucking elephant,' he said without taking it from his mouth.

'It is lamb, honest!' the foreman repeated, still chuckling.

But whatever it was, it was definitely dead and I wouldn't touch it for anything.

Night was dispersing like smoke when I left Smithfield and walked aimlessly through the blue dusk of the day's beginning. A water sprinkler pulled by a shaggy horse turned the street into a black river. The city was deserted, as if emptied by plague. I had the familiar illusion that my whole life was a dream from which I'd wake to find myself in another place, another time. Who was I? What was the purpose of my existence? I puzzled over these questions while sitting in the cemetery of Bunhill Fields eating Mrs Schiller's sandwiches near the grave of Bunyan. John Bunyan, 1628–1688. I'd never read any of his poems. Had he asked the same questions, and did he write down the answers in a way I could understand?

There were more immediate problems, almost as insoluble. How to pass the time, what to do for money, where to go? I gave up my last few pennies as soon as the cinemas opened and sat with musty old men and women who made their home in the cheap front rows. Hours passed in flickering sleep. Cowboys galloped off the screen and herded their cattle into the abattoirs of my dreams.

Night returned and I found myself in Soho, the first time for weeks. Bohemia congregated in the Dive, a cellar café in Frith Street where soup and bread could be had for fourpence. I believed it was full of painters and poets living in wickedness with girls whose bodies were given as generously as bread in Stalin's paradise. A drunken Canadian named Roger stood me a coffee. He was writing a serial, *The Black Hawk Swoops Again*, for a boy's weekly paper and laced my coffee with whisky from a hip flask because I was good at suggesting plots.

When the last loiterer left and even prostitutes had gone for the night, the waiter chucked us out. Roger looked at me with brimming eyes. 'You ought to be in your mother's arms,' he said in a choking voice, then waved goodbye and walked off unsteadily. I sat down on the kerb and began to cry, because the street was rolling like the sea and I had nowhere to sleep. Some time later, still drunk, I knocked several times on Mrs Schiller's front door. An upstairs window scraped open cautiously. 'Who's dere?' she called. 'Who's knocking in the middle of the *nacht?*'

She came down, an old fur coat thrown over her nightdress, and shrieked: '*Oy, Gott! Eyr is shicker!*' I staggered into the yard and was sick. 'A Yiddisher *kind*! A Yiddisher *kind*!' Mrs Schiller said, one hand pressed to her cheek, and, having led me to bed, undressed me as tenderly as if I was her own disaster. I think she loved me more than Feigelbaum, the upholsterer's apprentice, who gave her no trouble at all – and because of that love, she betrayed me.

Captain Diamond held a one-man court-martial the very next day and sentenced me to doom as a moral delinquent beyond regeneration. I was a disgrace to the community, I'd finish up in the gutter, the Board of Guardians for the Relief of the Jewish Poor entirely washed its hands of responsibility.

There was one gesture of rebellion left. I unbuttoned my jacket and threw it off. 'I'll have my clothes back, if you don't mind.'

'Your clothes? Leave here immediately!'

'I know my rights,' I said, standing my ground.

'You're mad, boy.' He shook his head hopelessly. 'Quite mad.'

They were found in the basement stinking of carbolic.

Someone had taken the precaution of getting them disinfected. Either I'd grown a bit or the clothes had shrunk, but the only things I retained of the Board's charity were the boots and some clean underwear.

The weather was still hot. I crossed over to the Salvation Army, hoping to find Trevor there. Downstairs in the canteen, as solitary as the first created man or the last, was my golden Chassid. Hunger burned like a flame in his transparent face.

'*Shalom.*' I gazed into his perilous eyes and my soul shivered.

He nodded gravely, lips shaping the ancestral prayers, and I knew we were living in different zones of time.

'Listen,' I said, 'this is no place for a Jewish boy.' I gripped his arm, stick-like under the sleeve, and led him outside.

'Go there.' I pointed to the Board of Guardians. 'Ask for the Welfare Officer.' The Chassid made no move. 'Please!' At last the urgency got through. He looked at me with a faint, patient smile and shrugged.

'*Shalom,*' he said, and began to cross the road.

12

Life Class

The day Chancellor Dollfuss was shot in Vienna Morry Spitzer and I joined the art class of the Bethnal Green Men's Institute. I wrote it down in a diary I was keeping at the time. 'July 25. Started to do Art. Modelled an egg in clay. The ovoid (egg) is life's basic form – Mr Snood. Death came to pocket Dictator Dollfuss today. *Blut fascisti*.[42] Capitalism cannot survive its own contradictions.' I wasn't sure at the time that I'd survive my own contradictions.

I began the diary in a mood of despair. Life was slipping out of my hands. It had to be trapped, somehow, held down. I prowled along Whitechapel Road, staring at wax dummies simpering in shop windows; drifted westward with the tide of the city to be washed up at Speaker's Corner, where men with virulent eyes spoke of the shipwreck of damnation; in Soho alleyways, stirred by a lonely thrill, I watched loitering women through narrowed eyelids, or turned aside to study tracts outside the Church of Christ Scientist. Nothing entered, neither good nor evil. All around life in its abundance was happening to everybody. I had to make it happen to me.

Morry Spitzer, my best friend at the time, a shy, left-handed boy to whom the world was the wrong way round, was masturbating too much and yearning his spare time away in the front row at the pictures. He worked in his father's kosher butcher shop, disembowelling chickens, although the trade disgusted him so much Morry concealed meat in his pockets rather than eat it and sometimes forgot to get rid of it before it began to stink. During this time, he was intensely absent-minded and was taking a course in Pelmanism[43] to improve his memory. But he couldn't remember to keep himself clean. His shirt was stained with chicken blood, dried spunk encrusted the front of his trousers and he never shaved the tufts of hair that were appearing on his otherwise smooth cheeks.

We were drawn together because we hated the same things and were depressed by our inadequacies. We hated our fathers first, most people afterwards. We were attracted and disgusted by the sexuality of women, and Morry had a vegetarian horror of their flesh. The stilted way they walked on their steep heels reminded him of hens lifting their feet in the farmyard. He was more passive than me. Where he was a reformer, according others the grace of improvement, I was a scornful and avenging angel, pronouncing the great guilty of corruption, the low of servility. Sometimes I raged to know the secrets of the world the better to destroy it before it reached out and crushed my life – through war, poverty, toil or neglect. And time was short. By eighteen, which seemed the crucial threshold, I aimed to master Karl Marx, become a powerful writer and arm myself with other intellectual weapons of superiority.

Because of this I was impatient with the teaching methods of Mr Snood. He had us sharpening pencils and drawing cubes, cylinders, circles and dead things like Woolworth vases. 'First learn the alphabet, my lads,' he said, 'and in time you'll work up to the poetry of the yuman figure,' pointing at a bench littered with plaster torsos. He talked in this condescending way as if to imply that teaching in Bethnal Green was his form of social service, but I'd seen him sitting alone in the eel-and-pie shop, rolled middle-class umbrella laid across his striped knees, eating a sixpenny sheep's head as if it was the first dinner he'd had in a week.

There were about twelve of us in his class. The two most advanced were a corporation dustman, Arthur Judd, who did watercolours of ships lying in palm-fringed lagoons, and an elderly Jew named Miskin, a grocer by trade, old-fashioned enough never to be seen without his skullcap. He stood in a reflective trance at the easel, smears of paint matting his grey beard, crowding the canvas with monstrously pregnant women, shy and stricken children, rabbis with the angularity of scarecrows brandishing torahs in the face of God. I used to hang around watching him work. He mixed colours so sweet and strong you felt you wanted to lick them, then applied his brush slowly, a stroke here, a touch there, and one face after another flared out as if picked from the darkness by a fire's reflection.

'Would you teach me to paint, Mr Miskin?' I asked him once. He responded with a lopsided smile. 'If I should split your head, God forbid, I couldn't teach you what you can see *mit* your own eyes.'

The more I used my eyes, the less I could fit the world together. Take the street we lived in, disorderly with light, colour, texture, voice, posture, movement, noise and silence. We jostled in that brick gulley as if we knew where we were going, but in the verminous night our lungs sucked at the used air as we struggled in a collective dream of suffocation. Panic pursued me behind closed doors. I stood in front of the mirror at home and interrogated my reflection. It was ill put together, the left side's innocence and the right hand's cunning. An abrupt resentful face shaped by an ancestry of misfortune; it looked back at me with disfavour. And behind us both, as daylight withdrew from the room, a shadow brushed the future with its wings.

After a few weeks, Mr Snood decided that we were ready for the human figure. He took down a clay model from a shelf and blew a cloud of dust from its scarred terracotta body. Its nose was chipped and a crack ran through its left breast. 'The female nood,' he announced, placing it reverently on a plinth. 'You can spend a lifetime studying the female nood.' He was working on a project of his own, a clay bust of a girl with jutting lips like something by Epstein, and periodically stepped back to examine it with pursed approval. Finally, he came and glanced over our shoulders. Morry's drawing was going well, but Mr Snood took a pencil and made swift corrections to mine. 'You've got the proportions of the 'ead wrong, lad. An eighth of the body. Don't give 'er water on the brain.' I showed it to Miskin when it was finished. He scratched the bony bridge of his nose and sighed. 'In Odessa,' he said, 'a boy can catch a sea fish *mit* a piece of string. A live fish, it moves beautiful.' He handed the drawing back with a deprecating smile. I tore the damned thing up and threw it in the rubbish bin.

There is an entry in my diary dated September 10. 'Drew another lousy piece of plaster. Felt like smashing it up. It's dead, dead, dead.' I was so obsessed with the idea of studying life at first-hand that I even conceived, and abandoned, the impractical idea of drilling a hole in our bedroom wall to watch Rita Schomberg when she got undressed. Rita was a fat girl of nineteen who wore tight sweaters and looked at me with sleepy concupiscence. She tormented my dreams but wasn't my type at all and I'd only study her naked in the interests of art. Hours on my knees peering through the keyhole as my mother fitted dresses on her customers gave me odd glimpses of female anatomy – broad bloomered bottoms, strapped thighs, flesh bulging over boned corsets. They came together to make a composite Rita Schomberg grotesquely armoured for sex, but I could not find in them the true lineaments of women, that slim yet voluptuous ideal that drew the leaping tides of lust.

I stood and watched Morry at work in the cubbyhole behind his father's shop. Sawdust and blood were sprinkled over the floor and there were feathers in his hair. He seized a dead bird, chopped its feet off at the knees and severed its neck with a swift blow of the axe. With bitterness and loathing, he threw the cock's head into a metal bin, then, ripping its scrotum with his forefinger, thrust his hand into the cock's body and pulled out a mass of steaming intestines. The warm mucous smell made me turn aside with nausea. Dead chickens, pierced through the throat, hung in rows on metal hooks. Morry rinsed his hands perfunctorily under the tap and we went off to the pictures.

One Sunday morning that autumn, we trailed two laughing girls in Victoria Park. They sat on a bench by the lake, rubbed their mouths with lipstick and looked at us in their tiny mirrors. One girl lifted her leg and slowly crossed her knees. Morry dug his hands deeply into his pocket and caught his lower lip between his teeth. He stared sadly and vacantly at the muddy green water.

'Did you notice that movement?' he said in a hoarse voice. 'She's got good legs,' I replied miserably. 'They swell up nice at the top.'

We shivered and became silent. The girl twisted her slender ankle, glanced at her friend and spoke in an undertone. They both laughed. I imagined more than I saw – thigh muscles joining the strong resilient buttocks and the groin, dark, tender and voracious as a Negro's mouth.

The girls departed as swiftly as migrant birds, leaving the park desolate. Brown leaves drifted over the surface of the lake. I ached like a bereaved bridegroom.

At the end of term, Mr Snood made an announcement. Two pictures by Arthur Judd were exhibited with distinction in the annual display of works by local government officers. His own *Jeune Femme*, which no doubt we'd all watched him model with profit, had been purchased by a private collector. Of the younger students, he particularly wished to congratulate Morris

Spitzer for his grasp of proportion, without which there could never be True Beauty.

'This class is ready for the yuman figure, the nood,' Mr Snood stated solemnly. His eyes shifted under our collective stare. 'The living nood,' he added quietly and impressively.

Morry and I exchanged a flushed and earnest glance. I scarcely heard as Mr Snood went on to warn us we must merit the faith invested in us by the Bethnal Green Men's institute, cast out all dirty thoughts and approach the living nude with fitting reverence. A dazzling image of Rita Schomberg plump and naked on a plinth had appeared in the centre of my mind and set off embarrassing physical reactions. In those days I was almost always tumescent. A poem, the lonely reflection of street lamps on wet pavements, unexpected news, saxophones, even a barrow high and aromatic with fruit, any of these could give me an unbearable erection.

We arrived early on the first day of the new term, but were not the earliest. About sixty men of all ages crowded the classroom. I recognized some as members of the Rabbit Breeders' Club and several elderly tailors from the English for Foreigners class. Mr Snood distributed sheets of cartridge paper and pencils with brisk excitement and everyone jostled for a place near the front. At the rear of the room, wearing an aloof constabulary expression, was the Principal. Mr Snood conferred with him for what seemed a very long time. We began to feel that something was not quite right. Where was the model? She could only be in the small adjoining office where the teacher did his paperwork and from which she must eventually make her astonishing appearance.

Mr Snood went fussily to the door, opened it, inserted his head and called: 'We're ready if you are.'

A figure emerged wrapped in a bathrobe and made its stately progress down the studio. There was heavy breathing followed by a collective groan. I still remember the shock: we'd been conned. The model wasn't even female. It was a ladies' hairdresser named Arnold, well known in the Bethnal Green Road as a tim-tum, a person of indeterminate sex, because of his mincing walk, his wrist bracelet and the tight seat of his trousers.

Arnold gave us a courtly nod and disrobed without hesitation. His genitals sagged limply below his hairy belly. I think we'd have been less embarrassed if he had been a woman. Nobody had ever seemed so naked. So unsightly a body should never have been exposed undressed to strangers. One by one men began to sneak out of the room. The Principal left after clearing his throat noisily. Mr Miskin went back to painting the picture in his head. I drew Arnold with the heroic proportions of a heavyweight champion as if somehow, obscurely, this mitigated the disaster.

It was after this that Morry and I decided we'd set up our own studio. The problem was where. He shared a bedroom with his fifteen-year-old sister and an unmarried aunt. In my own family you even had to fight for a corner of the kitchen table. Space was the ultimate luxury. There was a derelict cellar under Morry's shop, too damp for human habitation and less romantic than a poor artist's attic, but it was something and one Sunday morning we started to clear the place out.

In those days nobody threw anything away that could be patched, cannibalized or traded for a piece of china. Morry's cellar was a warehouse of such articles. There were mildewed boots with splayed uppers, stinking mattresses, empty bottles, upholstery stuffing, rags, splintered glass, a broken WC and other abject refuse. Luxuriant green mould had grown over a dilapidated leather sofa and when it was moved we found the decayed corpse of a cat. Its tiny yellow teeth were bared in a grimace of terror. It must have been dead a long time. Dark came before the mess was all shifted, leaving a space about ten feet square. A pauper's ration of moonlight filtered through the metal grating in the pavement. It would never be much lighter. Even a millionaire couldn't have brought the sky down to a cellar like that. But it was a place from which to climb. It was a beginning. We were ready to start.

At this stage I ought to explain about Morry's aunt. She was a handsome, bitter woman of twenty-eight who'd had a love affair with a man in a dry-clean business in Brick Lane. He'd disappeared suddenly and it turned out he had a wife in Poland. As far as people in the neighbourhood were concerned Morry's aunt was henceforth a soiled woman. At best she could only look forward to marriage with an elderly widower. There were ugly rumours that Morry's father only kept her in the house because she was loose, and she walked around the streets with a cold implacable fury as if daring some busybody to say these things aloud so that she might tear the slanderous tongue out of their head – man or woman. Morry was terribly afraid of this aunt. She was angry about everything he did. When he slept she searched his pockets and became even more furious for, of course, there was nothing to find – only packets of Woodbines, or loose change, or bits of meat he'd forgotten to throw away. He was afraid she'd come snooping into the cellar when we were there and catch us without clothes, because we intended to pose for one another, of course.

But it didn't deter us. All our beginnings used to be optimistic. We bought sticks of charcoal and new blocks of drawing paper and prepared to write a fresh chapter into our lives that grey Sunday morning the studio was inaugurated. It was now early winter. The November sky slid over the streets like an iron shutter. I arrived shivering with cold and excitement to find Morry tiptoeing around the cellar arranging things. 'Shush!' he cautioned me. 'They're all still asleep.' He'd smuggled in a couple of kitchen chairs and fixed a carbon mantle on the disused gas jet. It gave off a warm and comfortable glow. We grinned at one another with delight and, undressing quickly down to his jockstrap, Morry dropped to one knee and adopted an athletic pose.

We'd never imagined any place could be so cold as that cellar. The gaslight created only an illusion of cosiness. After twenty minutes Morry couldn't stop his teeth chattering and kept jumping up to slap his arms against his sides. I wasn't looking forward to my turn at all. When it came we were both getting a bit irritable. I sat numbly on the edge of the chair, my forehead propped up by a clenched fist, trying to hold the naked soles of my feet away from the icy concrete floor.

'What are you supposed to be?' Morry said, studying my pose from all angles.

'What do I look like? Jesus Christ?'

'You look as though you're having a crap.'

'If you know your Greek sculpture,' I replied cuttingly, 'you'll recognize Rodin's *Thinker*.'

He started to laugh and I was furious. Soon we were jumping about and pummelling one another, hilarious as a couple of maniacs.

Morry's father appeared, slippered and unshaven, a woollen nightcap on his polished bald head, and stared in astonishment. I put my trousers on as the old man carefully looked away. '*Boychik, boychik,*' he grumbled reproachfully to Morry. 'Fighting in the cellar, like a drunken *goy!*'

For a couple of weeks we didn't meet. Bad things were happening in Europe. People were on the move, trundling bundles in prams, and frontier guards played football with stateless Jews in the no man's land between Germany and Poland. Night after night I scuffled with Mosley's Fascists while Morry, who shirked violence, humped his loneliness into backstreet cinemas. I saw him once when I was walking down Brick Lane. He was eating chips out of a newspaper, staring dejectedly at girls' legs. It looked as if he'd mislaid himself somewhere and was wandering around with little hope of finding himself again. 'Hey, Morry!' I called. 'I'll come over to do some sketching on Sunday.' He turned, blinking vaguely.

'All right, I'll expect you,' he said in an embarrassed voice. 'Going to a meeting?'

'Sure. Wanna come?'

His eyes had the fixed stunned look that came from sitting close up to the screen in smoky darkness at the Pavilion. I hurried away to join my boisterous guerrillas in another skirmish.

On Sunday the weather had changed and a bright winter sun made it seem pointless to spend the morning in a dingy cellar. By the time I came Morry's family were already up and about. We could hear his father overhead scrubbing the bloodstained block on which he hacked and butchered his carcasses. Standing naked in the striped light that came through the cellar grating, I thought of the cold sun above Poland's frontier. Miskin's black rabbi stared at his God with slaughtered eyes. Oh, to be Lenin commanding the Revolution with an uplifted finger; Budenny speaking a terse soldierly message as his Red Cavalry galloped into the white Siberian desert. *Blut fascisti.*

'Would you fight against Hitler, Morry?' I said. 'Even if it was a capitalist war?'

He extended his pencil and measured my physical proportions with one eye. 'I'm a pacifist,' he replied. 'You know that.' He made some swift alterations to his sketch and showed it to me. There was a thrusting masculinity in the drawing. Thighs, shoulders and neck strained against an invisible obstacle and the penis was as supple and dangerous as a serpent's head.

'It's good,' I said.

The compliment pleased and embarrassed him. 'You really think so? Really?' He hurried out to pin it up in his bedroom.

I stood by the window smoking a cigarette when the door reopened. It was Morry's aunt. For a moment we stared at each other in petrified silence, then she half-turned distractedly and said: 'Oh, it's you! I'm sorry.' As I reached out stealthily for my clothes she appraised me with a direct, severe, yet passionate gaze. Her bosom strained against the cloth of her dress. My skin burned and I doubled up sharply to conceal my embarrassing erection, but she did not take her eyes off me for a moment. In that instant I knew that all the stories about her were lies. She had the sadness of small Jewish towns hemmed in by ancient curses, and she was afraid of me. It was as if I was twenty-one already and master of half the world. I stood up slowly and began to dress, not even pausing when she left the cellar and quietly closed the door.

Something happened to me about that time. Suddenly I wrote a poem. The words came to me unexpectedly one day during dinner break at work. I found a crumpled piece of paper in my pocket and wrote them down. 'Farewell O Queen of the Night, dark mistress of my cosmic dreams.' It was a strange thing to write and I wondered what it meant. But if I failed to understand how the words came, I knew with extraordinary elation that they were a message from inner space. Things would never be the same again.

Appendices

Prologue: The Day the World Came to an End

It came with the dry fierce wind which blew a tropical summer against the city. After the fortress of winter and the streets clamped in the fist of frost; after the doomed hope of April and the flooded sewers; after the rain's recession came the drought-bearing winds and the fever of July. Under a sky turned blue and solid and a sun scorching a slow arc of fire above the roofs, the desiccated city settled beneath dust and silence – not a silence of the ear but the silence of a heap of ashes buzzing with flies. And it was a terrible city, a mausoleum of dry bones set like stumps in the decayed mouth of the world, a desert moving with lethargic animals approaching the time of extinction.

Wilderness.

The sky blazed up ravenous with fire. On the second Monday of the month there was to be an eclipse of the sun above the rock desert of Arizona and the one sky of the world would be dark.

It was twilight of Sunday evening in the east suburbs of London. The street markets had dispersed: merchants, strongmen, vendors of medicine, charlatans and bargain hunters, all had vanished. Gone the dancers and the music. A litter of refuse decaying in gutters, the dim bleary windows of pubs, groups of tired children combing the beaches of the streets, grey buildings toppling slowly into darkness – these remained.

Trapped in the shadow between a tenement and a toy factory, some small boys talked heatedly towards midnight. They argued about school and girls and grown-ups; about how far each could run, spit, make water; they debated their scattered knowledge of the legendary world; they spoke with awe of the moon and stars and of how tomorrow there would be an eclipse of the sun. Someone said it would be the end of the world. They quarrelled bitterly with him but, because it was night-time and the dark was full of terror, they knew it to be true. 'It's not true!' they said. 'True! . . .' echoed the silence of empty alleyways and gloomy arches as they ran nervously home to their beds.

Daniel climbed the unlighted stairs of the tenement filled with apprehension. Grinning faces floated by in the gloom, secret and appalling voices whispered in each dark corner. Into his bedroom and the host of invisible eyes that stared at him from sinister objects that had lost the friendly and familiar aspects of daytime. They pursued him when he crouched under the bedclothes and for a long time he was afraid to go to sleep and abandon the watch on his body. The reassurance of morning was remote, unbridgeable. Tonight, the world would end tomorrow. He was in a train racing across a bridge suspended above a turbulent river. It was an arrow aimed into empty space, to nowhere. As it dropped he remembered the necessity of prayer. A great wind of voices sprang up round his ears, singing:

TOMORROW   *give us this day our daily bread*
THE WORLD   *for Thine is the Kingdom, the Power and the Glory*
ENDS   *for ever and ever, Amen . . .*

Separating from his dense body, he was carried aloft into sleep.

He woke up to the church bells beating the gong of morning.

It was the long moment in which dream and reality, time and eternity, I and you were all contained in the crystal stillness of not-being. Then the reverberations shattered the unity into splinters of consciousness and he ran to the window to see if the street was still there. The stone forest replied with its early-morning look, shuttered windows and long spears of shadow falling across the cobbled streets, and now he remembered he was eight and his name was Daniel; and the feel of the cool tongue of water as he washed under the running tap; and the taste of bread in the mouth; and how the white milk clouded the cherry-coloured tea with brown; and all the sounds of breakfast and the city at eight o'clock of a hot morning in July. The wonder of it caught in his lungs and carried him on a tide of excitement into the beginning of the day. It was Monday, the day of beginnings, and he quite forgot they said it would be the end of the world.

Going to school, the heat from the pavements came through the soles of his shoes and a trickle of sweat oozed down his back. He loitered in the shade of the striped shop blinds and, passing the grocer's store, paused to sniff the cool dark smells of paraffin and soap and yellow cheese, of soused herrings and green cucumbers pickling in brine, of dust and flour and sharp-smelling garlic sausages, and the cool sour smell of the big caskets of vinegar. The slow-moving carthorses from the railway stables passed by in dejected procession like a straggle of prisoners, leaving a trail of yellow droppings rank and steaming in the hot sunshine. Torn scraps of newspaper littered the road or drifted underfoot, blown by the foetid breeze. A train whistled and an engine trundled by on the elevated railroad, dragging a thick streamer of black smoke across the sky, its muscular piston thrusting in slow motion as the wheels climbed the gradient to the goods yard.

Ahead was the church of St John – gloomy brickwork, a

spire like a rusty needle, the sickly sweet and evil-smelling atmosphere of decay which filtered through heavy Gothic doors and contaminated the commonplace breath of the morning. He hurried by with averted eyes past the terrible stone christ, the drab and terrible christ whose marble corpse, disfigured by sores of grime, hung hideous with history in the eye of the Jewish street. It pursued him with a nameless and incommunicable fear. He remembered the stories his mother told of ominous, icon-worshipping priests, pogroms, child abductions, terror that blew up like a storm in the night and left the imprint of its thumbs on the closed eyes of the dead. The marble image annihilated the distance between mother and child, between Bethnal Green and the Black Sea of Russia. And suddenly he knew that this was the day the world would end.

The god would lift its sunken head and come down from its cross of wood to walk stiffly through the city; and wheresoever its shadow fell, the flowers of death would sprout from the cobbles; and whosoever looked on the blind stone face would turn to marble; and the clock of time would stop and the sky fall down on the earth; and the world would drop for ever into the pit of darkness . . .

He stood motionless, staring at his reflection in the window of a shop. A hundred – two hundred – times a year he passed the church, never without fear, sometimes at night with a naked terror of the evil power which inhabited the sad white figure of this alien god. He alone knew it for what it was, because he was Daniel and there could be nothing in the world unless he knew it and spoke its name, nothing. Until it was born in his mind it did not exist. He knew the stone christ and was afraid; and the stone christ knew he was afraid.

Once, hurrying by at night, he had revolted against his fear. Slowly he had crept back and, with a quick nervous glance at the bowed head, he muttered quickly: '*Yoshke pondrack! Yoshke pondrack!'*[1] then ran with a pumping heart, not stopping until back in the safety of his home. For days afterwards he had been afraid to pass the church, but after a while he thought the stone god had forgotten. Now he knew that it remembered. It was because of that terrible insult that the world was to come to an end.

Perhaps if he'd gone back some time and said . . . something, not an apology (only a coward would say, 'I'm sorry', to a wicked god), but something like: 'My name is Daniel and I'm not afraid,' perhaps if he'd done that the power might have been broken. But he couldn't. As soon as the words came out of his mouth the god would strike him dead – and – and maybe it wouldn't do any good.

'If I can keep on counting to a million,' he thought suddenly, 'I can stop it happening even now.' And immediately he was sure of it, an implicit believer in the potency of spells. 'One . . . two . . . three . . .' he began, catching the sound made by his running feet as they bounced off the pavement – and soon he was no longer counting footsteps but the pale procession of faces floating in the heat of the city, and the white surf of pigeons fretting the tide of morning, and the sneeze and snuffle of motors on the distant highways, and all the great minute movement of the universe contained in the womb of his mind. By the time he reached the red-brick building of the school he was engrossed in the dream of the city.

In the playground waiting for the bell a bundle of boys scrambled after a football made of paper. Others roamed in small packs, barking dangerously like young wolves loose among a flock of lambs, or exploded with loud noises like the eruption of fire-crackers. Daniel came in solemnly. He had forgotten the magic of numbers. Only the sound remained, echo of a lost meaning, and he was puzzled and vaguely dismayed, as if he had lost his own identity. The noise of the schoolyard remained distant and its shape was blurred and indistinct, the light striking the retina of his eyes filtering through thick green bottle-glass. He had forgotten the magic of numbers and he couldn't quite remember why it mattered.

Suddenly he became conscious of pressure in his bladder and went to make water. The natural function at once restored the balance between himself and the world and he came racing out, boisterous with high spirits, and plunged into a scrum struggling for the paper ball. Soon he was scampering towards the chalked wall, earnest and scarlet with the heat of play. The bell high up in the belfry clanged out on the summer air and startled the pigeons hovering on the edge of the school roof.

'The Lord is my Shepherd, I shall not want,' came the somnolent drone of children's voices, while the noisy traffic of the city rumbled by in the enduring, normal and ever-lasting world . . .

2

The sun came through the tall windows of the classroom striped and golden like a tiger. Its hot muzzle sniffed at the wilting gladioli which had been placed as an offering on the desk of Miss Baker, the goddess with mild blue eyes and yellow protruding teeth. It stained the blackboard and the big wall-map with its steaming breath and steadily consumed the afternoon.

Daniel sat drowsily in the back row of desks listening to the torpid voices of children chanting the poem of numbers. Miss Baker uncoiled her thin, lofty body and wrote on the blackboard. Her head nodded on the tall stalk of her neck. A high giggle of laughter rippled across the throat of the class. The cry of a street vendor floated into the closed world of the school. Far in the distance, the noise of an engine in the shunting yard, the slow clip-clop of van horses, the high intermittent whining of a sawmill. The music of the afternoon jazzed in his head. Then the school bell rang and the children swarmed into the street, a tidal wave of energy which swamped the desultory day with noise and excitement.

He went the long way home, avoiding the church. All the windows of the tenement were open, exposing its dwellers to the naked heat of the sky and the foetid breath of the city. Rows of washing hung from lines fastened to drainpipes and people leaned on windowsills, looking out at the street placidly and incuriously. The sight of their homely, unsuspicious faces revived Daniel's uneasiness. The sinister atmosphere of Sunday night began to revive in his mind. He went upstairs furtively, hiding the sin in his face, but he felt as if his body was covered with guilt as shameful and hideous as the rank hair that grew on the great genitals of men.

Becky (Mrs Mandelstein) was in the flat, breathing wheezily and shifting her bulk uncomfortably in the narrow wooden chair. Occasionally, she wiped her steaming face with her apron and sighed as if the burden of her mountainous flesh was too great to endure, as if her spirit were a caged bird beating its wings against the prison of her corpulence. Becky, big mother-bosom, big woman-voice rich with salty Yiddish, china teeth biting hard-boiled eggs with daffodil-yellow yolks, heavy with lamentation, a perpetual mourner at the feast of life. 'Ai, ai, ai! ... What a life it is! In winter it's so cold, it's like Siberia. In summer a person can die from the heat.' Her tongue slipped easily into the familiar soliloquy of death and disease, of childbirth and hunger, pogrom and persecution. 'Believe me, Rosa' – she fanned herself languidly with her apron – 'hot is not good for anybody. Even a dog gets such a fever from the sun, is like a *meshuggas*, a madness. And with *goyim* is no difference. You remember, it was just a day like this came the pogrom in Odessa. I remember like it was yesterday. First it was so quiet; if the whole world stopped all of a sudden it couldn't be quieter. And by us *Yuden*[2] is a thing like this. When it's quiet everybody holds his breath in fear.'

Daniel's mother nodded her head and sighed, leaning her elbows on the table and staring out far beyond the immediate cliffs of the city to some distant and dreamlike landscape. The lids of her eyes drooped like a child's lulled by the somnolent rhythm of a familiar lullaby. 'Sleep, my son, my little Jew. One day you will grow up and become a pedlar of raisins and almonds and live in a fine house. But always remember the sorrow of Israel.'

Becky rocked to and fro gently as she spoke. She was in Odessa in the unnatural quiet that surrounded the Jewish Pale.[3] It was the eve of Passover but instead of the customary rejoicing the blood of the people ran cold. A child's body had been found, flung like the corpse of a cat in the courtyard of a Jewish house. Outside the ghetto a whisper sprang up and ignited a small flame of rumour – Ritual Murder. The flame was fanned by the hot angry breath of the priests. Soon a fierce wind roared through the streets and the storm beat on the walls of the *Judengasse*.[4] Cringing in cellars, the Jews heard the thunder of Cossack cavalry and the long night of lances and rape began.

As he listened to Becky's soliloquy spoken in the traditional singsong like prayer, Daniel saw the city grow alien and huge with terror and the sky become stormy with the mad wind of horses and their demonic riders. Lances tore the membrane of the sky and darkness poured down on the earth in torrents of vodka and fire. That was the image of desolation that arose in him and he saw it with the eyes of the generations in his blood. His childhood stood steadfast and impervious against this tide of history. The two women filled the kitchen with their impregnable femininity and, while he was with them, drinking the milk of their words, the world that enclosed him was a womb, fleshy and unassailable; but one day he would emerge, a conqueror, and destroy that other world of his father's enemies, and in the future he would make sure they would be without honour.

He looked through the window of Becky's childhood at his own and what had been inexplicable in it was suddenly underlined with meaning. There was the stone christ and what it did to the Gentiles of the backstreets and to Old Meg, the mad gypsy, who lived in a room on top of a house facing the tenement. Old Meg with her beads, her frog's laugh, and her narrow, brown, secret face, which gave off a musty smell like old books, or cellars, or things shut up for a long time in a damp cupboard. She leaned on her windowsill, staring with narrow black eyes at the tenement, saying nothing, not missing a movement behind its front windows. Sometimes her sullen alien face opened in an unaccustomed smile at nobody in particular, as if it would swallow all the tenement in the genial cavity of her mouth. For six days of the week her silent watchfulness was an accepted part of the atmosphere of the street, but every Saturday evening she adorned her body with rings and bracelets and beads to visit the public house on the corner. Late at night she would stagger homewards past the people gossiping in doorways, the youths and girls flirting under the street lamps, and the children sitting on the steps of the toy factory, crooning: 'Nice little jewboys! Lovely little circumcised bastards!' and, reaching her room, would lean far out on the windowsill, screaming: 'You killed our Lord, but I'm not afraid! I'm not afraid!' then hurl her crazy frog's laugh at the lit windows of the sane.

And a queer silence would fall on the street. People stopped talking and closed their doors apprehensively. The youths and girls giggled and moved away, and the children, seated in the shadow of the factory, were moved by uneasiness in the dark . . .

Daniel framed the incident carefully in his memory and

returned to the present. Downstairs in the communal yard Mrs Marks from Number Five was emptying a bucket of refuse into the dustbin. His mother looked down and exchanged greetings with her. How was Mr Marks? . . . Oh, one mustn't grumble. The tailoring was slack again but, thank God, they could still live. She wasn't feeling too good herself, the heat was bad for her kidneys . . . She smiled and shrugged her shoulders as she went into the passage.

Becky was clairvoyant, with a habit of sudden prognostication. 'Poor woman! She's very ill, Rosa,' and she shook her head sadly. 'Who knows how long she's got?'

'She'll get better,' Daniel's mother said. 'It's not like she was an old woman, she's not even thirty.'

'*Nu*, we'll see. You know, it's a saying in my home town that more people die from kidneys than anything else.' She heaved herself up to talk more freely. Becky was the chronicler of her time, weaving a rare and commonplace tapestry of gossip out of her own and other people's lives. Ai, ai, ai . . . She knew what poor Mrs Marks suffered. Such a lump of a husband she had with his horses and his dogs and his story about how it was always slack in the tailoring. If he was more of a man – she spoke cryptically to conceal her meaning from Daniel – maybe his wife wouldn't even have kidney trouble. Last week she had taken the secret of her barrenness and confided it to the rabbi. The rabbi had given her a *brocha*, a prayer, to induce fertility. If only Mrs Marks had come to Becky she could have told her a better thing than a *brocha*. The *Rabboine Shel Oilem*, the Lord, had other things to do than bother his head whether Mrs Marks had a baby.

Thus the women drifted into talking of the commonplace acts of existence, closing the door on the dead and the past, and, though he paid no particular attention to what they said, their words were stored up in Daniel's memory. In this communion of the child with the women of his race was the tradition made manifest and passed on unto the coming generations.

3

As the day drew on the heat did not abate, indeed the atmosphere thickened and grew more stifling. Towards seven o'clock the men came back from work in the tailor shops, fur factories, cabinet-making works. Tired, dusty, faces spiky with beards and grimed with sweat, they came slowly down the street in their braces and tramped heavily up the tenement stairs. The drainpipes grumbled with water as they washed, and the daytime noise of the tenement, shrill and soprano with the voices of women and children, took on a deeper, harsher resonance. The tempo of existence changed. It lost the brisk, feminine rhythm of grating scrubbing boards, rattling saucepans, of clothes pegs, washing and the clatter of crockery, and became slower and more leisurely, filled with the pleasurable weariness that comes after the strict labour of a long working day. Lights began to appear in some of the windows and people could be seen in the kitchens eating supper, the men in shirt sleeves talking peacefully with a laconic economy of gesture, the women busy with pots, the children subdued and ill at ease in the confining company of their fathers.

There was to be a party in Number Six that evening. Twice a week, on Mondays and Thursdays, the little community became festive with cards, music and the quick interchange of Yiddish humour. Begun some years before when the men had returned from Russia after their compulsory service in the Tsar's armies, the practice had now become traditional. Becky and Daniel's mother went up together. When they had gone he walked disconsolately into the bedroom and stared out of the window. While they had been with him he had known he could not die, they and he and the world were invulnerable. He had been buttressed against hurt by the flesh of their bodies, and the story that the world was going to end was only a part of the nightmare that talking in the shadow of the toy factory about sex and violence and the strange mystery of the stars brought to his feverish imagination: a nightmare that vanished in the mundane arithmetic of morning and the geography of daylight. Now it was growing dark and he was alone and who knew, who knew? . . .

The lamplighter came down the street and dismounted from his bicycle, his long pole on his shoulder. As he cycled away, the unwinking eye of the street lamp discovered the boy's sombre thoughtful face and stared him out until he was driven away from the window and the sight of the half-deserted street. He went upstairs to Number Six, drawn by the magnet of his mother.

The parlour was dense and acrid with tobacco smoke and resonant with the impatient argument of men. They sat round a big table, each with a pile of money at his side, blowing streams of smoke through their nostrils, their faces flushed, growing tense as the game reached a climax. As soon as Daniel entered, Big Alec seized him. He was florid with heat and alcohol and sweat had made big damp patches under the arms of his shirt.

'Alright, Schreiber,' he roared, 'now you'll see a different story. I never lose when Danny's in the room.' He turned to the boy and said: 'Don't go away and if I win I'll give you a big kiss. Eh, what d'you think of that?' and, pressing Daniel against his hard, broad thigh, he winked slyly at the company. The boy stared with nervous fascination at his large bristly black moustache and the black hairs which grew out of his thick nostrils and, blushing painfully, managed an embarrassed smile. But Alec pretended to be angry. His voice rumbling up from the depths of his stomach, he thundered: 'What! You don't answer? So a kiss is not enough, *hein*? What's the matter? Anybody would think you was a gel. Alright, I won't give you a kiss, I'll give you sixpence!' The men laughed. Alec was a card.

'Believe me, Alec,' said Schreiber sardonically, 'if you got sixpence when the game is finished, I'll go back to Plotzk on the next boat.'

'Sh! . . . *mein frau* is in the kitchen,' said Alec in a hoarse whisper audible throughout the flat. 'You want all the rest of the week I should have to sleep on the other side of the bed?'

'In future,' said Schreiber, 'you'll have to pay in advance, otherwise your missus will make you sleep under the bed, never mind on the other side.'

For a few moments the genial laughter held up play entirely, then the cards were dealt out and there was an interval of silence while the men studied their hands.

'To the devil with it!' said Alec gruffly. 'What's the good of playing for monkey nuts? I'll buy another card for half a sovereign.'

'Half a sovereign it is,' agreed Schreiber.

Alec picked up the card, then threw his hand on the table. 'Ach! A black year on it,' he muttered with disgust. 'Today, if the sky was to fall down and break everybody's head, on Schreiber's it would drop gold.'

Suddenly the evening was deprived of its gay but frightening hilarity. Animation ebbed from the robust atmosphere of the room and Daniel stared through the drifting lifeless eddies of smoke at the stern, lonely faces of men set against time and decay and history. 'If the sky was to fall down . . .' From the formless chaos of sound, the image stood out with an apocalyptic clarity. It arrested time and immobilized the processes of living. They would be caught like this, unprepared, with the taste of pleasure on their tongues, their unaccomplished history toppling into an uncomprehended abyss . . .

He walked through their ghostly faces into the kitchen, where the women were congregated, bare arms folded over their deep, comfortable bosoms, drinking tea, chattering, laughing at times until the tears came into their eyes. Mrs Schreiber sat with her blouse open suckling a tiny, black-haired infant; Mrs Sam, who was modern and had bobbed blonde hair, walked backwards and forwards from the kitchen to the parlour to stare dreamily at the men; Becky, the continent of her body enthroned among the islands of women, dissected out the tissue of scandal from the meat of conversation and the small bones from a herring, eating the flesh delicately and wiping her greasy fingers fastidiously on her apron; Old Clara nodded and nodded her ancient head like a cork bobbing on the tide of gossip, wisps of grey hair escaping from under the traditional *sheitel*, a nut-brown glossy wig that was perched incongruously above the bony promontory of her eagled nose; Daniel's mother, who fed the story-tellers with the generous subsidy of her rapt, childlike attention, turned as he entered and smiled without speaking.

He went quietly to her side and took up a position by the window where he could see the deep well of the yard and the stone shaft of the tenement climbing sixty feet towards the sky. Over to the left, above the stacked timber of a woodyard, terraces of roofs erected a vast amphitheatre of slate around the circumscribed area of the street and the bloodthirsty face of the setting sun watched the spectacle of humanity playing out the small drama of its existence in all the rooms of all the houses of the lethargic city. A slow wave of darkness crept up from the east, where Wapping and Limehouse met the waters of the river, and began to engulf the unsuspecting city street by street, moving with the impetus of flood. In the distance there was a faint, almost imperceptible vibration of thunder. A flicker of lightning danced on the perimeter of roofs and the sound of thunder increased. The atmosphere became compressed and unendurable, a solid mass of air charged with the high voltage of storm. Inside the room, a curious mauve twilight refined the silhouette of forms until people and furniture became tenuous and insubstantial. Their voices dwindled away. Daniel moved into the dream of the storm and the nightmare of approaching calamity.

Suddenly the sky was ripped from end to end by a dazzling blade of lightning and an invisible mountain of thunder tumbled its boulders into the hollow bowl of the earth. The men and women turned startled faces to the window. Bemused and apprehensive, they left their chairs and stared out at the curious twilight and the sun, whose clotted, apoplectic countenance was now naked of brilliance to the eye. They were filled with awe and trepidation, as if it had been given them to look in the face of God. Hurriedly, they left Number Six to go down to the street. Old Clara, bent with the infirmity of her eighty years, tottered in their wake.

'*Vos is? Vos is?*' she moaned feebly to Daniel.

'The eclipse!' he shouted.

She did not understand, but as he ran down the stairs he could hear her reedy lamentation, the ancient, age-old accompaniment of calamity: '*Oy, vai! Oy, vai! Oy, vai! . . .*'

Oh, pain, pain, pain! . . .

The street was crowded with people. They stood in every doorway, crowding under the lintels as if to shelter from rain. The sky, no longer remote, pressed down so close upon the rooftops that it seemed impaled on the blunt chimneys. It exuded a mauve light which flowed with the consistency of milk down the gutter of the street, dissolving the hard contours of houses. And, sinking in the west, the dying sun, Lord of the Day, Father of All Living Things, Master of the Universe, had lost its fire and become dense and crimson.

The clock of time was slowing to a stop and Daniel stood in

the centre of the dying creation, imagining the quenched light of the stars and the barren spaces of desolation entombing the world and the brief memory of mankind.

A fine curved line of shadow began to erode the sun's rim and an incredulous gasp came out from the midst of the people. The supreme act of sacrilege had begun. The shadow ate further and further into the heart of the sun and a huge and terrible silence contained them utterly, heaven and earth, the world and its people, the great compact universe witnessing with awe the death of a god.

Instead of the sun, a black cinder rolled on the floor of the sky . . .

And then there was only darkness.

4

An intense stillness gripped the world at the moment of its extinction. It reached up beyond the desert of the heavens and deep into the motionless heart of the earth. Each man looked into the dark mirror of his spirit, into a depth so chasmic and profound that no image of light returned, and a primitive murmur rose up in the midst of the people. It was the murmur of a crowd awaiting a Voice, the Voice that had spoken to them in Egypt and in the Wilderness and from the holy peak of Sinai, from the caves of the dead and the mountains of the living, and that would now speak amongst them the final and utter revelation. But there was only silence.

Then suddenly Old Clara forced her way into the street, and out of her mouth issued a voice like brass: 'Moshe Rabbanu! Moshe Rabbanu! The Messiah is coming!' She stumbled into the intense apocalyptic dark and the trumpet of her words rang hard and clear in the silence: 'Rejoice, O Israel! The hour has struck! Messiah is coming! Messiah is coming! . . .'

And Daniel heard the Word and knew its power; and his loins were girded up with the spirit of his fathers; and all the generations of Moses marched like an army in his blood.

'Messiah is coming!' he shouted, running down the catacomb of lightless streets to meet the corruption of darkness. As he ran the streets began to fill with people oozing from the gloom of houses, tumbling in rivers out of tenements, cascading from subterranean alleyways. The air began to fill with cries as of myriad birds begging crumbs, and one voice, rising above all others, a voice of subtlety and seductive sweetness, crying: 'Buy my violets, sweet violets!' and then, 'Who'll buy my roses, white or red? Who'll buy my sweet roses?'

A whirlpool of bodies sucked him in and for a long time he lived through close and secret intercourse with them, so that he came to know intimately their hooded beings and the pain of their lives. And their faces were the faces of strange-brother, strange-lover, strange-child of his loins; of emperor, priest and beggar; of the brother on the far shore of a distant continent and the stranger on the corner of a familiar street. In the brief instant they possessed him was contained the prophecy of how all his life he would be possessed by strangers, as the sea possesses the river and its source.

He passed through them into the quiet graveyard of night, littered with the tombs of houses. The church advanced the monstrous magnificence of its spire into the cathedral of desolation. Daniel had come safely through the allegory of the city, mingling with its concourse of living dead, but it had exacted its tribute, taking so much of himself that henceforth the city was him and he was the city. Now he stood before the bowed figure of the christ that had pursued him with fear for many days of his years and burnt its stigma into the souls of his fathers.

Its body hung on its cross, a white bat with a drawn, human and suffering face. It looked down at him with a love so savage and terrible it was more destructive than hate. He had always known it would destroy him and it did, commanding the last utterance of his soul. He gripped the railings of the church and looked into the eyes of Christ; and the voice of Moses came out of his mouth:

'*Shema Yisroel Adonai Elohanu Adonai Echod* . . . Hear, O Israel! The Lord thy God, the Lord is One,' he cried, tears of exaltation running down his face, obliterating the sin in his eyes.

And he sent out the Messiah of his spirit to redeem the world of darkness . . .

Emanuel Litvinoff (second row, second from right, seated) at Wood Close School, early 1920s

A Jew in England*

Before me as I write is a school photograph: I am the fourth boy on the right. Forty-six of the other boys in the photograph are also Jews – Kantorovich, Zelinikoff, Cohen, Dubovsky, Shrebnik, Abramovich, Segal, and others whose names I cannot now recall. The one *goy* stands forlornly in the back row, and across the fading years I still remember how lonesome he was, the unreflective cruelty of our indifference.

Outside the school yard where we self-consciously pose are the backstreets of Whitechapel and Bethnal Green, a hard-working district of sinewy cabinet-makers, round-shouldered tailors, itinerant street-vendors hoarsely praising the goods on their barrows, furriers, button-hole makers, housewives battling the daily grime that seeps in from the littered pavements. Back-rooms vibrate to the noise of machines. There are shops heaped with rags, cracked gramophone records, chipped crockery, old iron, ancient magazines. Whatever it is, someone can make a living out of it. The district stinks of too many people occupying too little space, of drains ill-equipped to flush away the waste of so many bodies, and this effluvia of poverty is spiced with

* The first part of this article was originally delivered as a lecture at the Anglo-Israeli Writers' Symposium held in Tel Aviv during the summer of 1966 (as well as Litvinoff, British participants included Dannie Abse, Chaim Bermant, Karen Gershon, Jon Silkin and Jacob Sonntag). The second part, 'The Problem of Survival', was written after discussions that took place at the symposium.

the smell of sour pickles, herring, garlic and meat rotting in the open windows of kosher butcher shops. People stand on pavements speaking Yiddish, but they avoid the corners occupied by pubs, which are numerous, and they seldom stand for more than a few moments near the marble crucifix implanted on the grass-bearded forecourt of the Catholic church. East London 1929 . . .

I lived near the school in a street of small two-storeyed cottages, some with cellars under the pavement in which whole families spent their days in artificial light. My home was in the tallest building of the street, a tenement of sooty brick whose squalor in retrospect seems unbelievable. But conditions were much the same all around us, acreages of slums boiling with humanity, and we were not at all conscious of special hardship. Most of the people in our street were East European immigrants and even if they could afford the luxury of privacy I doubt if they would have thought it worth buying.

Life varied according to light and season. In summer, when it was hot, we were both more languid and more violent, occupying our doorsteps like the sands of a Mediterranean beach; in winter, we hurried indoors to jostle peevishly for a warm place near the fire. Twilight transformed people's faces and voices, enveloping them in a kind of loneliness. The sluggish movement of life at day's end made even us children reflective and philosophical, like old men on park benches; but when streetlamps lit up the night people came out to enjoy themselves, with a feeling that they'd earned it. The fat started to sizzle in fish-and-chips shops, thumping pianos sounded from pubs, brilliantined young fellows in sharp suits stared with insolent lust at the plump buttocks of high-stepping girls, and crowds skirmished around the picture-palaces trailing peanut shells wherever they went.

I have a habit of thinking about that past in collective terms, partly because my memories have become generalized but chiefly because in my childhood we were still members of a tribal community, our neighbourhood a village remote in spirit from the adjacent cosmopolitanism of the great city of London. The way of life was still much like that of the small Jewish towns scattered across the lands of Eastern Europe, from Poland in the north to the southern Black Sea town of Odessa, where my own parents had been born. We shared the same Sabbaths and festivals, ate the same food, sang traditional songs in the same minor key, laughed at the same Jewish jokes. We were a foreign colony, like the Italians of Saffron Hill or the Chinese of Pennyfields, but unlike them I do not think that as children we felt at all un-English, or regarded the *goyim* in the next street as more native than ourselves. If anything, we thought ourselves to be a superior kind of English, because we were also Jewish and, therefore, cleverer, cleaner, more industrious and sober, less a different race than another class, and any hostility we encountered was put down to envy of our superior qualities.

My first serious experience of antisemitism was in my fourteenth year when I won a trade scholarship. Successful candidates were allowed to nominate, in order of preference, the trades they wished to learn. I chose, first, a school of lithography, then one for catering and, finally, a study course in electrical engineering.

Object of Ridicule

The school of lithography rejected me without explanation after an interview, in which I had politely and correctly answered a number of simple general knowledge questions, submitted a short written essay and produced a decently carpentered towel-rack as an example of my handiwork. The one question

I did not apparently answer to the interviewer's satisfaction was that relating to my religion. The other schools granted me no interview at all. Instead the London County Council offered a place at a Cordwainers technical college, which turned out to be an institute for shoe-making near an offal yard in Smithfield market. I was the only Jewish pupil. From the very first roll-call the headmaster improvised variations on my name. It became Litintoott, Levypotsky, Levinskinoff, Litmuspaperoff and – on one hilarious public occasion – Lavatoryoffsky. For the rest of the term I endured ridicule and humiliation at the hands of both teaching staff and boys, the headmaster proving the most inventive of all. But I did not generalize from this experience. The barbarities of Cordwainers technical college seemed localized, like the stench of decaying offal which permeated its classrooms.

As far as I can recall, therefore, the problem of identity did not begin to arise until the onset of adolescence, with all its emotional and intellectual uncertainties. In my case, it coincided with the beginning of the thirties, as it must have done for many young Jews in Germany. I was then a young communist with a rather apocalyptic notion of political salvation and one day I was walking with another young communist, a big-nosed lad named Izzy Birnbaum, in the alien territory of Hoxton, where Jews were unwelcome. It was not politics that brought us there, but girls. Jewish adolescents had an idea that Gentile girls were complaisant and we skirmished the neighbourhood in the hope of finding it true. Rather unwisely, Izzy had made himself conspicuous in a jazzy pullover and my hair was glistening with a dressing of margarine. Instead of attracting female attention, we ran into a gang of youths who spread themselves across the pavement and told us to get back to Palestine. It wasn't the first time in my life I'd been given that advice. The usual rejoinder was 'go to Palestine your f—g self,' or 'this is my bloody country', or 'I'm as good a f—g Englishman as you.' But it was somehow no longer possible to say such things with conviction, and the Hoxton boys looked as if they wouldn't stop at trading insults. We got shoved around a bit and retreated from Hoxton bruised in body and self-esteem. Uneasiness had begun.

The day of Mosley and his fascists had arrived and a frightening change came over the East End. Snotty-nosed kids with whom one had exchanged fairly harmless abuse suddenly appeared buckled and booted in black uniforms, looking anything but juvenile as they tramped through the district shouting: *'We gotta get rid of the Yids, the Yids! We gotta get rid of the Yids!'* And it was even difficult to laugh at the bespoke-tailored fascists who came from the suburbs to officer these eager troops. Black was not the only para-military colour. A green-shirted organization which had practised woodcraft with religious fanaticism abruptly expelled its Jewish members and turned to antisemitism. Also green-shirted, the Social Credit movement took up back-street drilling with wooden rifles in preparation for armed insurrection against the international Jewish financiers of Whitechapel Road. Young communists marched to meetings in red; Zionist youth went around in blue; Jewish ex-servicemen paraded in their war-medals. Sir Oswald's bodyguarded visits to his stronghold in Roman Road, Bethnal Green, were ludicrous and, at the same time, sinister. He looked to us as we skirted the crowds with a prickly sense of peril like a comic 'toff' playing at Mussolini; and his hot-eyed, rigid expression suggested that he derived from the slum streets and shabby onlookers an onanistic illusion of conquest. As he stood on a platform orating in a prissy upper-class English voice he aroused more derision among us than fear. We could not hate him in the way we did his followers, because we could never take altogether seriously a man with an accent like that. What came across unmistakably was a kind of hysterical evil. It penetrated to the marrow of my Jewish bones. There was something inevitable about it all; it was as if all my life I had been waiting for it to happen.

Unwanted Inheritance

Every child of East European Jews has grown up with a working knowledge of persecution. When his elders exchanged reminiscences at the family table, there was usually a curse or two for the Tsarist police, government officials and Christian clergy. Antisemitism was a sort of unwanted inheritance: you were lumbered with it. Now it was on the doorstep again and if you were shocked, as I was, it was because it didn't seem possible that it could happen in England, the country of freedom, justice and tolerance.

When I was about sixteen or seventeen, I was abnormally sensitive about my appearance, having the notion that my nose was too long, my lips too thick and my walk flat-footed and ungainly. I tried to remember not to talk with my hands, but the moment I got excited they jumped out of my pockets and made un-British gestures. When I shoved them out of sight my tongue stumbled on the simplest phrases. At the same time, I had a secret conviction that people were justified in despising me.

This self-contempt made me intolerant of the imperfections of other Jews that I had begun to recognize with sickening frequency. Every time a woman with a foreign accent made a scene on a bus, or two men argued loudly in Yiddish over a business deal, or a music-hall comedian got a few laughs by jamming a bowler-hat over his ears and retracting his neck into his shoulders, I was miserably ashamed. I started to look at my surroundings in a different way, although all my life had been spent in the same neighbourhood. Now the foreign names on shop fronts seemed grotesque and provocative; the Kosher signs and Yiddish lettering were embarrassing advertisements of alienation; there was too much huckstering in street-markets; the flies crawling over exposed meat and groceries were proof of ingrained backwardness and squalor. I was equally affronted by the sight of a Hassid walking through the street in outlandish garb, impervious to the effect of his own strangeness, and of the herring-women down the Lane, plunging their chapped and swollen fingers into the open barrels of pickled fish.

Much had changed since those innocent days when I had taken it for granted that Englishmen were simply people born in England. Until the age of ten I had not seen a country lane, a field, or the sea. England's green and pleasant land was a green and pleasant conceit in a school poem. Reality was the ghetto of East London, the only England I knew, the only place in the whole wide world to which I was truly native. And if I ever thought of it at all, what else was I but English, and what else was I but Jewish, and why should the one be inconsistent with the other? True, a hostile English tribe lived on our perimeter incomprehensibly ordering us to go back to this or that place – anywhere but here. So we were intermittently troubled: but in our teeming streets we dwelt unchallenged and secure except for the ills of poverty. I have been asked, generally by other Jews who grew up as a separate people among the nations of Eastern Europe, if it did not occur to me to wonder how my forefathers fitted into the kind of history we were taught at school. I can only reply that it did not. We got little beyond those narratives in which Canute ordered the tide to halt and Alfred burned the cakes, and what, in any case, had history to do with a boy's dreams and disappointments?

But in my early years a line was drawn through your life

at fourteen and everything changed. One day you were a schoolboy in short trousers, the next a putative adult dressed like a man of forty, and shoved out to earn a living. You came abruptly into contact, and sometimes collision, with the complicated society in which people competed for work, advancement and opportunity at a time when these were not easily come by. It was then that I began to learn that some were more English than others. In the first place the lesson had a class character. The kind of occupations open to a working-class boy of little education were restricted. It goes without saying that in the thirties it was still unthinkable for anyone from Bethnal Green to aspire to become a bank-manager (or cashier), a newspaper reporter, a sanitary inspector or a commissioned military officer, even with a carefully adjusted accent.

Soon I discovered an additional handicap. Being reasonably intelligent and writing a fair hand, I hoped to break out of the tailoring, cabinet-making, fur-manufacturing, hairdressing circuit in which Jewish boys of my background sought a livelihood. Painstaking letters of application went out advising insurance companies, shipping lines, city commercial houses and similar respectable establishments that I had all the qualities required for the post of office-boy. No-one ever replied. I rushed to be first in the queue for direct interviews. Some people were frank enough to tell me that it was their policy not to employ people of the Jewish faith, others preferred ambiguity.

Not Quite British Enough

The 'Situations Vacant' columns of newspapers exploited the prevailing insecurity. We unemployed youths pushed and jostled around copies of the *Daily Telegraph* in public libraries, day-dreaming of wonderful opportunities for salesmen, of learning to make £6 a week in our spare time, of having a healthy and interesting career with free travel all over the world in the armed forces, of becoming masters of our fate by a short course in Pelmanism. One advertisement invited the reader to obtain lucrative employment in His Majesty's Civil Service as a Grade Three Officer or something through a correspondence school that guaranteed success in entrance examinations on a money-back basis. Not having more than a shilling or two at any time, I applied directly to the authorities for the conditions of entry in the hope that it would be possible to read for the examinations in the free library. This was how I made the dismal discovery that I was not quite British enough even to empty the waste-paper baskets in the civil service. Without British-born parents, I learned, they would have nothing to do with you as a postman, a policeman, a naval rating, a customs and excise officer, a government cipher clerk or a weights and measures inspector. In fact, you weren't particularly wanted, and it seemed quite obvious to you why.

So far, my experiences had been singularly parochial, not at all lessened by a growing sense of alienation. The people I best understood were those among whom I'd always lived, the East End Jews, and I knew little about others with whom I was linked by fate. But more and more of them were appearing in London, uprooted men, women and children, some with scuffed cardboard or wooden suitcases, some still showing signs of recent affluence, all subdued, apologetic, unwanted.

Many hundreds of other refugees were shuffling through the wintry streets of Paris. They queued in cellars for bowls of soup, huddled for warmth in cheap bistros, hoarded their misery. In Germany thousands of others bartered vainly for passports, scurried from frontier to frontier, crawled through thickets of clawing wire towards the rifle-muzzles of vigilant border-guards. One could not then know that after the migrant search for a chance to live would come the enforced migration of millions to certain death. In Paris it seems to me then that the symbol of rootlessness could be taken no further. A few months earlier, I had been down, if not out, eating in soup-kitchens and sleeping in doss-houses. But the umbilical cord of group and family belonging had not been severed: there was always the knowledge that friendship, or a new job, would put everything right. If Fascism conquered Britain, in what wintry city would I, too, seek transient companionship, bread, sex, forgetfulness?

A proletarian life could not prepare me for the society of the refugee artists, writers, musicians and scholars with whom I now occasionally came into contact and my East European antecedents made it even more difficult to understand them. In the Whitechapel ghetto we were never in any doubt about being Jews, but many of these new acquaintances had travelled far from their Jewish origins. Some were entirely deracinated, baptized Jews, Germanized Czechs, Marxist intellectuals, elite representatives of German culture, only the crude general-izations of Nazi racial philosophers could herd them into a common category. They were to prove far more adaptable than that earlier generation of Jewish immigrants from Poland, Russia and Lithuania who, by and large, left it to their children to assimilate. These newcomers swam in the mainstream of European culture: they had style, facility, sometimes erudition. All they required was a period of acclimatization. Within a decade, their accents perfected, there was little to distinguish them from born Englishmen, Frenchmen or Americans.

Changing Names to Order

During the war I was commissioned into an alien company of the Pioneer Corps composed of these Jewish refugees. There cannot be a single civilized language for which we did not have

an expert. We could easily have mustered the academic quali-
fications to staff a small university, assemble a decent orchestra,
script, direct and shoot a movie, or launch a newspaper. One
day an order came from the War Office authorizing alien
personnel to change their nominal identities in case they were
ever captured by the enemy. For some strange reason Scottish
clan-names were most favoured and few, if any, ever reverted
to their former titles.

The war, when it came, had unexpected benevolences. I
travelled north to an army depot in Glasgow with a draft of
conscripts from all parts of East London, young Cockneys
leaving the smoke with reluctance. When the train left Euston
a few of the Jews grouped themselves together, exchanging
glances of recognition and commiseration. There were other
regional groupings, for local patriotism used to be strong in
the poor districts of London. Bermondsey boys eyed natives of
Shoreditch with misgiving, Hoxton stared through Homerton as
if X-raying his backbone. Upper-class conscripts avoided conversation for fear of giving their class away by their accents. Once
battle-dress was on and square-bashing began we were as alike
as if hatched together from the same gigantic womb. For my
own part, this anonymity was convalescent. The army offered
little hardship. For the first time I was eating three square meals
a day and still feeling hungry. I got the first warm overcoat
of my life, free boot repairs and laundry, a primitive sense
of well-being. Without being a good soldier, I was skilful at
tempering the rigours of military discipline and kept out of
serious trouble. My Jewish neuroses vanished as I learned to
turn the occasional antisemitic remark against its perpetrator
with nonchalant good humour. Friendships took no account
of religion or race, anyway. There was an unbelligerent war
going on somewhere; if there were also rumours of cruelties,
practised upon civil populations in German-occupied territory,

little of it got into the newspapers, or we didn't think too much about it. In the gentle, soft-hued Ulster countryside troops played war-games and grumbled at the rain. In barrack room, canteen and village hall I stared at nothing, writing poems of frustration.

'We are the soldiers whom no gun awakes. / Whose living fades in dumb monotony of thought, / Whom pain gropes in the urgent thighs, / And in the breast lies numb. / Death is an angel who has passed us by / To grasp another hand sailing an ocean / Or a boy mocking the quiet stars / While we grieve and desire.'

My name appeared in anthologies with titles like *Poems From the Forces*, *Poets in Khaki*, and so on. This gave me modest status at Belfast (we had moved to Ireland) literary gatherings and may have had something to do with my subsequent selection for a commission: it did not change anything much at the time. The poems spoke of sexual deprivation and a melancholy longing for violence. It was a somnambulistic episode in many people's lives. Then came Dunkirk and one awakened to fear.

The horrible prospect that the Nazis might win the war brought home once again that I was involved in the Jewish fate. My friends, in the event of a German occupation, would have the choice of resisting or submitting to conquest. We Jews have no choice: we would die. We had not yet heard the term 'final solution' and the Germans were still conducting experiments to perfect the techniques of mass-murder. But the starvation and sadistic cruelties practised in Dachau, Buchenwald and other places were known even in 'peace-time'. It needed little imagination for a Jew to visualize what awaited him at the hands of the Nazis now that killing was licensed, hallowed by the requirements of war and patriotism.

Most Vulnerable of All

I began to be haunted by the sufferings of Jews in Europe because these unknown victims took on the features of my own family, of my mother, my young sister and my brothers, three of them soldiers like myself, four still schoolchildren and, therefore, most vulnerable of all. It is curious and, I think, significant, that I was less worried by the immediate danger they were experiencing in the London blitz than by the fear of their helplessness in the event of a Nazi invasion. Bombs falling from the sky made no discrimination between victims: everyone had an equal chance of doom or survival. What horrified me was the cold-blooded selections practised by the Nazis in the name of a warped ideology. I was no longer a soldier like any other soldier; I was a Jew in uniform.

About this time, a small group of Jewish fugitives – men, women and children – succeeded in escaping to the Dalmatian coast and were smuggled aboard an old cargo boat, the *Struma*. It must have seemed a miracle of deliverance. Again, miraculously, they survived a hazardous Mediterranean crossing and reached Turkey, from whence they hoped to travel overland to Palestine. But there was a legal obstacle. The British authorities refused entry certificates for Palestine on the grounds that the quota allocated to Jewish immigrants was exhausted. The fugitives then applied to the Turks for permission to stay in the country. This also was refused. They pleaded that the children, at least, should be permitted to stay, but again the answer was no, and the *Struma* was ordered to leave port. Where were the wretched people to go? Back to the Nazis, who would kill them? The British and Turkish authorities were sorry, but there were rules and regulations. *Struma* sailed. Some distance out at sea, there was an explosion and it foundered. Only one survived. No-one knows what caused the explosion. Some say the boat struck a floating mine, others that the fugitives chose to die at sea rather than face torture and death at the hands of the Germans.

The sinking of the *Struma* was desolating news. It blurred the frontiers of evil. Those stony-hearted British and Turkish officials who could send people to their death because their papers were not in order were Hitler's accomplices. They were doing the devil's work, refusing children the right to live because it would upset their book-keeping. No doubt they had consulted with superiors. Coded messages had gone from Ankara to Whitehall. Senior bureaucrats must have found it tiresome to be bothered in the middle of a war by a group of refugees who inconveniently turned up demanding to be let into Palestine. Before they escaped from the Nazis they should have found out if there was room on the quota for them. Didn't they know there was a war on?

Tragic Turning Point

After more than twenty years the memory is still painful. This is how I recorded it at the time in an incoherent poem of grief and bitterness.

'For everything the poets have a word. / To everything the soldier brings his sword, / And I who am soldier and poet only bring, / A crushed heart and my tribal suffering. / Too heavy are my eyes for tears, I am dumb of grief. / They mouth the usual promises but I am deaf . . . / Today I invoke Christ in his heavenly mansion / To come down from the mountain and the sun / And walk into my lowly dwelling place, / My house of mourning, to seek out and bless / Me for my dead, my dead for peace. / I am Matthew, I am Luke, I am twelve Jews / Against many whom my Master knows. / Arrogance of Caesars and Hitlers, lies / Streaming dark through many centuries, / Have stormed and taken many forts of strength, / But mine shall

hold until my ally cometh . . . / Today my khaki is a badge of shame, / It's duty meaningless; my name / Is Moses and I summon plague to Pharaoh. / Today my mantle is Sorrow and O / My crown is Thorn. I sit darkly with the years / And centuries of years, bowed by my heritage of tears.'

If it were possible to point to one single episode as a decisive turning point in one's life, the tragic sinking of the *Struma* would be that for me. Never again would I be able to think of myself as an Englishman, or face uncertainty about my identity. In the middle of this century any Jew in Europe was condemned as surely as if he was born with an incurable disease. Only the accident of geography, or astronomically lucky odds, determined his survival. And when the war was won, for me it was also lost six million times over. This exclusive sense of injury lacks generosity, even imagination. It was some time before I was able to recognize that there was no less depravity in the indiscriminate slaughter by mass bomber raids than in the selective killings practised by the Nazis, that both techniques derived from an increasing tendency on the part of people to regard other people as abstractions. But that is not my theme. I am concerned here with my education as a Jew, and it was the *churban*, the destruction, which largely completed it.

Yet England made me. When the State of Israel was established in 1948 it confronted me with a clear-cut choice and I found that I would not willingly emigrate from the English language, spoken in English ways by mild, tolerant English people. In reality I have encountered little antisemitism, most of it inconsequential, some of it the chemical reaction of oversensitivity. I live in an urbanized English village and am not conscious of segregation from my neighbours, whose reputation for insularity has been exaggerated. I belong to them a little and they belong to me, yet they would probably be faintly astonished to learn that I feel in some ways an outsider having more in common with certain people in New York, Tel Aviv or Moscow than with themselves. They might not understand why I am sometimes overtaken by desolation watching my small daughter playing in the sunshine, why a child's discarded shoe can germinate terrible images in my dreams. But if they ever guessed these things, I would be confident of their compassion. Most of them, anyway.

The Problem of Survival

First of all, I will answer the two or three personal questions that were put to me in the course of the discussion. I was asked if I had expressed my experience in print. My output happens to be rather small but, insofar as it exists at all, I have dealt with precisely the kind of things that were intimated in my opening statement yesterday evening – in poetry, in a novel and in articles in the Press.

Then there was the more serious question: What will happen to your grandchildren? This is the kind of question that one is always being confronted with in Israel. I would like to reverse that question . . . I would like to say: What will happen to *your* grandchildren? Now it seems to me that we do face a very serious problem of Jewish survival; that the Jewish people are suffering – and it would be incredible to expect otherwise – the appalling after-effects of the death of six million people, particularly the almost complete erasure of large sections of Eastern European Jewry; and that Israel suffers this disease – the effects of this tragedy – every bit as much as anybody else.

This problem of Jewish survival is one that you face in Israel just as much as Jews face anywhere else in the world. I would like to summarize it for you in one rather revealing experience I had some time ago in England. There was a young Israeli girl who told me that she had been briefly engaged to an Irish poet. Now she told me, with some relish, that he didn't like Jews. So I said to her, in some perplexity: Well, how did you feel about that? How on earth could you reconcile yourself being engaged to somebody who's an antisemite? She said: Well, he liked Israelis – he thought they were wonderful! So here was a curious kind of fracture of consciousness where a Jewish girl – and she is clearly a Jewish girl (her parents are East European Jews) – can *completely* dissociate herself from the common predicament of Jews, wherever they are . . . because the problem is both regional and international.

I cannot see how you can possibly talk in terms of a meaningful Jewish survival in Israel, at the present moment, when it is in extreme doubt. First of all, there is the conflict between the whole European tradition and the Oriental Jewish tradition – which is not resolved, which sharpens in many ways and which cannot yet be determined in terms of what kind of Jewish survival you will have in Israel. After all, I think Herzl envisaged the new State of Israel as speaking German or some other European tongue. So if it hadn't been for the fanaticism of a Ben-Yehuda, you might even have had a German-speaking nation in this country, who would be no more Jewish than we are in England or than we are likely to become in the course of the next century or so.

If you merely have a Hebrew-speaking nation in Israel, the kind of nation that Moshe Shamir has begun to sketch out in outline for us . . . they won't be Jewish in any sense that I would accept at all. The fact that they use the language of the Bible would mean very little to me; there are Christian clergymen who use the language of the Bible – that doesn't make them Jews in my eyes.

Jews – the Most Rooted People

Now it seems to me that this is a very simple situation because we are facing a problem of Jewish survival. Now I don't want to talk in terms of literature, the dialogue between writers, because it doesn't get you very far. We have established that we don't understand one another very well because we don't read one another's works . . . What I would like to say is this: Clearly I don't think anybody here would endorse the idea that it's a good thing for a kind of vast steam-roller to iron out the national differences, the national distinctiveness in the world. We're not looking forward, I hope, to the creation of some kind of super-nation, which would be one step before we created the Earth-man, without individual national characteristics. Human society is immensely enriched by national distinctiveness of all kinds; and human society has been immensely enriched – and I'm not saying this in a missionary way at all – by the existence of a Jewish nation.

When people talk to me about the rootlessness of the Jews in different countries . . . I am astonished; because they equate rootlessness with lack of a geographical centre. But the Jewish people have existed for a very long time without a national geographic centre, and I would not say that their existence has been rootless at all. I would say that their existence has been deeply rooted: they are one of the most deeply rooted people in the history of the world. It's as simple as that.

Now I was asked: What conclusions do I draw from what I said about my early experiences of life? I do want to emphasize again that it sounded much more than it was; that, in fact, by the compression of these incidents it sounds as though all my life I've been harried by antisemitism. It isn't true! But, nevertheless, supposing I was: What conclusions do I draw?

I have faced this question in 1948. I wrote a poem about it

called 'The Dead Sea'. It seemed to me then, when I thought about it very carefully, that what I identified with clearly was not Zionism and the return to Israel: I identified with the exile; I felt all my responses were to the kind of conditions that existed in the exile. My responses, if they were to another language, were to the Yiddish language and the Yiddish tradition. I couldn't take the Zionist view that the whole exilic history was bad, or even the last few centuries of it was bad . . . It was extremely rich, extremely creative; it had great happiness as well as great tragedy. And *to discard* it as an unwanted piece of baggage seemed to me to be absurd . . . and tragic.

I know a number of Israelis extremely well and I've had this dialogue with them consistently. After all, Zionism – the return to Palestine – was only one of the remedies advocated for a solution of a certain historical crisis in the Jewish people. There were various solutions: There were the people who believed that once a communist society was achieved, this thing couldn't exist because racialism, differences of nationality would become unimportant. There was a socialist view that – particularly a Jewish socialist view – the Jews could exist in a socialist society without antisemitism and still retain their distinctiveness. That also seems to me to be valid. And there was the Zionist view which said: We have had enough of centuries of persecution. We turn our back on Europe and we go to Palestine and we rebuild ourselves as a new Jewish nation. Well, that's also absolutely valid – but it's only one reaction to a certain crisis in Jewish history, and it's not necessarily the *only* one or the right one.

In fact, it's rooted in a rejection of Jewish history – and this is where I quarrel centrally with the more dogmatic Zionist ideologists. Their dislike of Jewish history was so extreme that they outlawed the Yiddish language: the Yiddish language became a stigma. It was a language of pedlars, of people who cringed, who were afraid of dogs and policemen and '*goyim*'. And there they jettisoned possibly the most exciting creative achievement of the Jewish people for a thousand years. How could you do that? I ask you: How could you do that? Unless you incorporate the Jewish tradition of Eastern Europe, intrinsically, into your tradition and into your future – what kind of Jews are you going to be? You're merely going to be a different variant from American Jews. You're not going to be superior because you're speaking Hebrew and living in a Hebrew-speaking country, in a Jewish State. You are merely going to be a different variant of Jew – not necessarily a better variant of Jew.

We, in England, may face a more specific problem. In time, it is possible that Anglo-Jewry may cease to exist. I think it is an arguable proposition. But I don't think that the solution for the survival of Anglo-Jewry is in this *carte blanche* statement that if you want to remain Jews you should come to Israel. It's only when I come to Israel that I am confronted with the dilemma of being Jewish. It's not a problem for me at all in England. In England, I know very clearly that I'm a Jew. When I come to Israel I begin to wonder: What sort of a Jew am I? I mean, obviously an Oriental Jew regards me as a European; a kibbutznik regards me as not quite a member of the family. I don't belong to Mapam, Mapai, Herut, Rafi. I'm not a religious Jew – they regard me as a 'goy'. So where am I? I find in the end that I identify myself with *precisely* the same people in Israel as I identify with in London: those East European Jews with my common background, who speak my kind of language, who have my concern for the survival of the Jewish people . . . So I might as well stay there, from that point of view.

Of course, there is a personal issue at stake, always. A writer finds it very difficult to emigrate from his language. I mean this is the intrinsic problem of being a writer: he lives within his language – and my language is English, as it is the language of the other people on this platform. And I should imagine that's an important consideration for all of us who have ever thought of the question of settling in Israel . . . that, in a sense, we would be emigrating from the English language – which we are not prepared to do.

So, finally, I would like to say that there should be just a greater sense of the fact that Jews are a universal people; they are an internationally distributed people. The Torah has not descended yet on Israel, the new Torah. Moshe Shamir found a very elegant way of stating one of the oldest clichés in this discussion when he says: (a) We are more Jewish than you; and (b) We are not Jewish at all now. And there it is. I think, in fact, the nub of the whole debate, for me, is the debate between Moshe Shamir and Abraham Kariv, in many ways. It shows you that your debate with us is your debate with yourselves. It's also our debate with ourselves and until we understand that I don't think we'll be talking to one another at all.

In terms of this very interesting debate between Mr Kariv and Mr Shamir, let me state categorically, without going into details, that I am entirely on Mr Kariv's side. In Moshe Shamir I hear the thin screech of chauvinism, and it sounds awfully ugly.

Yesterday Mr Shamir suffered very seriously from the sin of pride, because yesterday he was telling us that in Israel you have Jewish trees and Jewish streams and Jewish rivers; I am waiting for Mr Shamir to tell us when the Jewish trees of Israel are going to march against the Arab trees of Jordan. That would be something indeed, when we begin to nationalize the trees and the rivers in quite that sort of way, and I think that perhaps nationalism is beginning to run mad.

When he addressed a number of remarks to the Anglo-Jewish writers here, I heard the authentic voice of the cultural commissar. For whom are you writing? To whom will you give an account? Are you writing for the reviewers in next Sunday's

Observer? There, in fact, is the clear note of envy for the first time, because the reviewers in the Sunday *Observer* don't review Mr Shamir, because they don't read Hebrew, so clearly there is a kind of sin in being reviewed in the Sunday *Observer*. But I can assure him that no writer on this platform writes for the reviewer on the Sunday *Observer*.

But what I would like to say is to add to what Mr Aharon Megged said so eloquently: For whom are you writing? Ultimately you are writing for yourself, the only person you can be sure of as an audience; you can't even be sure that someone else is going to read what you are going to write. You may be able to read it to your wife, but there is no certainty that anyone else will listen. It requires a certain arrogance, I feel, for a writer to feel like Mr Shamir does, that he is writing for posterity, that the Jewish people in centuries hence are going to say: 'Ah, Moshe Shamir was addressing us, he is asking us to call him to judgement.' There is a very serious danger for all of us, including Mr Shamir, that the Jewish public, even a century hence, may never have heard our names, may never have even known that we existed, and this kind of humility seems to me to be a very essential element in the make-up of a writer.

There is, unfortunately, in the course of all these dialogues, a kind of hectoring note, which one could almost call after today's exhibiton the 'Shamir note' which is addressed to the guests; and I say very seriously to you that it immediately terminates any kind of practical or concrete or constructive discussion, because it completely alienates you – you begin to feel that you have to defend yourself. And there should be no need for us to come here and feel that we have to speak in our own defence.

You can't judge a writer on account of the place he lives in; a man isn't guilty because he chooses to live in London or New York or Moscow or even Berlin. You judge him as a writer, on what he writes, and that's all. And you cannot ask him on the platform here to account for the reason why he will not join what some people here call 'the mainstream of Jewish history' by settling in Israel; why he is not going to guarantee to you that his grandchildren will also be in the mainstream of Jewish history in Israel, and so on. This is absolutely pointless, and mildly insulting.

A Long Look Back

London's my town and proud of it
I am, though born in a street of it
more like a ditch,
with a smell like a Polish Baghdad
that bothered the rich.

Me, I was one of a big quarrelsome family,
We could swear in lots of languages
and thought grass
was something delicate, very uncommon,
a rare place

To make love in a shut park
but not to dance on even in the dark;
sort of a paradise,
gates open to let you out and closed to keep you out
sunset to sunrise.

Something was always happening in our street.
We had a genuine witch, Chaya,
and a black-eyed rascal, Meyer.
Chaya hadn't a crust
but could stop babies;

Meyer gambled and got bust
but made babies.

We even had a murder once
when Yossel, the tailor,
stabbed his missus's sailor
with a scissors.
But mostly the only thing that got murdered
was English,
and the only thing that got in the papers
was fish.

It's all different now, like after a revolution.
You don't have a wash there, but an ablution,
if you don't mind!
You can even walk on the grass anytime,
and the gates are gone
like any respectable place in London.

Chaya, poor old witch, dead,
they say. Meyer married.
The old faces all gone, only
sometimes a ghost shuffling by,
talking to the wind and lonely.

To T. S. Eliot

Eminence becomes you. Now when the rock is struck
your young sardonic voice which broke on beauty
floats amid incense and speaks oracles
as though a god
utters from Russell Square and condescends,
high in the solemn cathedral of the air,
his holy octaves to a million radios.

I am not one accepted in your parish.
Bleistein is my relative and I share
the protozoic slime of Shylock, a page
in Sturmer, and, underneath the cities,
a billet somewhat lower than the rats.
Blood in the sewers. Pieces of our flesh
float with the ordure on the Vistula.
You had a sermon but it was not this.

It would seem, then, yours is a voice
remote, singing another river
and the gilded wreck of princes only
for Time's ruin. It is hard to kneel
when knees are stiff.

To T. S. Eliot

But London Semite Russian Pale, you will say
Heaven is not in our voices.
The accent, I confess, is merely human,
speaking of passion with a small letter
and, crying widow, mourning not the Church
but a woman staring the sexless sea
for no ship's return,
and no fruit singing in the orchards.

Yet walking with Cohen when the sun exploded
and darkness choked our nostrils,
and the smoke drifting over Treblinka
reeked of the smouldering ashes of children,
I thought what an angry poem
you would have made of it, given the pity.

But your eye is a telescope
scanning the circuit of stars
for Good-Good and Evil Absolute,
and, at luncheon, turns fastidiously from fleshy
noses to contemplation of the knife
twisting among the entrails of spaghetti.

So shall I say it is not eminence chills
but the snigger from behind the covers of history,
the sly words and the cold heart
and footprints made with blood upon a continent?
Let your words
tread lightly on this earth of Europe
lest my people's bones protest.

Notes

Journey Through a Small Planet

1. *Menjavinder!*: Mend your window!
2. *Arbeter Fraint Institute*: The *Arbeter Fraint* (Worker's Friend), a Jewish socialist organization, ran an office and club room in Jubilee Street.
3. *shtetl*: a small town or village
4. *Nu* . . . ?: So . . . ?
5. *yeshiva*: (pl. *yeshivot*) Hebrew school
6. *schvitz*: a steam bath
7. *kaddish*: Hebrew prayer for the dead
8. *yok*: the name given to a coarse, ignorant non-Jew
9. *Shmackel*: penis
10. *Toochus*: bottom
11. brown Russian cigarettes: The *papirosa* referred to later, these incorporated a hollow cardboard tube.
12. *Yideneh*: Jewish woman
13. *Kinder*: children; also *kind*, child, and *kindelech*, small children
14. *Gehenna*: Hell
15. *goyim*: non-Jews
16. the local *Talmud Torah*: This was held in Hare Street, round the corner from Fuller Street.
17. *Aleph, Bet*: the Hebrew alphabet, *aleph* and *bet* being the first two letters
18. made *pish*: pissed; also *pisherle*, pisspants
19. *meshuggah*: crazy

20. Rudolph Valentino: a great and handsome star of the silent cinema

21. *gantze*: whole

22. *mitzvah*: a religious good deed

23. *shiksa*: a non-Jewish woman or girl

24. *knish*: an obscene term for a woman's genitals

25. *Shickerve a goy*: Drunk like a goy; also *Eyr is shicker*, he is drunk

26. Peruvians: Dutch Jews referred disparagingly to Polish Jews as Peruvians.

27. *Boobele*: little baby

28. Mogen Dovid: the Star of David

29. George Raft: A famous film star who played very attractive villains, or occasionally heroes, he just crossed over into the talkies at the end of the silent era. As Litvinoff recalls, in one much-remarked scene he was shot, and the way he fell led people to say, 'My God, *how he died*,' in reverential tones, conveying his excellent acting abilities.

30. David: Litvinoff's half-brother was born David Levy. He later adopted the name David Litvinoff and became associated with the Kray twins and the Rolling Stones.

31. *dybbuk*: the devil

32. *sheigetz*: an abomination

33. *chuppah*: the bridal canopy under which the bride and groom stand during the marriage ceremony

34. *Liebchen*: darling, sweetheart

35. *Tzu sein . . . frage*: To be or not to be, that is the question.

36. Ted 'Kid' Lewis: boxer (real name Gershon Mendeloff), known as the 'Aldgate Sphinx', who was world welterweight champion in 1915, 1916 and 1917–19

37. Mickey Lerner: a real, rather than a fictional, individual who perished in the Spanish Civil War

38. Shabbos: Sabbath

39. *shmock*: idiot, fool

40. *pogromchik*: one of those taking part in a pogrom

41. Sir Abraham: Sir Abraham Mendoza was a Jewish aristocrat,

descended from the Jews who were driven out of Spain by the Inquisition. The Mendozas settled principally in Holland, but eventually took up residence in England, after the period of the expulsion was lifted.

42. *Blut fascisti*: Kill the Fascists, blut meaning 'blood'

43. Pelmanism: A correspondence course which was widely advertised in magazines etc., Pelmanism claimed to increase people's ability to think, rationalize and remember.

Prologue: The Day the World Came to an End

1. *Yoshke pondrack*: Yoshke shitbag

2. *Yuden*: Jews

3. Jewish Pale: the Pale of Settlement, the area in which Jews were allowed to live

4. *Judengasse*: (lit. Jewish street) the district where Jews lived